D0321963

Money in Africa

Edited by

Catherine Eagleton, Harcourt Fuller and
John Perkins

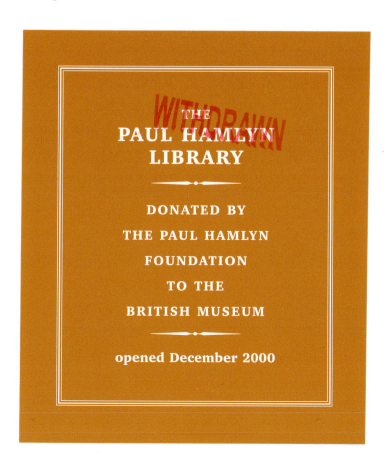

THE
WITHDRAWN
PAUL HAMLYN
LIBRARY

DONATED BY

THE PAUL HAMLYN

FOUNDATION

TO THE

BRITISH MUSEUM

opened December 2000

737.496   EAG

Publishers
The British Museum
Great Russell Street
London WC1B 3DG

Series Editor
Josephine Turquet

Assistant Editor
Margarita Luna

Distributors
The British Museum Press
46 Bloomsbury Street
London WC1B 3QQ

Money in Africa
Edited by Catherine Eagleton, Harcourt Fuller and John Perkins

Front Cover: Four cowrie shells given to the explorer, Mungo Park, by Mansong Diara, ruler of Bambara, West Africa, in 1796

ISBN 978-086159-171-8
ISSN 1747-3640
© The Trustees of the British Museum 2009

Note: the British Museum Occasional Papers series is now entitled British Museum Research Publications. The OP series runs from 1 to 150, and the RP series, keeping the same ISBN preliminary numbers, begins at number 151.

For a complete catalogue of the full range of OPs and RPs see the series website: www/the britishmuseum.ac.uk/
researchpublications
Order from www.britishmuseum.org/shop

For trade orders write to:
Oxbow Books,
10 Hythe Bridge Street, Oxford, OX1 2EW, UK
Tel: (+44) (0) 1865 241249
e-mail oxbow@oxbowbooks.com
website www.oxbowbooks.com
or
The David Brown Book Co
PO Box 511, Oakville
CT 06779, USA
Tel: (+1) 860 945 9329; Toll free 1 800 791 9354
e mail david.brown.bk.co@snet.net

Printed and bound in the UK by 4edge Limited, Hockley
www.4edge.co.uk

Contents

Introduction

Catherine Eagleton

In March 2006, the British Museum hosted a conference on the theme of money in Africa, which brought together scholars from 10 countries and from a range of academic backgrounds. The aim of the conference was to take an interdisciplinary view of this rich and complex subject, and to generate new ideas for future research. The papers published in this volume are a selection from those presented at the conference, and show some of the range of approaches taken by, and areas of focus of, the participants in the meeting.

The study of monetary systems in the history of Africa is a subject that by its nature crosses disciplinary boundaries, covering more than 4,000 years of African history and a huge and varied geographical and cultural area.[1] There is a clear need to bring together evidence from fields of study including numismatics, ethnography, archaeology, geography, politics and history, as well as linguistics, literature, religion, and other disciplines. In some of these areas the empirical evidence needs building, and in others there is a need to develop better theoretical understanding.

At the heart of this subject is the concept of money, which is still shaped by past ideas. This basic problem of definition complicates interdisciplinary approaches to the study of African currencies. At the heart of many definitions is the idea that money can, at least in part, be defined as a medium of exchange, but it is clear in the African contexts considered at the conference that this central concept needs rethinking, and redefining. One very influential definition of money was developed by Karl Polanyi, who distinguished between general-purpose and special-purpose money. General-purpose money, Polanyi argued, was that which could be used as a medium of exchange, a unit of account, a store of value, and a standard of future payments, whereas special-purpose money met only some of those criteria.[2] This definition has been shown to be problematic, not least because even the European-style coin currencies that should, according to Polanyi, be defined as general-purpose, can be seen a special purpose money.[3] Other authors have, through examination of particular case-studies as well as through consideration of trade routes and markets, redefined the idea of money.[4] However, these definitions remain focused on the functions of money – what is does rather than what it is. Broadening the idea, money can be a symbol, it can be linked to power, and it can be defined by space and time as well as by form. It can be a metaphor – a concept that defines our experience of the objects used as money,[5] and it can be a symbol as well as an object with a particular function or value.[6]

Perhaps, then, a flexible definition of money is needed – one which allows us to recognise the multiplicity of monies, and the overlapping and complimentary significances they have. A relativist definition of money can open up new perspectives on money and the markets in which it is used,[7]

but it brings with it methodological challenges. In an important article published in 1982, James Webb discussed the problems with the application of neoclassical monetary concepts to the study of West African currencies, arguing that there is a need to question our assumptions about money supply and economic growth, as well as to start to understand African currencies in their own terms in order to then integrate them into the same theoretical framework as western coin-type currencies.[8] More recently, Gareth Austin has argued that there are dangers in importing neo-classical economic models and European concepts into the study of African economic history; he argues instead for a new model of reciprocal comparison, which acknowledges the specificity of African history at the same time as exploring ways that this can be used in contrast or comparison with other histories or other models.[9] Jane Guyer's book, *Marginal Gains*, begins from a similar concern that current economic and anthropological approaches have enabled only a small part of the complexity of African monetary transactions to be explored and understood.[10] These challenges have begun to be taken up by scholars, but there remains much work to do.[11]

This volume, and the conference from which it began, has as its aim the opening up of some of these debates across disciplinary boundaries. The papers published here are a selection from those presented at the conference, and they cluster around three key areas discussed at the meeting. The first three papers each focus on a particular type of currency object, and consider the ways that these objects were made and used, how they circulated and were inscribed with values and significances. Laurence Garenne-Maro points out the need for detailed accounts of currency objects, rather than reliance on a few 'hotspots' of evidence. Her work on the metal wires and copper ingots used in the trans-Saharan trade shows how archaeological evidence can supplement the rather limited evidence available from the written record, and open up the possibility of a new understanding of these types of money. Carlos Liberato takes as his focus the textile currencies of West Africa, and considers the ways that Portuguese traders tried to control the use of this money, as well as indicating the extent to which cloth currencies were adopted by the Portuguese traders. Karin Pallaver, looking at the trade routes running inland from the East African coast, shows how beads were used to pay taxes and caravan personnel, as well as to buy food and other necessities. Looking at the ways that demand in Africa affected the Venetian glass industry, she indicates how the choices made by Africans could impact on European interests.

The second group of three papers all focus on modern-day Nigeria, each taking a different approach to the evidence available, and using a different type of evidence as primary sources. Between them, they highlight the challenge posed by the sometimes patchy evidence for currencies and monetary systems in Africa, and show the value of looking carefully at the sources on which our studies are based. Simon Heap, in discussing the use of gin as currency in colonial Nigeria, draws on colonial records to construct his account, describing the ways that gin worked as currency, including in payment of court fines. Jane Guyer, working with a single document, considers why the document was prepared, and in doing so changes her initial assumptions about how it could be used as a source. The document provides important evidence for the links between money and authority, and the legitimation of that authority; as well as giving insight into the practises of calculation and record-keeping, and the interweaving of price and value. Foluke Ogunleye brings a literary approach to the subject, discussing the depiction of wealthy women in historical plays, and the light that such representations can shed on attitudes to money and wealth.[12]

The final four papers in this volume are focused on British West Africa in the early 20th century, although all take different approaches and subjects within this temporal and geographical frame. At the conference, these were part of a group of papers which focused on colonial monetary systems, and showed this area of study to be a highly active one.[13] Chibuike Uche focuses on the commercial banks in British West Africa and their relationship with the West African Currency Board. He describes the tensions between the aims of the colonial authorities and the banks, and the importance of the indigenous banking system alongside the colonial banks. Harcourt Fuller considers the issue of coins and banknotes by the colonial government of British West Africa, using the colonial records held in the National Archives of the UK and of Ghana to show some of the motivations behind the establishment of the colonial monetary system and the West African Currency Board, and the challenges faced by the WACB in encouraging people to make use of the new currencies. Adebayo Lawal's paper takes as its focus the same issue of coins and notes, considering the problems with the supply of currency to all parts of this large area. The final paper in this volume, by Ayodeji Olukoju, focuses on the counterfeiting of colonial currency, focussing in particular on the case of Ernest Adisi. Constructed from the colonial records, this paper provides a different angle on the accounts given by Fuller and Lawal of the introduction and circulation of colonial currencies.

These papers between them show some of the work is currently being done on this subject, but they also point to the scale of the task remaining. The title of the conference, Money in Africa, is deceptively simple, since it is clear that both 'money' and 'Africa' are shifting concepts that are redefined in each particular case. However, despite the fact that only a flexible set of definitions can encompass all the currencies and monetary transactions of African history, it is clear that there is much to be gained by keeping the definitions open, to enable conversations to continue across disciplinary boundaries, and to shed new light on the complex histories of African currencies.

Notes

1   This conference focused mainly on the period after AD 1000; a workshop meeting at the British Museum in November 2008 discussed the currencies and trade routes of ancient North Africa.
2   Polanyi in Dalton 1971.
3   Melitz 1970.
4   See, for example, Curtin 1975, Lovejoy 1974, and Webb 1982.
5   Cribb 2005.
6   Hart 1986.
7   An excellent example of this is Akinobu Kuroda's paper on the Maria Theresa dollar (Kuroda 2007), which considers the Maria Theresa dollar in East Africa and the Middle East, and shows its role in linking local and international markets. This complementarity between currencies and markets illuminates our understanding of both currencies and systems.
8   Webb 1982.
9   Austin 2007.
10   Guyer 2007, 7.
11   See, for example, the special issue of *African Studies Review* devoted to responses to *Marginal Gains* (50:2, 2007).
12   There are many other approaches and types of evidence that can be fruitfully brought into the study of money in Africa, and, indeed, it is part of the nature of the subject that a range of sources is used. In a paper presented at the conference, but published elsewhere Lutz Marten and Nancy Kula show how linguistic evidence from the choices of names for currencies can add to our understanding of the introduction of new currencies after African nations gained their independence from colonial rule (Marten and Kula 2008).
13   In addition to the four papers on British West Africa published here, Robin Hermann discussed money in colonial Nigeria. Moving the focus to Eastern Africa, Torbjörn Engdahl (University of Uppsala, Sweden) discussed the establishment of the colonial monetary systems of East Africa, and Terrence Ryan (Central Bank of Kenya / Strathmore University, Kenya) discussed the monetisation of modern-day Kenya.

Bibliography

Austin, G. 2007 'Reciprocal Comparison and African History: Tackling Conceptual Eurocentrism in the Study of Africa's Economic Past', *African Studies Review* 50:3, 1–28.

Curtin, P.D. 1975, *Economic Change in Precolonial Africa: Senegambia in the Era of the Slave Trade*, Madison.

Cribb, J. 2005, 'Money as Metaphor 1: Money is Justice', *Numismatic Chronicle* 165, 417–438.

Dalton, G. (ed.), 1971, *Primitive, Archaic and Modern Economies: Essays of Karl Polanyi*, Boston.

Guyer, J. 2004, *Marginal Gains: Monetary Transactions in Atlantic Africa*, Chicago.

Hart, K. 1986, 'Heads or Tails: two sides of the coin', *Man,* new series 21:4, 637–656

Kuroda, A. 2007, 'The Maria Theresa dollar in the early twentieth-century Red Sea region: a complementary interface between multiple markets', *Financial History Review* 14, 89-110.

Lovejoy, P.E. 1974, 'Interregional monetary flows in the Precolonial trade of Nigeria', *Journal of African History* 15: 4, 563–585.

Marten, L. and Kula, N.C. 2008. 'Meanings of money: national identity and the semantics of currencies', Zambia and Tanzania, *Journal of African Cultural Studies* 20, 183–199.

Melitz, J. 1970, 'The Polanyi School of Anthropology on Money: An Economist's View', *American Anthropologist,* new series 72:5, 1020–1040.

Webb, J.L.A. 1982, 'Towards the comparative study of money: a reconsideration of West African currencies and neoclassical monetary concepts', *The International Journal of African Historical Studies* 15:3, 455–466.

Acknowledgements

The editors wish to thank the peer reviewer, whose thoughtful and useful comments very much improved this publication, and Josephine Turquet, whose assistance with editing the articles was very much appreciated.

'Fils à double tête' and Copper-based Ingots: Copper Money-objects at the Time of the Sahelian Empires of Ancient Ghana and Mali

Laurence Garenne-Marot

Introduction

In reconstructing African monetary history, Webb has stressed the importance of working in depth with money-objects, non-minted 'coins', of sub-Saharan Africa, of placing them in their wider context and thus to clarify what they really represent in terms of monetary systems.[1] We support this goal. Economic anthropologists and historians, however, have mostly concentrated on explaining the true 'behaviour' of African money and have tended to put all pre-colonial money-objects into a single framework without taking into consideration the local history specific to each region. For example the functioning of all pre-colonial West African copper-based currencies has been explained solely through an account of the Niger Delta situation, or of the specific manilla story.[2] In the long term, local, precise, historical studies of West African copper currencies still need to be done, such as the one on the cowrie.[3]

Such in-depth work can only be carried out by drawing data from different fields of evidence – the archaeological record is one major field to take into account. The work of P. de Maret on data from Central Africa is a good example. Before his work, the evidence for the copper currencies of Central Africa came primarily from chance finds of ingots and ingot moulds, many of them undated, and from travel and ethnographic accounts. Through de Maret's thorough archaeological study of 300 graves of the Upemba depression covering 1,000 years, drawing upon data that relate to date and sequence, he was able to reconstruct the monetary history of central Shaba, showing how the H-shaped crosses, the croisettes, evolved from items limited in circulation to the prestige sphere (objects of value) to a commercial, all-purpose currency (monnaie polyvalente).[4]

Concerning West Africa at the time of the Muslim trans-Saharan trade and of the great Sahelian empires of ancient Ghana and Mali, E. Herbert recalls Ibn Battuta's account of the copper currency of Takadda and the confirmed presence in West Africa in the 14th century of copper rods – not just ingots for barter but true means of exchange – true currencies – and in doing so evokes the important work done by R. Mauny in tying Ibn Battuta's text to actual archaeological data.[5]

The analysis does not, however, go far enough: both textual and archaeological evidence should be placed in the wider historical context, following in this manner what had been in general advocated by Webb (as cited above). One has to take into account the influence of the weighing and fiduciary systems of North African Muslim courts (through the merchants) on sub-Saharan imperial polity-ruled entities at the time when trans-Saharan trade brought these worlds into contact. One also has to take into account what went on in sub-Saharan areas not in contact with North African customs and in which barter was the usual form of economic exchange.

Ibn Battuta's text and another account by an Arabic author of the 14th century explicitly demonstrate that copper-based objects identified as probable currencies occurring at the same time may, however, have been endowed with different qualities in order to serve different monetary purposes. Archaeological records shed light on this debate by revealing tangible money-objects, which, due to their aspect and composition, imply different usages, showing clearly the coexistence in western-most Africa (as early maybe as the 11th century), of money-objects expressing completely different 'behaviour' and, thus, involved in separate monetary systems.

A. Money-objects in copper-based material in West Africa: the evidence from 14th-century records

During his visit to Takadda (identified as the site of modern Azelick in Niger) in 1352 Ibn Battuta recorded:

> The copper mine is outside Takadda. They excavate the earth for it and bring it to the town and smelt it in their houses.… When they have smelted it into red copper they make bars of it a span and a half long, some thin and some thick, of which the thick are sold at 400 bars per gold mithqal and the thin at 600 or 700 for a mithqal. This is their currency. With the thin ones they buy meat and firewood and with the thick ones male and female slaves, sorghum, butter and wheat.[6]

Herbert drew attention to this 'standardization of the rods' and 'the "minting" of two different sizes' adapted to cheaper and more expensive purchases, which made these rods 'true means of exchange, not simply ingots for barter'.[7] Mauny has already noted that these 'bars' (or rods) were an extremely small division of the mithqal, and therefore currencies with a very low purchasing power; in other words, their values were given in terms of the mithqal of gold.[8] In consequence, one should not be opposed to the definition of these 'bars' as standard monetary units (based on the mithqal, thus, on the Muslim monetary – or at least weight– system).

In the same text Ibn Battuta tells us that the copper is not only used in the city of Takedda but is also meant to be 'carried to different lands and among these to the lands of infidels'. Certainly, this would be for the purpose of exchange for other goods, even if this is not precisely indicated in the text. Another text, by the Arabic writer al-'Umari, may clarify what could have been the purpose of the copper bars. Al-'Umari, who interviewed many Egyptian officials who had met the Mansa Musa (then the Emperor of Mali) during his visit to Cairo in 1324, reported what the Mansa had said about a copper mine he had within his empire which seemed to have brought him significant revenue.

> We send it [the copper] to the land of the pagan Sudan and sell it for two-thirds of its weight in gold, so that we sell 100 mithqals of this copper for 66 2/3 mithqals of gold.[9]

The text from al-'Umari shows that the copper sold to the gold suppliers, the 'pagans of the forest', yielded enormous profits. They accepted a totally unfair trade if one considers the values of the same metals in the northern Sahelian region indicated by Ibn Battuta. Such a discrepancy in metal 'values' was so hard to grasp that the debate over the true nature of the 'bars' recorded by Ibn Battuta lasted decades. Lhote started the debate by arguing that the price indicated by Ibn Battuta (400 or 600 bars for 1 *mithqal* of gold) was extremely low, considering al-Umari's mention of copper being sold for two-thirds of its weight in gold. For him, the rate quoted by Ibn Battuta would fit salt better and he therefore suggested that what Ibn Battuta saw in Takadda were, in fact, salt bars.[10] This continued even after Mauny drew attention to archaeological evidence of copper mining in the region of Azelick.[11] Finally, Bernus and Gouletquer ended the debate by providing definitive proof, not only of the presence of copper mines, but also of the transformation of this copper on the Azelick site and its vicinity.[12]

From these texts one may deduce that in 14th century West Africa different values were ascribed to copper and this was so in relation to the cultural context. At Takedda/Azelick the situation was that of a local exploitation of copper resources with prolonged contact with northern African customs. In the gold-producing regions the situation was different, with people geographically distant from the copper mines and with no direct contact with northern African merchants. Apart from this question of the discrepancy (and the reasons behind it) between the 'values' of copper and (subsequently) gold – an extremely small division of the *mitqal vs* a product worth two-thirds of its weight in gold – which has been reviewed at length by Bucaille, as well as by Garenne-Marot and Mille,[13] there is the question of the same copper product being 'used' differently. In one situation the copper bars were 'currencies' or 'coins' – non-minted coins – in a set accounting system. In the other, copper bars were monetized or bartered goods that could be used or 'consumed' as commodities. It is therefore of interest to consider whether it was the very same copper product, such as the 'bars' of Takkada, which was used in backing various transactions or if, on the contrary, specific copper 'money-objects' served specific purposes, some as monetized goods within a bartering system, others as true 'currencies' or 'coins' within a set accounting system.

Ibn Battuta's text is not very explicit on the matter. Although he describes at length the bars used in Takadda for local transactions he only mentions 'copper' as the 'product' that leaves the town for the purposes of trade.[14]

Despite Ibn Battuta being precise regarding the 'thick' and the 'thin' bars, no factual data can be drawn from the text in relation to either their measurement or weight.[15] Mauny has discussed the possible value of the 'palm', but he comes to no conclusions.[16] What about the archaeological data? Two kinds of copper 'bars' have been collected on the Azelick archaeological site,[17] though not in the context of controlled stratigraphy. On the one hand there is a collection of some 200 'wires' of copper based metal – around 50–70mm long when unbroken – either with an angular (usually square) section or a flat ribbon-like section, and, on the other hand, a collection of short copper bars – the term 'ingots' would be appropriate – 7mm thick, though their fragmentary state does not permit their original length to be estimated. Either the 'wires' or 'ingots' could be Ibn Battuta's 'rods' of Takadda.[18] However, the presence on the same site of two kinds of copper-based objects – clearly distinct in shape – that could both be some kind of commodity/currency raises the question of the possible co-existence of differently 'shaped' copper-based materials embodying distinct money-objects meant for different purposes. Still more data has to be drawn from the archaeological field in order to document clear copper money objects and then gather new elements to ascertain the possibility of the co-existence of differently shaped copper-based materials meant for different purposes. We must therefore turn to two other Sahelian sites, which date from slightly earlier than Takadda and Ibn Battuta's and al Umari's descriptions and examine a situation on the ground, which is comparable in some ways to that of Takadda. Kumbi Saleh and Tegdaoust owed their economic development to the Muslim trans-Saharan trade, for both the presence of North African merchants and the use within their markets of the Muslim weighing system are firmly established and, at least in the case of Tegdaoust, there was exploitation of the local copper resources.

B. The archaeological evidence: the *'fils à double tête'* of Kumbi Saleh – a probable money-object

In the course of their archaeological work in 1949–1951 at the site of Kumbi Saleh, in the south-east of present day Mauritania, very close to the border with Mali, R. Mauny and P. Thomassey uncovered many small wire-like objects.[19] These minute objects, varying in length and weight (most of them 30–40mm in length and 2–8g in weight), unlike ordinary copper wires, have a very characteristic shape. The wire, which is frequently flattened in the middle, has thickened rounded ends (see **Fig. 1**). Bucaille, who examined some of them in 1976 in their corroded state of conservation, came up with a very vivid description of them: 'a match burned entirely that would have had two thickened rounded ends'.[20]

Their ubiquity on the site – in all the soundings and excavations that were conducted – and Ibn Battuta's report led Mauny to characterize these *fils à double tête* as a currency – a fractional 'coin' of low purchasing power based on the *mithqal*.[21] His assumption has been widely accepted in regard to both the very wide distribution and diverse contexts on the Kumbi Saleh site, to the point where Berthier adopted the term *fils-monnaies* for them.[22]

As a matter of fact, some *fils à double tête* of Kumbi Saleh can be dated to the 14th century and were found in what is

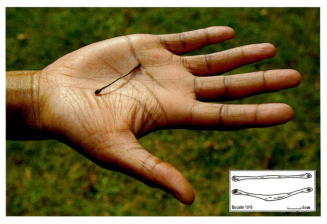

Figure 1 A 'fil à double tête' (photo: J. Polet) and line drawing of another by Bucaille (1976)

thought to have been the quarter of the Muslim merchants of the town (called also the 'urban tell' because the accumulation of collapsed stone buildings caused this area of about 44ha to really stand out in the general landscape of the site). The *fils à double tête* seem to have appeared even earlier at Kumbi Saleh but the problem is that most of those recovered before the careful excavation conducted by Berthier in the 1980s of a habitation unit in this quarter were not precisely dated. The chronological sequence established by Berthier shows that although copper remains occur in the earliest levels (9th century), the first *fils à double tête* appear only at the end of the 11th century, thus coinciding with the setting of the urban framework on this area, the stone buildings and the occurrence of artefacts of more distant North African origin such as carnelian beads, glass weights, glassware similar to those from Raqqada.[23] After this period the *fils à double tête* are found in all subsequent levels up to level Vb with a peak in level III (13th century). In summary, thus far the proven use of the *fils à double tête* on the Kumbi Saleh site seems to have lasted for at least three centuries – from the end of the 11th century to the end of the 14th century or beginning of the 15th century.[24]

Kumbi Saleh is the presumed site of the capital of Ancient Ghana, the first Sahelian Empire recorded in Arabic texts (8th to the mid-13th century). The emergence – or at least the development – of this empire is linked to the trans-Saharan trade and the control of exchanges. North African products, and among those Saharan salt, were exchanged for gold from countries located upstream on the Niger and Senegal rivers, with Ancient Ghana exploiting its position as an intermediary between the suppliers of gold and the trans-Saharan traders[25] (see **Fig. 2**). The decline of the Empire of Ghana and the later control of this region by a hegemonic power of Malinke origin, leading to the Mali Empire, did not seem to affect the urban development of Kumbi Saleh, as shown by the architectural features of the area excavated by Berthier. Thus, the archaeological data from Kumbi Saleh documents the existence of copper money objects in Sahelian West Africa in the 11th to the 13th century, which, in a sense comparable to

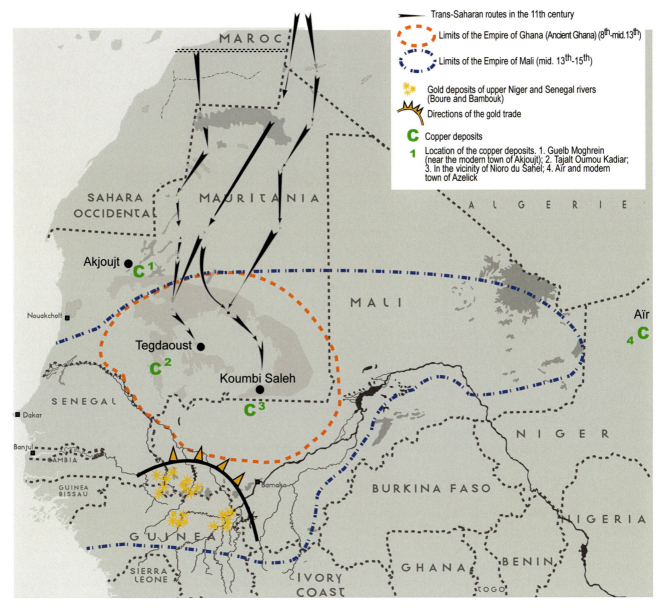

Figure 2 Map of the western part of Africa, showing: the trans-Saharan routes heading to Awdaghust (Tegdaoust) and Ghana (Kumbi Saleh) as recorded in the writings of al-Bakri (11th century) and al-Idrissi (12th century). All known routes are indicated and mapped without taking into account the fluctuations in the frequency and in the itineraries, which occurred between the 11th (time of al-Bakri) and the 14th century AD; the (estimated) limits of ancient Ghana (8th–mid-13th century) and Mali (mid-13th–15th centuries); the gold deposits of upper Senegal and Niger rivers; the copper deposits bearing evidence of ancient workings; the location of the sites cited in the text. (Graphic: Geoatlas maps modified by L. Garenne-Marot)

that described by Ibn Battuta at Takkada, certainly correspond to the definition of 'standard monetary units'. What remains to be documented, however, is the possibility of the coexistence of different copper money-objects meant to embody different monetary or transactional functions. The town of Tegdaoust/ Awdaghust and the data from its copper workshops might provide elements of a response to this question.

C. The archaeological evidence: copper-based ingots of the Tegdaoust workshop and the transformation of the trans-Saharan brass rods

Tegdaoust (the modern name of the site of the ancient town of Awdaghust), situated at the end of one of the main western-most trans-Saharan roads, was a major centre of trans-Saharan trade, a place of unloading and exchange, from its settlement at the end of the 8th century until the mid-11th century. Its relation to the capital of the Empire of Ghana fluctuated during this period but in the 10th–11th centuries at least it was a tributary town of the capital of Ghana. Excavations during a 12-year period in the 1960s–1970s yielded a good overview of the organization of the town with its residential quarters and workshops.[26]

Important workshops were unearthed in a quarter separate from the residential parts of the town in which artefacts related to copper metallurgy were recovered. Several ingot-moulds and 16 ingots or fragments of ingots of copper-based material were found beside three large furnaces.[27]

In order to understand the importance of the copper workshops of Tegdaoust in this discussion about copper money-objects, some broad overview of the contextual situation is required. Arabic texts from the 9th century onwards mention that along with desert salt the trans-Saharan caravans brought copper, both red copper (non-alloyed) and coloured copper (alloyed copper such as brass, which has a golden tint).[28] As tangible proof, 2,085 long bars (around 70cm in length and 500g in weight) of copper-based metal (see photographs of the bars in **Fig. 3**) were recovered from an abandoned load of a caravan buried in a sand dune in the Majâbat al-Koubrâ, the most arid part of the Mauritanian Sahara.[29] This load has been dated to between the 11th and the beginning of the 14th centuries.[30] Interestingly, the bars were made, not of unalloyed copper, but of brass with high zinc content (20% of the total weight).[31] The difference is significant, because the brass was certainly imported. Brass originated at that time from North Africa, certainly from the mines of the Sus and Daï valleys (in present day Morocco), famous then for the production of 'coloured' copper. Unalloyed copper may have been imported but also could have been local to the regions just south of the Sahara. There are the copper deposits in the Aïr region of modern Niger (where Azelick is situated), as we have seen. Mauritania is also rich in copper, for example there are the well-known deposits around the modern town of Akjoujt and those of Tajalt Omou Kadiar closer to the archaeological site of Tegdaoust. Finally there are deposits in present day Mali, close to the border with Mauritania, around the modern town of Nioro du Sahel.[32] Thorough archaeological investigations of the mines around Akjoujt have shown that copper was smelted there as early as the beginning of the 1st millennium BC.[33] Direct dated evidence for 'medieval' exploitation – especially in the Tajalt Oumou Kadiar area – is lacking due to an absence of

research but numerous clues (among them geological reports of ancient workings) suggest that local copper smelting was still going on at the time of the Muslim trans-Saharan trade.[34] Some of the conditions experienced by Azelick/Takkada on the ground in the 14th century thus existed already in Tegdaoust/ Awdaghust in the 11th century, including exploitation of local copper resources and prolonged contact with North African customs.

The ingots recovered next to the three furnaces in the copper workshops of Tegdaoust are of special interest. Of the three complete ingots, two were about 25cm long and the other 14cm long. The analyses show an alloy of leaded brass with very unusual iron content.[35] By combining the data from the archaeological remains, the composition of the analyzed ingots and that of the bars from the Ma'den Ijâfen, it was possible to deduce what transformations of the copper material were made in the workshops.[36] The ingot-moulds showed that the ingots of copper based material were manufactured there. The hypothesis is that the long bars like those from the Ma'den Ijâfen, of an ideal size for camel transportation through the desert, were transformed into shorter rods (25–26cm long). This was a more convenient size for transport by donkeys and for the trade with the South, certainly as far south as the gold mines. Moreover, the composition of the metal was certainly also modified there. Mike Wayman, metallurgist at the university of Alberta, Canada, and the author were able to show through a careful reading of the elemental analysis of the ingots that not only was lead possibly added there, as had been previously thought,[37] but that the Moroccan brass was diluted with locally smelted copper in the workshops of Tegdaoust[38] (**Fig. 3**). Considering the amount of income that the taxes on copper transactions represented for the King of Ghana – more than double those on salt (as mentioned by al-Bakri writing in 1068)[39] – it would have been very lucrative to mix northern imported brass with local copper without altering the golden colour of the metal, and thus increase the mass of metal to be traded with the South. The colour was important there and has certainly helped to clearly distinguish imported from local material.

In all probability, the Tegdaoust workshops were destroyed at the time of the Almoravid raid in 1054–1055, according to al-Bakri.[40] They were not rebuilt (destroyed furnaces, discarded ingot mould and ingots were left *in situ*) and so this dramatic event gives a *terminus ante quem* date of mid-11th century to all the material recovered there.

D. Copper-based ingots and *fils à double tête* of Tegdaoust: copper-based bars of different shape and metal composition found in the near vicinity

Some *fils à double tête* were also found at the Tegdaoust site. Still, as they were recovered in disturbed, non-stratigraphic contexts, they were mostly discarded and not archaeologically recorded. Interestingly, the three precisely recorded ones were all situated within the workshops area and close to the discarded ingots and ingot moulds.[41] No indication of their local manufacture was evident. They simply lay close to the furnace in the same mid-11th century environment as the previously cited leaded brass ingots.

So, here we have in the same contextual environment two copper-based objects of different shape: on the one side, ingots,

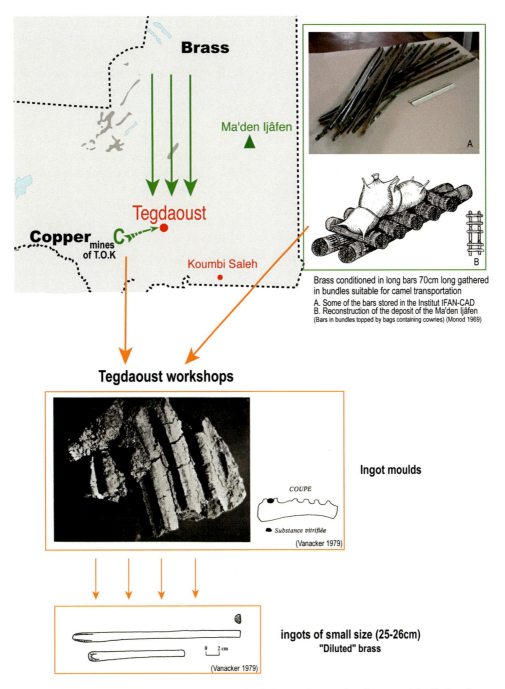

Figure 3 The workshops of Tegdaoust: transformation of copper-based material with the manufacture of small ingots and the dilution of Moroccan brass with locally smelted copper. (Photo of the bars and graphic: L. Garenne-Marot)

rods, about 25cm long and on the other, some tiny, wire-like objects of a length and weight about 1/60 of that of the ingots. The shape of the ingots meant that they could easily be transformed – either bent with hammering work into ready-made anklets or bracelets or else re-melted and the fused metal cast into a wide range of objects. The *fils à double tête* are, however, completely different, being so tiny that it would have been difficult even to work them into rings.

The composition of the metal of the ingots and the *fils à double tête* is also different. The metal of the three Tegdaoust *fils à double tête* was not analyzed, but analyses on examples from Kumbi Saleh show that their composition varied.[42] This is only to be expected when one considers their use over three centuries, but interesting patterns may be seen. Copper – not brass – is always the base metal. This copper base is alloyed with lead, sometimes in very high proportions – up to a quarter of the metal in some cases. In the cases with a high lead

content, the alloy is quite standardized in its composition revealing a regular pattern of impurities. Leaded copper has none of the aesthetic and workable qualities of brass. Thus both their metal composition and their size mean that the *fils à double tête*, could not be transformed into other consumable objects, unlike the leaded-brass ingots.

E. Leaded-brass ingots and *fils à double tête* of Tegdaoust: monetized goods versus standard monetary units

Both the shape and the quality of the metal of the leaded-brass ingots of Tegdaoust made them items that could easily be transformed into secondary products. They fit nicely with the definition of goods with a high level of consumption, which, in the process of regularized exchange, acquire the properties of money – that is, to serve as a medium of exchange, store of value, standard of deferred payment and above all standard of measurement,[43] and thus become monetized. They are exemplary items within any monetary system of barter transactions. However, both the size and the composition of the metal of the *fils à double tête* give a final product with a low to negligible rate of consumption – favouring the hypothesis of the *fils à double tête* as standard monetary units.

The political centre of the Empire of Ghana was distant from the gold mining areas. The control of the gold was mostly through the control of transactions. Al-Bakri mentions the taxes that were imposed to insure the state income.[44] Transactions on the Tegdaoust market were done with gold powder, again according to al-Bakri.[45] Weights in unalterable glass bearing Fatimid inscriptions of the 10th–early 11th centuries were found, testifying to the use of, if not a fiduciary, at least a weighing system comparable to that of the Egyptian Fatimid court.[46] If we accept the *fils à double tête* found in the Tegdaoust workshop as *fils-monnaies* – standard monetary units – this would mean that already in the mid-11th century, there was some centralized control of money, with the creation of a local standard unit, a division of the *mitqual*. This would not be inconsistent with the imperial polity of regulating all exchanges.

Lead, a by-product of the extraction of silver from galena ores, was certainly an import from the North. Galena mines are abundant in Morocco and were intensively exploited at that time.[47] The problem is that, apart from the few that emerge from Berthier's excavations, the analyzed *fils-monnaie* cannot be put into a chronological sequence and so it is not possible to determine if there was a fluctuation of the lead content over time. It would have been interesting to see if a fluctuation did exist over time, from a standardized alloy with a high lead content to a mixed composition with lower and lower lead additions. If such a fluctuation did exist, it could reveal an interesting pattern. At the beginning of the period, the *fils-monnaie* might have been imported as finished products directly from the Maghreb, as standard monetary units at the demand, perhaps, of the local state power –the King of Ghana – in order to facilitate taxation and to reduce flexibility in currency substitution. The ease of manufacturing the *fils-monnaie* might have led to local production with a lower and lower standard quality of metal. It might be significant to note that, along with the brass bars of the caravan of the Ma'den Ijâfen were heavy bags of cowrie shells. Were those intended to 'replace' the devalued *fils à double tête*, which no longer fulfilled their role? The cowries also had the same characteristic advantages of smallness in size, durability and ready divisibility together with the added advantage of being impossible to counterfeit.[48] Ibn Battuta made precise reference to them as standard monetary units in the 14th century: 'these cowries are also the currency of the Sudan in their countries. I saw them sold at Mali and Jawjaw at the rate of 1,150 to the gold dinar'.[49]

F. Tegdaoust and Kumbi Saleh: same monetary systems?

Why are the *fils-monnaie* mostly restricted to the Kumbi Saleh site, considering the relations that existed, at least in the 11th century, between Tegdaoust and Kumbi Saleh?

The dramatic events that took place at Tegdaoust with the Almoravid raid and the destruction of the copper workshops were the beginning of a series of changes that occurred in the second half of the 11th century in the westernmost African sector of trans-Saharan and interregional trade. The Tegdaoust copper workshops were not rebuilt and one sees subsequently a

major change in the trans-Saharan routes: the road that led to Tegdaoust was abandoned.[50] Tegdaoust no longer played a major role as an unloading place and a redistribution pole between the North African merchants and the gold traders. From then on, the economic activity of the town declined dramatically. Tegdaoust (Awdaghust) is described in 1154 as a small town in the desert in which there is no large trade.[51]

Changes certainly occurred in the town of Ghana, the capital of the Empire, after the Almoravid episode, but there is little to be gleaned from the Arabic sources. A century later, we learn from al-Idrissi that the king of Ghana claimed descent from the prophet's family. So a Muslim king perhaps of Arabic descent had succeeded the animist king of Soninke origin described by al-Bakri in the mid-11th century. It is interesting that the period following the end of the Tegdaoust workshops corresponds to the period of development on the site of Kumbi Saleh of the quarter around the mosque to which belongs the habitation unit excavated by Berthier. This habitation unit continued with little disturbance for three centuries (the end of the 11th–14th century) but it did display embellishments.[52] The city of Ghana seemed to have remained economically and politically active even during the Mali dominance. Al-'Umari, in a chapter entitled 'the Kingdom of Mali and what appertains to it', recalls that even if Ghana is a province of the Kingdom of Mali, 'In the whole kingdom of his sovereign there is none who is given the title of "King" (*malik*) except the ruler of Ghana who is like a deputy to him even though he be a king'.[53]

It appears that the decline of Tegdaoust gave new impetus to the economic development of Kumbi Saleh. It is after that time also that the *fils-monnaie* are found in numbers in the levels of the urban tell of Kumbi Saleh (see **Fig. 4**). Kumbi Saleh might have taken over the industrial transformation of copper-based metal formerly carried out in the destroyed workshops of Tegdaoust. The copper mines in the vicinity of Nioro du Sahel, already mentioned, are very close to Kumbi Saleh. Geological survey reports have shown the importance of ancient workings in these mines, and many authors, beginning with Mauny, have related this data to the copper mine mentioned by the Mansa Musa which, as we have seen, was very profitable.[54]

It is therefore due to both political and economic circumstances that the *fils-monnaie* are only rarely found at the Tegdaoust site after mid-11th century. Still, the Tegdaoust evidence may point to the fact that money-objects in copper – not minted coins but with the same properties as minted ones – may have existed already at the beginning of 11th century. This was due to the special circumstances prevailing at the time – Sahelian empires in close contact with monetary and weighing systems indissolubly identified with the nation-state, and with large transactions taking place with a centralized control of money. We could advocate the existence of polities exercising monetary powers as early as this time, although economic historians like Webb only evoke the existence of a true correlation between nation-state and monetary control with the Asante or the Hausa states.[55]

Conclusion

In tying together the archaeological findings of copper money-objects and the remains of copper metallurgy of the Tegdaoust/Awdaghust workshop destroyed in the mid-1050s, copper money objects of Kumbi Saleh (late 11th to 14th century) and

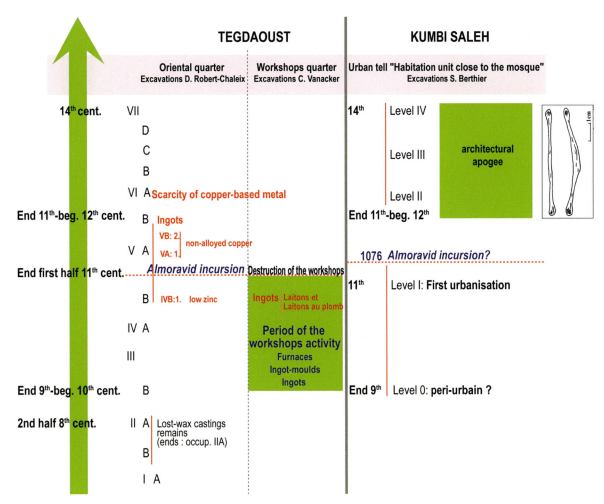

Figure 4 Comparative chronostratigraphies for Tegdaoust (residential and workshop areas) and Kumbi Saleh (habitation unit excavated by Berthier on the urban tell) in relation to the copper material, ingots and *fils à double tête*. (Graphic: L. Garenne-Marot)

Arabic accounts of copper products used as 'monetary items' in 14th century West Africa, it has been possible to show that money-objects in copper, not minted coins, but with the same properties as minted coins, may have existed already at the beginning of the 11th century. This supports the argument that a true correlation existed between nation-state and monetary control before the Asante or the Hausa states.

Furthermore, the evidence shows that two 'monetary' systems in which copper money objects played a major part might have co-existed at that time within the most western part of Africa: first, in towns in close contact with monetary and weighing systems identified with the nation-state, a system with large transactions taking place with a centralized control of money and, second, in regions with no contact with these monetary systems identified with the nation-state, another system in which copper was a medium of exchange within a monetary system of barter transactions (including transactions for gold).

Through the data from Tegdaoust/Awdaghust (backed up by data from Kumbi Saleh) it was possible to show that specific copper-based money objects correspond to each 'monetary' system. In the Tegdaoust copper workshop, within the same archaeological unit, both items of standard monetary units – the *fils à double tête* – and items that could relate to standards of measurement – leaded-brass ingots – were found.

Acknowledgment
Special thanks to John Dryden who, in correcting much of the style and syntax of the text and refining the expression, helped the author to express her thoughts in a more accurate way.

Bibliography
Bates, M. L. 1981. 'The function of Fatimid and Ayyubid glass weights', *Journal of the Economic and Social History of the Orient* XXIV (1), 63–92.
Bernus, S. and Gouletquer, P. 1976. 'Du cuivre au sel. Recherches archéologiques sur la région d'Azelik (campagnes 1973–1975)', *Journal des Africanistes* 46 (1-2), 7–68.
Bernus S. 1983. 'Découvertes, hypothèses, reconstitution et preuves: Le cuivre médiéval d'Azelick-Takedda (Niger)', in N. Échard (ed.), *Métallurgies Africaines, Nouvelles Contributions,* Mémoires de la Société des Africanistes 9, 89–107.
Berthier, S. 1997. *Recherches archéologiques sur la capitale de l'empire de Ghana, Étude d'un secteur d'habitat à Koumbi-Saleh, Mauritanie. Campagnes II-III-IV-V (1975–1976)-(1980–1981),* Bar International series 680, Oxford.
Bucaille, R. 1976. 'Une probable monnaie sahélienne de la période des Grands empires: Les fils de métal cuivreux', *Notes Africaines* 151, 74–77.
Devisse, J. (ed.), 1993. Catalogue '*Vallées du Niger*', Réunion des Musées Nationaux, Paris.
Devisse, J. 1972. 'Routes de commerce et échanges en Afrique occidentale en relation avec la Méditerranée. Un essai sur le commerce africain médiéval du XIe au XVIe siècle', *Revue d'Histoire Économique et Sociale* 1 et 3, 42–73, 357–397.
Devisse, J. 1990. 'Commerce et routes du trafic en Afrique occidentale', *Histoire Générale de l'Afrique,* III. *L'Afrique du VIIe au XIe siècle,* ch. 14, Unesco/NEA, 397–464.
Garenne-Marot, L., Wayman, M.L., and Pigott, V.C. 1994. 'Early copper and brass in Senegal', in T. Childs (ed.), *Society, Culture and Technology in Africa,* supplement to vol. 11 of MASCA Research

Papers in Science and Archaeology, Philadelphia, 45–62.

Garenne-Marot, L. and Mille, B. 2005. 'Les fils à double tête en alliage à base de cuivre de Koumbi Saleh: valeur du métal, transactions et monnayage de cuivre dans l'empire de Ghana', *Afrique: Archéologie & Arts* 3, 81–100.

Garenne-Marot, L. and Mille, B. 2007. 'Copper-based metal in the Inland Niger delta: Metal and technology at the time of the Empire of Mali', in S. La Niece, D. Hook and P.T. Craddock (eds.), *Metal and Mines, Studies in Archaeometallurgy*, Archetype Publications and British Museum, London, 159–168.

Herbert, E. 1984. *Red Gold of Africa. Copper in Precolonial History and Culture,* The University of Wisconsin Press.

Hogendorn, J.S. and Gemery, H.A. 1988. 'Continuity in West African monetary history? An outline of monetary development', *African Economic History* 17, 127–146.

Johnson, M. 1970. 'The cowrie currencies of West Africa, part 1', *The Journal of African History* 11(1), 17–49.

Lambert, N., 1983. 'Nouvelle contribution à l'étude du Chalcolithique de Mauritanie', in N. Échard (ed.), *Métallurgies Africaines, Nouvelles Contributions,* Mémoires de la Société des Africanistes 9, 63–88. Société des Africanistes, Paris.

Launois, A. and Devisse, J. 1983. 'Poids de verre découverts à Tegdaoust, chronologie du site et histoire des étalons de poids en Afrique occidentale', *Tegdaoust III. Recherches sur Aoudaghost. Campagnes 1960/65. Enquêtes générales.* Éditions Recherche sur les civilisations, 'mémoire' 25, 399–419. Paris.

Levtzion, N. 1973. *Ancient Ghana and Mali*, London.

Levtzion, N. and Hopkins, J.F.P. (eds) 2000. *Corpus of Early Arabic Sources for West African History*, trans. J.F.P. Hopkins, Princeton.

Lhote, H. 1955. Contribution à l'histoire des Touaregs soudanais, *Bull. IFAN*, B. 17, 334–370.

Lhote, H. 1972. Recherches sur Takedda, ville décrite par le voyageur arabe Ibn Battouta et située en Aïr, *Bull. IFAN*, B 34(3), 435–470.

Maret, P. de 1981. 'L'évolution monétaire du Shaba central entre le 7e et le 18e siècle', *African Economic History* 10, 117–149.

Mauny, R. 1961. *Tableau géographique de l'Ouest africain. D'après les sources écrites, la tradition et l'archéologie*, Mémoires de l'Institut Français d'Afrique noire 61, IFAN-Dakar.

Monod, T. 1969. *Le Ma'den Ijâfen: Une étape caravanière ancienne dans la Majâbat al-Koubrâ*, Actes du premier colloque international d'archéologie africaine, Fort Lamy, 286–320.

Robert-Chaleix, D. 1986. 'Nouveaux sites médiévaux mauritaniens: Un aperçu sur les régions septentrionales du Bilad as-Sudan', in *L'histoire du Sahara et les Relations Transsahariennes*, Bergamo: Gruppo Walk Over, 46–58.

Robert-Chaleix, D. 1989. *Tegdaoust V. Recherches sur Aoudaghost. Une concession médiévale à Tegdaoust,* Éditions Recherche sur les Civilisations, 'mémoire' 82, Paris.

Rosenberger, B. 1964. 'Autour d'une grande mine d'argent du Moyen Âge marocain: Le Jebel Aouam', *Hespéris Tamuda*, V, 15–78.

Rosenberger, B. 1970. 'Les vieilles exploitations minières et les anciens centres métallurgiques au Maroc', *Revue de Géographie du Maroc* 17, 71–108, and 18, 59–102.

Thomassey, P. and Mauny, R. 1951. 'Campagne de fouilles à Koumbi Saleh', *Bulletin de l'Ifan*, B, 438–462.

Thomassey, P. and Mauny R. 1956. 'Campagne de fouilles de 1950 à Koumbi Saleh (Ghana)?', *Bulletin de l'IFAN*, B, 117–140.

Vanacker, C. 1979. *Tegdaoust II. Recherches sur Aoudaghost. Fouille d'un quartier artisanal.* Mémoires de l'Institut Mauritanien de la Recherche Scientifique 2, (résumé en arabe). Institut Mauritanien de la Recherche Scientifique, Nouakchott.

Vanacker, C. 1983. 'Cuivre et métallurgie du cuivre à Tegdaoust (Mauritanie Orientale)', in N. Échard (ed.), *Métallurgies Africaines, Nouvelles Contributions,* Mémoires de la Société des Africanistes 9, 89–107. Société des Africanistes, Paris.

Webb, J.L.A. Jr. 1982. 'Toward the comparative study of money: a reconsideration of West African currencies and neoclassical monetary concepts', *International Journal of African Historical Studies* 15(3), 455–466.

Werner, O. and Willett, F. 1975. 'The composition of brasses from Ife and Benin', *Archaeometry* 17(2), 141–156.

Notes

1   Webb 1982.
2   Hogendorn and Gemery 1988.
3   Johnson 1970.
4   de Maret 1981; see summary in Herbert 1984, 186.
5   Herbert 1984, 195.
6   Ibn Battuta, in Levtzion and Hopkins 2000, 302, ref. manuscript B 697, 440.
7   Herbert 1984, 195.
8   Mauny 1961, p. 311.
9   Al-'Umari, in Levtzion and Hopkins 2000, 272, ref. manuscript B 67, 36a.
10   Lhote 1955.
11   Mauny 1961, 139–141 and 308–313; Lhote 1972.
12   Bernus and Gouletquer 1976 and Bernus 1983.
13   Bucaille 1976, Garenne-Marot and Mille 2005 and 2007.
14   Ibn Battuta, in Levtzion and Hopkins 2000, 302, ref. manuscript B 697, 440.
15   Bucaille 1976, 74.
16   Mauny 1961, 311.
17   As cited by Bucaille 1976, 74.
18   Bucaille 1976, 74.
19   Thomassey and Mauny 1951 and 1956.
20   Bucaille 1976, 75.
21   Mauny 1961, 312.
22   Bucaille 1976; Berthier 1997, 75.
23   Berthier 1997, 75, table 17 and Berthier 1997, in passim.
24   See Garenne-Marot and Mille 2005.
25   Levtzion 1973
26   See references to the numerous publications about the archaeological work at this site in Robert-Chaleix 1989, Berthier 1997 and in Devisse 1993.
27   Vanacker 1979 and 1983.
28   See complete references in Herbert 1984.
29   Monod 1969.
30   Monod 1969. (I-2769) : 785±110 BP et (Dak-1) : 860±108 BP. The dates which appear in Monod's publication and were repeated inchanged in any subsequent publication have been recently revised using calibration curves (Stuiver and Reimer 1993, Radiocarbone 35), see Garenne-Marot and Mille 2005, 89, note 16.
31   Werner and Willett 1975.
32   Cited in Mauny 1961, 310. Recent researches on the copper mines in this region around Nioro (Mali) have been conducted by Sylvain Badey (université de Paris 1 Panthéon-Sorbonne).
33   Lambert 1983.
34   See Vanacker 1983 and Robert-Chaleix 1986 for the copper deposits of Tajalt Oumou Kadiar and Mauny 1961, 308 for those of Nioro.
35   Length (and weight) of the complete ingots were given in Vanacker 1983. Elemental analyses done on the Tegdaoust ingots were published in Vanacker 1983. The results are graphically expressed in Garenne-Marot and Mille 2005, 91, fig. 4.
36   Vanacker 1983; Garenne-Marot *et al.* 1994; Garenne-Marot and Mille 2005.
37   Vanacker 1983, 100.
38   Garenne-Marot *et al.* 1994
39   Al-Bakri, cited in Levtzion and Hopkins 2000, 81, ref. manuscript 176.
40   Al-Bakri cited in Levtzion and Hopkins 2000, 73, ref. manuscript 168.
41   Vanacker 1979 and 1983.
42   See results and tables in Garenne-Marot and Mille 2005.
43   Webb 1982, 457.
44   Al-Bakri, cited in Levtzion and Hopkins 2000, 81, ref. manuscript 176.
45   *Idem*, 68, ref. manuscript 158.
46   Bates 1981; Launois and Devisse 1983.
47   Rosenberger 1964 et 1970.
48   Johnson 1970; Hogendorn and Gemery 1988, 128.
49   Ibn Battuta cited by Levtzion and Hopkins 2000, 281, ref. manuscript 122.7.
50   Devisse 1972 and 1990.
51   Al-Idrissi, cited in Levtzion and Hopkins 2000, 118, ref. manuscript N108.
52   Berthier 1997.
53   Al-'Umari, cited in Levtzion and Hopkins 2000, 262, ref. manuscript 26b.
54   Al-'Umari, in Levtzion and Hopkins 2000, 272, ref. manuscript B 67, 36a.
55   Webb 1982, 462.

Money, Cloth-Currency, Monopoly, and Slave Trade in the Rivers of Guiné and the Cape Verde Islands, 1755–1777

Carlos F. Liberato

Introduction

Historical research has yet to do justice to the role of cloth-currency within the mechanisms of the Atlantic slave trade and corresponding power struggles among its principal protagonists, the local and colonial powers of West Africa. This chapter shows that the monopoly exercised by the Grão Pará and Maranhão Company over the production and trade of cloth strips in the Cape Verde Islands was one of the most important factors in preserving Portugal's position in the region known as the Rivers of Guiné[1] throughout the second half of the 18th century. To do this, it explores commodity-currencies and the company's activity related to the Atlantic slave trade, the use of slave labor in Cape Verdean plantations, and the relation between cloth-strip production and trade.

In the geography of pre-colonial currencies in West Africa, Senegambia was the heart of a cloth-currency territory. The use of cloth strips as money was well established by the 16th century and the use of cloth as money was still expanding in the 18th century. It is also clear that many other commodity currencies were in use alongside cloth: cattle were a standard of value in the north of this zone; dates were sometimes used in the Sahara; measures of millet were common in the Sahel, and bars of salt were used at certain times in the interior. As discussed in this chapter, much of the cloth currency was made locally in Senegambia, and increasingly also in the Cape Verde Islands. Locally-made cloth used as money was called *pagne* in Senegalese French, country cloth in Gambian English, *soro* in Pulaar, *tama* in Soninke, and *panos* in Portuguese. This cloth money was the dominant currency along the upper Guinea coast when the Portuguese first arrived, and it had spread eastward along the sahel and throughout much of the region of Mandinka and Fulbe culture. When *soro* was first used in the Fuuta Jallon highlands is not known, but the Fulbe made it the dominant currency there in the 18th century. Cloth currency had spread to the coastal zone well before the 18th century and was even produced in the Cape Verde Islands by the 16th century.[2]

Information on cotton cultivation in the Cape Verde Islands demonstrates that the use of cloth strips as money on the upper Guinea coast was well established by the late 15th century. Indeed the growth of a local industry to produce cloth strips in the Cape Verde Islands was closely associated with Portuguese trade on the upper Guinea coast and the Rivers of Guiné, it also competed with locally produced cloth for use as a currency. By the early 18th century, however, French merchants had introduced a standard piece of Indian cloth from Pondichéry, usually referred to by French authors as a *piéce de Guinée* or simply *guinée*, which competed with locally produced cloth and cloth strips produced in Cape Verde. The spread of the Pondichéry *guinée* as a monetary unit actually represented the substitution of an imported cloth for locally produced cloth, although never replacing local production. Hence the wide-spread adoption of Pondichéry cloth strips in the 18th century was an innovation that earlier had been achieved with the introduction of *panos* from the Cape Verde Islands. As the activities of the Grão Pará and Maranhão Company in the 18th century demonstrate, Cape Verde Islands *panos* continued to supply strips of cloth for use as money on the mainland well into the late 18th century.

The required skill for textile production was brought to the Cape Verde archipelago by slaves transported from Senegambia to work on the plantations and in port cities. This process is vividly depicted by Christopher Fyfe:

> Some of the slaves were weavers by profession, and wove the cotton into country cloths as they had done on the mainland. New elaborate patterns of North African type were introduced, and from the middle of the 16th century Cape Verde *panos* were regularly exported to Guiné to be exchanged for slaves. As elsewhere in West Africa, European traders were forced to adopt African methods of accounting, and *panos* became recognized as units of account, just as bars and cowries were in other regions.[3]

In the Cape Verde Islands and the Rivers of Guiné region four or more cloth strips sewed together were generally called a *pano*. In Cape Verde a variant of *pano*, called *barafula* or *berafula*, became the standard currency on the islands and in the Portuguese trading zone of the West African coast.[4] From about 1510 to the first half of the 19th century cotton cloth constituted a privileged medium of exchange for the acquisition of slaves by Portuguese and Cape Verdean, as well as other European slave traders, in Guiné. The Portuguese obtained their supplies from two regions, the Cape Verde Islands and some areas of the coast, especially the region known as the Rivers of Guiné, or simply Guiné. For the period of existence of the Grão Pará and Maranhão Company (1755–1777), it is possible to give concrete indications as to amounts and destinations for the *panos* manufactured in the Cape Verde Islands. Few such statistics exist for the ones produced by local weavers in Guiné, though it is known that they had similar patterns to those from Cape Verde. In both cases the company used cloth-currency to buy slaves and other local goods, to pay taxes to local authorities and to pay its representatives, soldiers, and workers. Nevertheless, amounts and prices of the *panos* acquired by the company in Guiné are largely unknown. The agents of the company in Cacheu and in Bissau obtained *panos* in exchange for European money and, more commonly, for imported goods. The *panos* were then shipped to areas of higher demand and exchanged for slaves and other goods. It is possible to demonstrate this use of *panos* as money, similar to the use of other commodity-currencies.

Commodities as money during the era of the Atlantic slave trade

Before anything else it would seem to be propitious to present a definition of money and how to interpret the use of different media of exchange, other than metal coins, within the African context. This study adopts Marion Johnson's definition, as presented in her examination of various currencies in African history:

> Money is essentially what can be used to buy things; unlike payment in kind, payment in money involves the expectation that the recipient will probably use the money for further payments, rather than consuming it himself. So the first requirement of anything to be used as money is general acceptability.[5]

Sometimes this acceptability can come from a convention supported by state authentication (silver, gold, coin, cowries) or by external market demand (gold dust). In other cases, such as cloth, acceptability can 'derive from the usefulness of the currency itself, so that the recipient knows that someone will always be wanting it'.[6] Other characteristics of money are its capacity of subdivision or to form part of a system of related units. It also may be used to reckon prices and to act as a 'store of value'.[7]

Recent decades have witnessed increasing interest in historical research related to money in Africa.[8] Correspondingly, historians working specifically with the Atlantic slave trade have examined currency mechanics and terms of purchases, as well as what Africans received in return for slaves and other exports. Stanley B. Alpern has shown that European input is important for the reconstruction of the material culture of Africa during the era of the Atlantic slave trade.[9] He combats two myths of recent African historiography about the Atlantic slave trade. The first of these myths proclaims that Africa received nothing that had not been produced by well-developed local industries, while the second, nicknamed the 'new gewgaw myth' by Philip Curtin, claims that Africa only received from Europe defective arms, cheap trinkets, poor quality alcohol, and useless luxury articles.[10]

Alpern's viewpoint is quite different; for him what dominated the Atlantic slave trade from beginning to end was African importation of 'practical cloth' and 'metal goods'. By working from an impressive number of sources Alpern has compiled a partial list of commodities that were used as money and exchanged for African slaves and products. The list includes cloth (Indian, European, Turkish, other African regions, etc.); clothing (kerchiefs, hats, caps, etc.); other clothing products (bedclothes, table linens, carpets and rugs, etc.); un-worked or semi-processed metal (iron bars, copper or brass bracelets, copper rods, lead, tin, gold, and silver); metal containers (basins, pots, kettles, cauldrons, dishes, plates, tankards, bowls, cups, jugs, buckets); other metal-ware (knifes, cutlasses, swords, razors, scissors, pins, needles, thimbles, fishhooks, bells, locks, keys, tools, nails, weights, trumpets, etc.); firearms (guns, muskets, pistols, cannons, gunpowder, lead balls, shots, and gun flints); beads (glass, crystal, pearls, semiprecious stones), coral, and cowries; alcohol (brandy, rum, gin, wine, beer, etc.); tobacco (rolls of *Nicotiana tabacum* and smoking pipes); glassware (mirrors, drinking glasses, etc.); ceramics (European, Chinese, and American earthenware vessels); paper; seasoning (salt, sugar, garlic); exotic foods (preserves, butter, cheese, candied fruits, salt beef or pork, etc.); drugs (tea, coffee, chocolate, sarsaparilla, etc.); non-metal containers (chests or trunks, goods containers, barrels, bags, sacks, etc.); and pompous trappings (satin robes, silk mantles, gold-trimmed hats, embroidered uniforms, European flags, umbrellas, silver-headed canes, silver tobacco pipes,

watches and clocks, music boxes, silverware).[11] This long list demonstrates that almost any commodity could be used as money.

On a theoretical level, this list establishes the relative importance of a variety of commodity-currencies, among which European weapons are cited, in the Atlantic slave trade. For years numerous historians concentrated their efforts on describing the process by which Africans used European arms to procure captives who were traded in order to obtain more European weaponry for further slave raiding or self-protection against slave raiders, calling it the 'gun-slave cycle'.[12] However, in recent years well-documented studies have demonstrated that guns were indeed important, but not enough to overshadow the impact of other imported goods.[13] The same seems to apply to the dynamics of the slave trade in the Rivers of Guiné, where the significance of weaponry should also be put into a wider context, as the many firearms received in exchange for slaves were often melted down to make farm implements and tools.

Walter Hawthorne, in his solid analysis of how small-scale and decentralized societies located in Guiné were transformed under the impact of the slave trade, stresses the importance of European guns as a source of iron for both agriculture and warfare:

> the need to obtain European weapons for defensive purposes may not have compelled Africans to conduct slave raids, but the need to obtain iron from which to forge practical defensive or offensive weapons – as well as cutting edges for digging tools – did compel 'coastal' Africans in Guinea-Bissau to produce and market captives.[14]

Thus European guns were imported, in many cases, for their metallic content and used more as a source of iron than as effective weapons in warfare. To a certain degree this situation is similar to the use of other commodity-currencies of the Atlantic slave trade, such as iron bars, copper or brass bracelets, and copper rods. The present study contributes to this debate by reviewing available documentation on the production and commercialization of cloth strips in the Cape Verde Islands, and by presenting *panos* as one of the most important commodity-currencies utilized by Portuguese and Cape Verdean traders for the obtaining of slaves in the Rivers of Guiné during the second half of the 18th century.

Cloth strips as money in West Africa, Cape Verde, and the Rivers of Guiné

There is no consensus about when cotton, the loom, and the techniques of weaving were introduced into sub-Saharan Africa, although cotton textile production was well established before the trans-Atlantic slave trade.[15] The most commonly accepted idea is that cotton seeds and weaving techniques came from the Mediterranean world. If it occurred through trans-Saharan routes in the times of Carthage or, more recently, through Muslim traders, is a matter of controversy. Yet one point seems to be clear: Muslims spread the use of cotton clothing south of the Sahara.[16] As Charles Monteil demonstrated, cotton textiles were common in sub-Saharan courts of the 11th and 12th centuries.[17] The introduction of the loom in the African sub-continent is still partial and incomplete, but evidence suggests that looms arrived through trans-Saharan routes.[18]

In the 1970s Marion Johnson opened a wide spectrum of possibilities for the history of commodity-currency in Africa, especially in her discussion about measures of cotton cloth as money and their competitiveness with respect to imported textiles during the colonial period.[19] In more general terms, Marion Johnson noted that

> Cloth has been used in Africa for most of the purposes it serves in other parts of the world – for clothing and headwear; for wrappers to carry the baby; for bedding, carpets and rugs and curtains; for bags and sacks of all sizes; for tents and sails; and for a variety of ritual, ceremonial and decorative purposes. In addition it was widely used as money.[20]

More recently, Colleen Kriger published a comprehensive study of the changes that occurred in the production of textiles in West Africa, showing that foreign competition occurred much earlier than previously assumed and certainly before the 20th century.[21] By studying particular groups of artisans during the eras of Muslim and Atlantic trading, she has shown how the importation of textiles from India and Europe affected craftsmanship in West Africa. As Kriger notes,

> along the way, technologies were transferred to new locales, centers of manufacture arose and declined, specific textile products were imitated or revised, and prices were affected by a variety of production and transport costs.[22]

Her observations may be applied to the Cape Verdean cotton cloth industry during the era of the Atlantic slave trade.

Despite these important contributions there are still few references to the use of cloth as money for the Cape Verde Islands and Guiné.[23] The extensive catalogue of the Berlin Museum's textile collections, edited by Brigitte Menzel, includes some fabrics from Guine Bissau, but there is no mention of textiles used as money.[24] Along the same line Rénée Boser-Sarivaxévanis published a classification of West African textiles according to history and techniques, containing examples from Portuguese Guinea; although at times she mentions that cloth was used as money, she does not include an analysis of the fact.[25] Similarly, Venice Lamb surveyed West African weaving processes, paying special attention to their artistic value and offering a particularly interesting historical survey, but she does not study the use of cloth as money.[26]

A noteworthy exception is António Carreira, who has dealt specifically with the *panos da terra* manufactured in Guiné and Cape Verde.[27] Carreira has stressed the important role these textiles played in this region's trade.[28] For more than three centuries the *panos* were the principal medium of exchange for the acquisition of slaves in Guiné and they were an essential part of almost all transactions. This chapter recognizes Carreira as the main expert on this subject and seeks to enhance and further his work, particularly as it relates to the use of cloth strips as money by the Grão Pará and Maranhão Company.

Despite the difference in the nomenclature and past and present variations in the *panos*, António Carreira has presented a well documented study of cloth production in Cape Verde and Guiné based on surviving data and examples. Carreira describes the *panos* used by the peoples of Guiné as being

> composed of strips, cotton bands of woven threads [called *bandas*] in widths that vary from 7 to 21 cm. The bands are in number of four to thirteen – in some areas even more – sewn together lengthwise, thus forming a whole to be used as a garment, as

protection for the body, as a funeral shroud, and to transport small children on one's back.[29]

Depending on the type of fibre, artistic value and the work needed to weave the bands, a *pano* could fall into one of two broad categories: *panos simples* or *singelos* (that is, ordinary cloth) and *panos d'obra* (that is, cloth involving much work). The *panos simples* were considered to be

> the ones formed by a number of off-white (natural color of the fabric) bands or those simply dyed with a single color, as well as the ones formed by bands woven with limited and simple linear adornments that do not demand much specialized weaving technique.[30]

In the 18th century, this category of *panos* was called *barafula* or *berefula*, *cates* or *ascates, bantans, xereos*, and *sabos*, or generically *panos da terra* (country cloths). On the basis of their artistic and commercial values, these *panos* were sold at different prices.[31]

The *panos d'obra* had more complex patterns that were defined by Carreira as being

> the ones formed by bands whose weaving involved complex loom creations (defined vaguely as ornaments in relief, brocade techniques or floating - for lack of a more appropriate or expressive technical term), alternately using black and white cotton threads or multicolored fibers of cotton and silk, forming geometric designs, objects, houses, churches, boats, insects, symbols like Christ's cross, stars of various points, rose-like ornaments and others.[32]

In this category there were four types: *bixo* simples; *bicho cortado*; *boca branca*; and *pano de vestir* (cloth for clothing), *oxós* or *oxó*.[33]

In a more generic classification, based on complexity and the quality of the yarn, the *panos* manufactured in the Cape Verde Islands could be divided into three broad categories: *grossos* (rough), *ricos* (intricate), and *tecido fino* (delicate) fabric. The *panos* made of wider bands (approximately 35cm) belonged to another category because of their practical use. Their main purpose was to protect against the cold, serving as a wrap or bed clothing. This kind of *panos* can be divided into three types: *colcha* (bed covering), *manta de lã* (woolen covering), and *manta de retalhos* or *manta de farrapos* (patchwork quilt).[34] While the *colcha* (bed covering) was entirely made of cotton fibers, the warp of the *manta de lã* (woolen covering) was made of wool with the weft made of cotton.[35] Used as bedding, the *manta de retalhos* (patchwork quilt) was made of the remnants of local and imported fabrics.[36]

In the Rivers of Guiné, the value of cloth surpassed the level of practical and immediate consumption, serving as a medium of exchange, as well as a display of wealth and superiority in life and death. The *panos* served as garments for men as well as women, probably more for the latter than for the former. *Panos* were also commonly used at funerals, as a shroud for the corpse. Sometimes the deceased went to his or her grave wrapped in *panos* the number of which could range from 12 to 100. It depended on the wealth of the departed's family, or better, on social rank. For respected elders, powerful authorities or religious figures, funerals required many more *panos* than the ones used to wrap other people.[37] The use of *panos* visually expressed the differences between the members of the various social levels that stratified the African population.[38]

Not only were *panos* used to buy slaves, but Portuguese

officials also used the cloth to pay soldiers and workers. In Guiné, weavers and their families manufactured fabrics made of local cotton and using local dyes.³⁹ On the cotton plantations of Cape Verde, from the end of the 16th century on, slave weavers worked under the supervision of their masters. The production from both areas was distributed among the Portuguese trading posts on the West African coast. The *panos* were the distinctive commodity used as money by Portuguese and Cape Verdean traders in the slave trade of the region. During the existence of the Grão Pará and Maranhão Company, difficulties related to measurement and the subdivision of pieces of cloth made civil and military authorities working in Portuguese trading posts oppose the official use of cloth as currency.⁴⁰ However, they were unable to convince the Portuguese government that some other form of colonial money should be introduced for the sake of commercial enterprise and for better control over the payments to troops and workers stationed in Guiné and Cape Verde.⁴¹ Despite sporadic attempts to create a Cape Verdean currency, also valid in Guiné, it was only in 1864 that in Portuguese overseas territories a provincial currency was introduced with the creation of the Banco Nacional Ultramarino.⁴²

The Cape Verdean *panos*: history, characteristics, and craft

When the first Portuguese arrived on the West African coast, its peoples were already cultivating cotton and using it to weave cloth. The oldest European sources that allude to weaving practices are probably the two narratives of Alvise Cadamosto, who visited the region in 1455 and 1456. He reported the existence of extensive cotton cultivation and weaving among peoples living in the region between the north side of the Senegal River and the Gambia River, notably the Wolof, Serer, and Mandinka.⁴³

A half century later, Duarte Pacheco Pereira found that most people did not wear cotton clothing. They mostly used animal skins, while the use of cotton was restricted to nobles and wealthy people.⁴⁴ In his description of the Senegambian coast between 1506 and 1510, Valentim Fernandes noticed that Wolof nobles wore good cotton clothing brought to their country overland by Muslims and by sea by European traders. He also reported the harvesting of cotton on the Cape Verdean island of Santiago, but he did not mention any kind of cotton weaving on the islands.⁴⁵

The first Portuguese settlers arrived on the uninhabited Cape Verde archipelago during the 1460s. From then on settlers gradually developed commercial, social, and cultural ties with the *lançados*⁴⁶ and with the African societies of Senegambia and the upper Guinea coast. Afterwards, European (mainly Portuguese, Italian, and Spanish) and local-born traders based on the archipelago conducted an increasing proportion of the Portuguese commerce with West Africa, from Senegal to the Gulf of Guinea. The islands of Santiago and Fogo seem to have had sufficient rainfall to support plantation agriculture. In consequence, slaves were brought to cultivate cotton, sugar, and indigo. Slaves were also introduced to herd livestock, where rocky terrain or meager rainfall ruled out the cultivation of commercial staples. During the 16th century, Cape Verde-born Portuguese and, increasingly, Cape Verde-born Luso-Africans became more numerous than peninsular Portuguese who were living as *lançados* in Guiné. These individuals

acquired immunity or resistance to endemic diseases in West Africa, such as malaria, dysentery, and others. Another advantage was fluency in Kriol, the language of the islands, and which, together with Mandinka, enabled commerce with Senegambia and the upper Guinea coast. During the 16th century the principal commodities exported from the islands included salt, horses, tobacco, alcohol, and other agricultural products. Most of the commerce conducted by these Cape Verdean traders was illegal.⁴⁷

Parallel to the increase in the population of the Cape Verde archipelago during the first half of the 16th century, the Portuguese crown issued a series of regulations seeking to boost cultivation of cotton and cereals, breeding cattle, and the colonization of new lands. In this period, production of cotton developed on the islands of Santiago and Fogo, cultivated by slaves and mostly sold for export.⁴⁸ For the most part, the Cape Verdean cotton production was exported in raw form to Europe and the African coast.⁴⁹ During the initial years of colonization, it seems that Cape Verdean cotton was exported to Guiné, where it was exchanged for *panos* produced locally by African peoples. Based on Portuguese sailors' oral narratives, Valentim Fernandes published a description of the Portuguese trade on the West African coast between 1506 and 1508. In this description, it is possible to read that on the West African coast people preferred the 'red cloth from Alentejo, the cotton that had been transported from the Cape Verde Islands, and horses each one of which could buy seven blacks'.⁵⁰ Fernandes's description gives details about transactions on the Cacheu and the Casamance rivers, to which 'ships came from Cape Verde to trade their cotton for *panos*, as there are Christian dwellers here, like in *Casa Mansa*'.⁵¹

Although there is no concrete evidence of weaving activity throughout the first half of the 16th century in the two most populated Cape Verdean islands, Santiago and Fogo, the existence of a developed cotton industry in Guiné is well established. Mandinka, Balanta, Brame, Banhun, Felupe, and other peoples produced undyed and dyed cotton fabrics, which were sold in markets throughout the region. On the Cacheu River (then called São Domingos), Portuguese and Cape Verdean traders acquired large quantities of cloth in exchange for European goods and indigo produced along the southern Nuno River. On 26 January 1582, Francisco de Andrade reported that the main production along the Nuno River was of bricks of indigo. These indigo bricks were sold to neighboring peoples, who used them to dye cotton fibers and create elaborate patterns. He is probably one of the first Europeans to report on the monetary importance of *panos* in regional trade:

> nothing is traded [along the Nuno River] other than loaves of dye, like sweet bread, that are then loaded on ships that go to the São Domingos River [Cacheu], to be used by the Negroes to color their cloth black so it [the dyed cloth] can be used as money all along the other Rivers of Guiné.⁵²

By the end of the 16th century, the island of Santiago was producing cotton cloth fashioned according to African patterns and techniques. The sale of *panos* in Guiné increased as a result of the intensification of European trade. Moreover, the importance of Islam in the hinterland also favored the sale of cloth because of the emphasis on clothing in Muslim society. In the Portuguese ports and trading posts European, Muslim, and Creole populations disseminated the taste for cotton clothing among local peoples. Although Portuguese accounts report little about commerce by Cape Verdeans on the West African coast, because of the need to protect trading secrets, it is clear from Dutch accounts around the turn of the 17th century that Portuguese commercial activities in the region relied on Cape Verdean cloth as an important element in their trade. In 1623 the Dutch shipmaster Dierich Ruiters described how Cape Verdeans developed a prosperous business 'out of nothing':

> The trade we called 'coastal' is mostly undertaken in small ships, *pinnaces* and launches, by Portuguese who live on Santiago Island. First they load these with salt, which they conveniently obtain for nothing on the islands of Maio and Sal (Cape Verde Islands) and they sail to Serra-Lioa with the salt and trade it for gold, ivory and kola. Then from Serra-Lioa they sail again to Joala and Porto d'Ale (in Senegal), where they trade a portion of the kola for cotton cloths. They also sometimes trade ivory obtained in Serra-Lioa for Cape Verde cloths [so called because many are made at Cape Verde]. From there they sail again east to Cacheo where they trade the rest of their kola and their remaining goods for slaves. They acquire fifty to sixty slaves in exchange for the goods they have obtained by trade along the coast, and each slave is worth 150 *reals* to them, or pieces-of-eight. So they make 9,000-10,000 *reals* out of nothing, in a matter of speaking.[53]

However, above all other merchandise, the *panos* were the most important item in the bundle of merchandise used as money by Portuguese and Cape Verdean traders to acquire slaves in West Africa. By putting a cotton industry in place on the archipelago of Cape Verde the Portuguese spurred growth of the local economy and aided the expansion of trade in Guiné, as reflected in the coastal trading activity and particularly in the transport of kola nuts, a local stimulant, from Sierra Leone to Cacheo.[54] On occasion, European ship captains who did not have Cape Verdean *panos* could not buy slaves in Guiné. Cape Verdean predominance in the slave trade reached its apex in the last decades of the 16th century and remained an important factor in coastal trade, being challenged only in the second half of the 17th century.[55] The Cape Verdean *panos* acquired transaction value due to their good quality and innovative patterns that allowed the cloth to be used for purposes other than as money. Portuguese accounts referred constantly to the superiority of Cape Verdean fabrics in relation to other imported goods in the region.[56] At various times, once before 1687 and again in 1700, the Portuguese crown issued laws and regulations prohibiting the sale of Cape Verdean *panos* to foreign ships. The offenders were to suffer capital punishment, though not even that impeded many impoverished islanders from taking the risks and trading extensively with Dutch, British, and French captains.[57]

John Picton suggests that the most important criteria in evaluating fabric included the type of loom used to produce it, its weave structure, the raw material of the cloth, and the characteristic configurations of its pattern.[58] According to Philip Curtin's description, it seems that looms and individual work processes in Cape Verde were similar to those in the Senegambia region. Within Senegambia, the techniques of weaving differed little and only the horizontal, narrow-band, treadle loom was used. The weaver used to sit 'under shelter or in the open shade, with one end of the warp fastened to a weight which was gradually pulled closer as the weaving progressed'.[59] The difference in Cape Verde was that most of the stages of the weaving were done by slaves that worked side-by-side with other slave weavers.

António Carreira established that cotton in Guiné was commonly grown on small tracts of land by women, children, and slaves of the family.[60] Generally the fields were located in the backyards or in the areas next to the family compound, called *morança* in Kriol. Cotton debris and other household scraps were thrown onto these lands to fertilize the soil in order to obtain better production. Women, aided by their children or slaves, were responsible for plowing, sowing, weeding, and harvesting the family's cotton fields. In much more recent times, in the areas where the cotton was destined for trade, the preparation of the soil, cultivation, and harvesting fell to the men, sometimes aided by their relatives. The activities around ginning, carding, and spinning were also considered women's obligations. Once the thread was put onto reels, the women delivered them to the weaver. The weaver would then manufacture the cloth strips that were later divided into two equal parts. Half of the bands belonged to the weaver, and the other half to the woman or women that supplied the thread. Weaving appears to have always been done by men in the Rivers of Guiné. With the intensification of the slave trade it gradually became more and more the occupation of slaves, of slaves' descendants or, more recently, of freedmen.[61]

In general, it can be said that Carreira's description of the stages of production of the *panos* in Guiné is also valid for Cape Verde. However, in the latter case, small domestic production on the plantations was substituted by production on a larger scale, conducted by slaves. And all the output was appropriated by the slave owners.

In the Cape Verde Islands the making of *panos* was traditionally a domestic activity in almost all the homes of the rural areas and even in the backyards of the elegant residences in the villages and towns. Cloth served as garments for the free and slave populations, and was sold or used as money to buy food and other staples. Some planters possessed dozens of looms and many slave weavers that worked side-by-side under the supervision of their masters. On the larger plantations cloth production assumed a much more entrepreneurial character. There, *panos* were produced in great quantity for local use and much more so for the slave trade on the West African coast.[62] However, this production and relative trading freedom would drastically change after the creation of the Grão Pará and Maranhão Company.

Panos within Portuguese monopolistic trade practices in Cape Verde and Guiné, 1755–77

The Grão Pará and Maranhão Company was founded in June of 1755 with the intention of reorganizing the trade between Portugal, West Africa, and Portuguese Amazonia, then called the State of Grão Pará and Maranhão.[63] When the company was created the development of Portuguese Amazonia with slave labour was the ultimate goal of the Portuguese authorities and traders that were involved in its foundation.[64] José I, King of Portugal, himself acquired a good amount of the company's shares. He, along with friends and partners, reaped steady profits for more than 20 years until the Grão Pará and Maranhão Company was dismantled in 1777, after the King's death. Sponsored by the Marquis of Pombal,[65] the enlightened prime minister of Portugal, the company unsuccessfully attempted to impose monopolistic trade practices over an extensive part of the African coast from Senegal to Angola. In addition, the crown granted to the company fiscal, political, and military powers. The company could then collect taxes and appoint civil servants and military officials to Portuguese trading posts in Guiné and Cape Verde. In exchange for these prerogatives, the company would be responsible for the payment of the personnel and had to fortify Portuguese trading posts. However, in reality, the presence of the company in Africa did not weight heavily except within the Rivers of Guiné, especially in the ports of Bissau and Cacheu.[66]

In Guiné, with variable grades of success, the company tried to achieve three main goals. First, the company was able to impede the activity of ship owners in the service of Brazilian traders and planters that were directly obtaining slaves from the region, evading legal contracts formerly allocated by the Portuguese crown to metropolitan traders.[67] Second, it tried unsuccessfully to grant its monopoly over the whole trade in the region, where English and French traders disregarded alleged Portuguese rights over its trade. Finally, the company attempted, but was also unable, to impose Portuguese control over international trade practiced by the peoples that lived next to its trading posts in Bissau and Cacheu. The last two goals were interconnected, since neither English nor French ships stopped trading directly with the peoples of Guiné, nor did the latter discontinue trading with foreign vessels.[68]

Because panos produced in the Cape Verde Islands were highly valued in Guiné when dealing for slaves, the Portuguese crown granted a monopoly over the commercialization of panos in the archipelago. Its agents also imposed financial terms that gave the company a virtual monopoly over the purchase of panos on the islands. Both small and large producers had to deliver to the company's warehouses all or a significant percentage of their panos to satisfy debts and tax collection.[69]

The means that allowed the company to obtain most of the Cape Verdean cloth production included three parallel or concomitant processes. Firstly, the company would make contracts with families that owned looms and slave weavers, the company advancing the cotton thread, the dyestuffs and other necessary implements. Sometimes it even provided foodstuffs to sustain the whole household for a certain time period. The return payment was compulsorily effected in cloth, at the ordinary price or at the price agreed upon at the moment the contract had been negotiated. Secondly, the company would acquire panos from wealthy land owners, who usually possessed a great number of looms and slave weavers. Finally, the company would receive cloth as payment for taxes, rent, tithes and other duties, and sometimes for the repayment of company loans or other debts at fixed prices that were imposed on the general population or on small merchants. These arrangements were already common practices among the population, even before the company adopted them. The cloth was normally bought at a 'small' price. Later, the company would profit by re-selling it for a higher price at local or regional markets, especially along the West African coast.[70] The low buying price paid by the company in the islands was the result of its own unfair trading policies when dealing with locals and, above all, of its 'not altering the custom of the country'.[71]

Thus, buying panos cheaply in Cape Verde and selling them at the market price in Guiné, the company was able to furnish for its representatives in Guiné thousands of low-cost panos. In this way the company succeeded in competing with its English and French rivals that also disputed commercial supremacy in the Rivers of Guiné. Considering that the panos produced in Cape Verde were the highest valued articles for slave trade in the region, and in most cases actually necessary for the closing of any business deal in the slave markets of Guiné, the company held a clear advantage in relation to its foreign competitors. However, it is necessary to say that English and French competition did not disappear before the second half of the 19th century.[72] This study seeks only to suggest that, by virtually monopolizing both production and commercialization of the Cape Verdean panos, the Grão Pará and Maranhão Company assured Portugal's leading position in trade in the Rivers of Guiné throughout the second half of the 18th century, not being driven out of the region by the more powerful French and English rivals, as had occurred in Senegal, Gambia, and Sierra Leone.

Throughout the period of its existence (1755–77) the Portuguese Grão Pará and Maranhão Company had to adapt its business to the employment of different kinds of currency and goods used as money for trade transactions already in practice in the Rivers of Guiné and the Cape Verde Islands. In attempting to solidify profits and exercise its monopoly, besides cloth strips the company had to deal with several metropolitan and colonial currencies from a number of European countries, gold and silver colonial coins from the Americas, iron and copper bars, firearms and gunpowder, alcohol, beads, and many other commodities from Africa, Asia, Europe, and the Americas, all of which were used to buy slaves in West Africa.

Nevertheless, most scholars who have studied the economic development of the relations between Portuguese and Africans on the West African coast are unanimous in saying that, in relation to the prices of a number of European goods, there were relatively stable prices in the markets of the region and that there was a nominal value for each item. Their nominal value suffered slow, little or no variation throughout the years. In the case of cloth units in Senegambia, Philip D. Curtin states that

> wherever these different currencies met, they were usually integrated by a recognized exchange rate or equivalence, but these rates of exchange were not true market prices. They were, rather, part of a more complex set of equivalents that began with the cloth itself, taking fractional parts of the whole cloth as fractional units of currency.[73]

In a detailed account of Portuguese trade in Guiné during the 1760s and 70s Bernardino António Álvares de Andrade stated that in Bissau a banda, or strip of ordinary cloth, had the nominal value of 100 réis.[74] It was possible to buy a cow weighing approximately 240kg for the nominal price of 4$000 réis, putting together the following goods: a flask of aguardente (alcohol made from sugar cane), a flask of gunpowder and a bundle of beads.[75] Between Bissau and Geba, there was a significant difference in the nominal value of imported goods. This difference becomes even more important if we take into consideration the nominal prices of the same goods in Lisbon. In Geba, in exchange for an iron bar with the nominal value of 6$000 réis, it was possible to buy 24 sheep.[76] More important yet, the nominal price for a slave was established based on the following terms:

Goods and nominal prices of a slave in Geba – hinterland of Bissau, 1770s

Quantity	Goods	Lisbon (réis)	Bissau (réis)	Geba (réis)
1	Ordinary gun	1$200	4$000	8$000
2	Pieces of ordinary cloth	1$000	3$000	8$000
2	Bars of iron	2$400	4$000	8$000
12	Flasks of aguardente*	3$600	12$000	24$000
1	Barrel of gunpowder**	5$760	15$000	30$000
2	Bundles of beads	400	2$000	4$000
100	Flints	300	1$000	1$500
100	Bullets	300	1$000	1$500
2	Panos of Cape Verde	3$000	4$000	8$000
1	Ordinary hat	200	2$000	4$000
1	Bottle of aguardente***	220	500	1$000
	Total	18$380	48$500	98$000
	Difference		+30$120	+79$620
	Profit		163.8%	433.2%

Source: Andrade 1952; 66.
* Alcohol made from sugar cane, commonly known in the Portuguese world as *aguardente* (Portugal), *cachaça* (Brazil) or *gerebita* (Angola).
** In the original, '1 Frasqueira de agua ardente de 12 frascos de 5 quartilhos cada hum'.
*** Probably a bottle of 1 litre.

With this intricate colonial math goods that in Lisbon[77] had a nominal value of 18$380 *réis* could buy a slave in Geba for the nominal value of 98$000 *réis*, while in Bissau the same slave would have a nominal value of 48$500 *réis*. However, contingencies such as bargaining between the parties, implications of a bad harvest, sickness or defect could change the customary ideal equivalent measures or quantities of goods needed to buy a slave. Andrade is clear when he addresses this subject:

> The slaves bought in the dry backlands ordinarily cost this price [98$000 *réis*]; often, however, a slave might have a much lower price, because of the vendor asking for certain goods, in which case the buyer pays less than a half of the above price. If the slave does not measure four hand spans, or if he has the slightest defect, be it from birth or later acquired, he can be bought in the backlands for no more than 20$000 *réis*.[78]

It is important to recall that all values were only nominal, since transactions conducted in metropolitan currency were rare. In fact, merchandise prices were determined by an amalgam of customs, bargaining, supply and demand. Most African goods held relatively steady prices, but, likewise, the bargaining ability of African, Cape Verdean, and European traders bore heavily on the final composition of prices. Paul E. Lovejoy and David Richardson state that to produce slave-price data for Africa, historians have generally adopted two methods. Firstly, in order to estimate slave prices at initial cost they used data on slaves shipped from along the coast and the value in Europe of goods bartered for them. Secondly, they relied on contemporary reports to produce price data on slaves in Africa.[79]

Since information on the prices for slaves in Guiné are rare the information provided by Andrade[80] is particularly important, especially since he spent more than a decade residing and traveling throughout the region. Citing a letter dated 19 May 1766, he declared that 'the Spanish *pataca* is all over these islands [Cape Verde and Guiné] with the exchange value of 750 réis'.[81] In Portuguese the terms *pataca*, *patacão*, or *peso*, refer to the Spanish silver coin valued at 8 *reals*.[82] In the English world it was known as the Spanish dollar and came to be called the Spanish-American dollar from the 16th century on, following the establishment of colonial mints in Mexico (1535), Peru (1572), and Bolivia (1575). It was also known as the 'piece of eight' and it is a well-studied currency, along with other similar coins, such as the *peso*, the *peso duro*, the Mexican dollar, the United States dollar, and the Maria Theresa thaler. Each had a slightly different silver content, but in Africa, generally speaking, all were accepted as equal.[83]

Based on the exchange rate between the Spanish dollar and the Portuguese *réis* (1/750), according to information provided by Andrade, it is possible to advance a tentative estimate of the average real price of a regular slave in Guiné. By considering that a regular slave was bought in Bissau for 48$500 *réis*, and by dividing this amount by 750, we reach the amount of 64.6 Spanish dollars. This calculation sounds about right and is consistent with the calculations by Paul E. Lovejoy and David Richardson, for whom the real price for slaves on West African coast was 74.8 silver dollars in the period 1783–1787.[84]

During the whole period of operation of the Grão Pará and Maranhão Company, the production of cloth in Guiné and Cape Verde was insufficient to meet the demands of the African market. António Carreira presents the following figures:

Exportation of *panos* from the Cape Verde Islands to the Rivers of Guiné, 1757–1782

Year	Destination			
	Cacheu	Bissau	Sierra Leone	Total
1757	143	/	/	143
1758	1,560	720	169	2,449
1759	1,551	/	/	1,551
1760	4,600	979	/	5,579
1761	695	3,029	/	3,724
1762	1,967	2,610	/	4,577
1763	2,366	750	/	3,116
1764	2,200	1,599	/	3,799
1765	2,536	1,939	/	4,475
1766	4,576	4,311	/	8,887
1767	2,160	2,752	/	4,912
1768	1,975	8,414	/	10,389
1769	4,107	7,231	/	11,338
1770	2,990	6,888	/	9,878
1771	3,862	1,352	/	5,214
1772	4,859	3,234	/	8,093
1773	4,790	4,200	/	8,990
1774	2,606	1,675	/	4,281
1775	6,287	6,472	/	12,759
1776	5,600	4,555	/	10,155
1777	1,889	1,831	/	3,720
1778	1,629	1,590	/	3,219
1779	/	366	/	366
1780	/	1,010	/	1,010
1781	/	203	/	203
1782	/	438	/	438
Total	**64,948**	**68,148**	**169**	**133,265**

Source: António Carreira 1968; 125.

By considering these 26 years, it can be seen that the annual average number of *panos* exported from the Cape Verde Islands was approximately 5,125. However, if we take into account that the year 1757 is the first effective year of operation of the company on the West African coast, and that 1780–82 were the years of the closing sales of its entire business, then during the 22 years of the company's full operation (1757–78) the annual average peaks at about 6,000 *panos*. The high point of exportation was in the years between 1766 and 1776, when about 95,000 *panos* (70% of the total) were shipped to Guiné, with an annual average of 8,635 pieces. The registers of the company record exports of almost the totality of cloth pieces for Bissau and Cacheu. Only 169 were registered as going to Sierra Leone in 1758. This small amount may be explained by the fact that the company did not have representatives in Sierra Leone. Transactions with this area were registered in the account books of the agency in Bissau, reflecting the supplies taken for trade to Sierra Leone, as well as the goods and slaves that were extracted from there. Afterwards, the headquarters of the company in Lisbon listed everything on the books as being transported by the agents at Bissau. Besides a small number of slaves it seems that the company had brought from Sierra Leone not much more than seahorse 'teeth', bricks of glue and indigo, and other such goods, though they represented substantial profits.[85]

As a means for achieving its commercial objectives, in particular its trade in slaves, the company had to increase the manufacturing of cloth in the Cape Verde Islands. When the supply of cloth dwindled there were problems with the acquisition of slaves and staples in Guiné. The company used cloth, gunpowder, muskets, swords, pistols, knives, beads, alcohol,[86] and other commodities to purchase slaves, wax, ivory and other goods produced locally in Guiné. In each region the amount of those goods that conventionally would correspond to the price of a slave, a certain amount of wax, so many ivory tips, etc., was previously established by custom and market value. Unfortunately, it is now difficult to find concrete indications of those amounts.[87]

In terms of types of cloth and their average prices, Carreira presents the following figures for the shipments from Cape Verde:

Exportation of *panos* from Cape Verde to the Rivers of Guiné 1757–1782 (according to type and average price, with totals)

Type/Denomination	Pieces exported	Average price in réis	Total in réis
Ordinário [ordinary]	62,039	1$500	93:058$500
Bicho and Bicho superior	46,985	8$625	405:245$625
Various	8,398	7$000	58:786$000
Agulha	6,257	3$000	18:771$000
Fio de lã and Vermelho	2,047	6$000	12:282$000
Agulha e Vestir	1,719	3$000	5:157$000
Vestir	1,699	3$000	5:097$000
Quadrado	1,436	3$000	4:308$000
Retrós	1,384	12$250	16:954$000
Obra	412	10$600	4:367$200
Preto and Preto superior	238	13$500	3:213$000
Cordão	192	2$000	384$000
Galã or Galam	188	3$000	564$000
Superior	132	13$500	1:782$000
Boca-branca & Boca-preta	85	6$100	518$500
Oxom & Oxom quadrado	13	10$000	130$000
Barafula	12	3$000	36$000
Preto de sorte	10	3$000	30$000
Lambú de retrós	6	6$000	36$000
Lambú	4	3$000	12$000
Colcha	3	3$000	9$000
Cortado de bicho	3	3$000	9$000
Sabalé	2	3$000	6$000
Riscado	1	3$000	3$000
Totals	**133,265**	**/**	**630:758$825**

Source: António Carreira 1968: 127

The above types or denominations obey the orthographic forms adopted by the Grão Pará and Maranhão Company. As it can be seen, the enormous volume of remittances was not limited to the lower-cost cloth. As might be expected, the cloth denominated *ordinário* (or *barafula*), used by the less-wealthy buyer, was the most popular, representing more than 46% of the total number of pieces exported. However, the more expensive ones, called *bicho*, *bicho superior*, *retrós*, and *fio de lã*, were also in great demand, for which reason they appear together, with 50,416 units exported, amounting to more than 33% of the total. These 'fine' fabrics were probably destined for the elders, notables, spiritual leaders, and other elements of the wealthy classes, as garments for their daily life and shrouds for burial, as well as for bridal gifts, and for comfortably securing children to women's backs.

The name of the Cape Verdean island that supplied the cloth did not always appear on the accounting registers of the company. Only occasionally were there clear indications as to the origin of the *panos*. Of the total of 133,265 *panos* that were acquired and exported to Guiné, the accounting books recorded the origin of only 64,681 (48.5% of the total): 19,272 from Santiago, 43,696 from Fogo, and 1,713 from Brava.[88] The total that was produced and exported was surely much higher. Despite all legislation to the contrary, an uncertain yet high number of *panos* was sold by impoverished islanders and smuggled to the African coast by other European ships.

The total value of 630:758$825 *réis*, although obtained without absolute certainty as to the accuracy of the figures, points to the importance of textile manufacturing for the economy of the Cape Verde Islands. It is necessary to pay attention to the fact that cloth prices in Guiné were at least 100% higher than in Cape Verde, which granted large profits to the Grão Pará and Maranhão Company, even taking into account costs with shipping and storage. In the last years of the 18th century the re-sale price of cloth produced in Guiné was at least twice as high as its original price in Cape Verde.[89]

As for numbers of slaves bought by the company in Bissau and Cacheu, António Carreira presents the following figures:

Slaves bought by the company in Bissau and Cacheu, 1756–89

Period	Total of slaves purchased	Total original cost in réis (approx.)	Annual Average of slaves purchased	Average original cost in réis (approx.)
1756–60	2,027	120,961$000	405	59$675
1761–65	4,183	308,959$000	837	73$861
1766–70	5,294	371,336$000	1,059	70$143
1771–75	4,637	329,480$000	927	71$055
1776–78	2,498	177,251$000	833	70$957
1778–89	1,805	119,715$000	164	66$324
Total	**20,444**	**1,427,702$000**		

Source: António Carreira 1988, 112

Of the total number of slaves bought by the company, only 105 were embarked in Cape Verde. At Bissau and Cacheu 1,920 slaves died before embarkation or escaped from the barracoons; a fact that reduced the shipments from both these ports to 18,419 during the whole period.

These last two tables show that there was an important increase in both figures, for *panos* exported from the Cape Verde Islands and for slaves purchased in Bissau and Cacheu. By taking into consideration that cloth from Cape Verde was an essential part of exchange for slaves and that the average price of a slave in Bissau was 48$500 *réis*, it is possible to assume that the cloth exported from Cape Verde during the period, valued at 630:758$825 *réis*, could have bought approximately 13,000 out of the total of 20,444 slaves during the whole period (1757–82). Even taking into account variations in individual slave prices, specific demands for particular fabrics, and the payment of taxes in cloth by the Portuguese to African authorities, the approximation of the number of slaves seems about right. Such credit input should have had a significant impact on the Portuguese slave trade in the Rivers of Guiné, which surely helped Portugal to maintain its position as a colonial power in the region, against English and French interests.

Conclusion

This study has explored some aspects of the use of cloth as money on the West African coast especially during the second half of the 18th century. In examining the activities of the Portuguese Grão Pará and Maranhão Company, it can be seen that cloth played a major role in the slave trade practiced by the Portuguese in Guiné. Cape Verdean cloth was important for the slave trade in Guiné and the company secured a virtual monopoly over its production and commercialization. Therefore, this chapter suggested that, largely financed by Cape Verdean cloth together with monopolistic and fiscal privileges, the company allowed Portugal to assume colonial influence in Guiné during a period when its power was decreasing in other regions of West Africa.

Each one of these aspects has countless implications, for fabrics had not only commercial value but also cultural and social significance for West Africans. In Guiné they were prized possessions as a display of wealth and social prominence. Even poor people tried incessantly to acquire as many pieces of cloth as they could during the course of their lives in order to provide for themselves a decorous burial and to arrive with some 'capital' at the other side of death.

The intensification of the slave trade during the 18th century occasioned ferocious competition among European traders over the coastal and riverside markets of the region. The Portuguese had to develop a series of measures to reinforce and protect their positions in the commerce of West Africa. This was a costly endeavour and the Portuguese crown placed the responsibility in the hands of the Grão Pará and Maranhão Company. In its turn, the company, seeking to solidify profits, cultivated overseas transactions looking to buy cheap goods at points of origin and sell them at a large profit at their destinations.

Under such circumstances, the monopoly granted to the company over the commercialization of *panos* produced in the Cape Verde Islands also gave it virtual control over the production of cloth on the archipelago. The company, empowered by taxation prerogatives, debt collection, and financial dealings, appropriated almost the entire production by local craftsmanship and large-scale manufacturing. Considering that the demand for cloth was increasing in Guiné, it is probable that the *panos* from Cape Verde should be credited with a role of great importance in the permanence of the Portuguese in the region, despite English and French pressure to expel them.

As far as scholarship can determine at this time, there are no records of how many of these *panos* were used by the company to pay taxes to African authorities, to buy slaves and other goods, and to make payment to soldiers and workers in Bissau.

Definitive research on the role of cloth as money in the region of Guiné is still to be written. This survey only found and knocked on some of the doors that will need a stronger hand to open them up to curious eyes. Among the many questions that deserve further examination are: what are the specifics of the migration of looms, slave weavers, and weaving techniques from the West African coast to the Cape Verde Islands; how a traditional household activity turned into an assembly-line production with European traits in the hands of wealthy planters in the Cape Verde Islands; how many pieces of cloth were actually produced in Guiné, and what were their destinations; what amount of cloth was smuggled from Cape Verde by other Europeans; how many slaves were effectively exchanged for cloth in West Africa; what is the level of personal involvement of soldiers and workers in the slave trade at Bissau, and what happened to them when they turned into Papel relatives? It is probable that many of these questions will remain unanswered for years to come, but the search for responses is still imperative for those who are committed to the unveiling of African history.

Acknowledgements
I would like to express my deepest appreciation to the Fundação Calouste Gulbenkian, Lisbon, which generously funded my trip to Portugal, where the idea of this chapter was conceived. I would like to thank Paul Lovejoy and José Curto for reading my early drafts. My gratitude also goes to Janis Jordan who assisted me with translation of the most difficult passages. And, as always, I wish to thank Rita and Ravi Liberato for their loving encouragement at all moments.

Notes

1   The term Guiné or *Guinea* depends on time, space, and authors. For some it refers to the Greater Senegambia, the region in between the Senegal and the Sierra Leone rivers. In Arabic it means the 'Land of the Blacks', while in English documents and texts it is called Gynny and upper Guinea coast, see Hall 2005, 80–82. In this chapter the Portuguese term Guiné was adopted following the example of René Péllissier (1989) in order to avoid confusion with other Guineas (Conakry and Equatorial) and to delimit the region to the area of Portuguese influence, which through renunciations and amputations became today's Guinea-Bissau. The name Portuguese Guinea is also unacceptable because colonial rule in the region only became reality in the 1930s. Therefore, to maintain closer coherence with the sources, the pre-colonial appellatives Guiné and the Rivers of Guiné seem to be more appropriate for the 18th century.
2   Meillassoux 1971b, 185; Curtin 1975, vol.1, 237.
3   Fyfe 1980, 21.
4   Curtin 1975, 237.
5   Johnson 1980, 193.
6   Johnson 1980, 193.
7   Johnson 1980, 193–194.

8   See Gregory 1996; Hogendorn and Gemery 1988; Hogendorn and Johnson 1986; Curtin 1983; Webb Jr. 1982; Lovejoy 1974; and Hopkins 1973.

9   Alpern 1995.

10 Alpern 1995, 5–6.

11 Alpern 1995, 6–32.

12 Inikory 1977; Richards 1980.

13 Curto 2004 showed that for Luanda and its hinterland an extremely close relationship developed between imported intoxicants and slaves exported by thousands to the Atlantic world.

14 Hawthorne 2003, 97.

15 Johnson 1977.

16 Cornevin 1962, I, 294–302, and 1966, II, 216–268.

17 Monteil 1927.

18 Montandon 1934.

19 Johnson 1974.

20 Johnson 1980, 193.

21 Kriger 2006.

22 Kriger 2006, 5.

23 Vogt 1975 is a brilliant exception, but his analysis is restricted to Portugal's cloth trade, mainly between Morocco and the Gulf of Guinea in the period 1480–1540; with just a couple of sentences referring to cloth trade on the Cape Verde Islands and the upper Guinea coast.

24 Menzel 1972–1973, II, images 700–708.

25 Boser-Sarivaxévanis 1972, 51–56.

26 Lamb 1975, 73–102.

27 Carreira 1968.

28 Carreira 1972, 1983a, 1983b, and 1988.

29 Carreira 1968, 83.

30 Carreira 1968, 84.

31 Carreira 1968, 84–95. In this category at least 17 types or denominations were produced in Cape Verde: *barafula* or *berafula*; *cate* or *ascate*; *bantan*; *xereo*; *sabo*; *preto*; *ordinário*; *lista de fora*; *agulha*; *gallam, galão,* or *galã*; *guluzan* or *golosam*; *jugulado*; *else*; *sor*; *dampé*; *sake*; and *lambu* or *bambu*.

32 Carreira 1968, 95.

33 Carreira 1968, 95–97.

34 Carreira 1968, 98–103. The *colcha* (bed covering) was usually made of white or colored cotton threads. Sometimes, silk and wool threads would be incorporated into the fabric, but the most common type used only cotton. These coverings were typically manufactured with white, black, yellow, green, or blue thread. The dimensions of the coverings were approximately 1.96m by 1.50m and they were composed of six bands, each about 25cm wide, and occasionally a fringe of approximately 4cm sewn all around as embellishment. For an extensive survey on dyestuffs in the 18th century see Fairlie 1965.

35 Carreira 1968, 98–99. In terms of dimensions, a woolen covering could vary from 1.90m to 2.25m in length and from 1.05m to 1.75m in width. It might be composed of three to five bands, each with a width ranging from 35cm to 50cm. In natural color, the woolen coverings presented a rough appearance. The wool was not previously softened by any means. The final product depended entirely upon the quality of the fibers provided by the archipelago's sheep herds.

36 Carreira 1968, 99–101. On the Cape Verdean island of Santo Antão, this kind of quilt received the name *clabedatche*. Its dimensions varied from 1.74m to 2.10m in length, and 1.50m in width, being composed of four to five bands, each with a width of 35cm to 50cm.

37 Carreira 1983, 208.

38 For a detailed account on cloth as a basic resource in another context see Martin 1986.

39 For an extensive survey on dyestuffs in the 18th century see Fairlie 1965.

40 Feijó 1797, 20–26 and Pusich 1810, 74–82.

41 As an example of this kind of petition made by Portuguese representatives in Guiné see Andrade 1952, 122.

42 Lereno 1942, 181.

43 Godinho 1956, III, 98–227; Peres 1948, 141–202.

44 Pereira 1954, 97.

45 Fernandes 1951, 12.

46 The term *lançados* refers to Portuguese individuals that, from the 16th century on, established themselves among African communities along the West African coast, adopting African spouses and customs; all despite constant regulations issued by the Portuguese crown against European settlement on the West African coast. The word comes from the Portuguese 'lançar-se,' which in the West African context may be translated as 'casting one's lot' among African societies. See Brooks 1980a.

47 Brooks 1993a and 1993b.

48 Barcelos 1905, III, 122.

49 Pereira 1954, 56.

50 Fernandes 1951, 42. Unless otherwise stated, all translations from the Portuguese were made by the author with the assistance of Janis Jordan.

51 Fernandes 1951, 42.

52 Brásio 1963, II, 10.

53 Translated from Dutch by Hair 1974, 51–52.

54 At this point it is important to make particular reference to the kola nut, for it also was a traditional African commodity that was largely used as money for many centuries and, like the *panos*, is still today highly prized in West Africa. Although other varieties were commercialized, *Cola nitida* nuts were the most appreciated. Red, white, or shades in between, the nuts were chewed and were credited with numerous properties such as medicinal, mouth asepsis and source of energy. Chewing kola nuts was a luxury, but it was also used at naming ceremonies, weddings and other occasions. Wealthy people offered kola to visitors as a sign of hospitality and affluence. Kola was grown only in the Equatorial forest, but it was traded almost everywhere in West Africa. At least from the end of the 16th century on Portuguese and Cape Verdean traders started to ship kola from the Scarcies River (Sierra Leone) north to the Gambia and the Rivers of Guiné, competing with kola brought overland to the coast and obtaining excellent profits. For a detailed account on the kola trade of the upper Guinea coast see Lovejoy 1980, 97–98 and 117–118; and Brooks 1980b.

55 Carreira 1968, 20–21.

56 Coelho 1953.

57 Lereno 1942, 59–63.

58 Picton 1992, 23.

59 Curtin 1975, 214.

60 Carreira 1968, 77–78.

61 Carreira 1968, 78.

62 Carreira 1983, 207.

63 Dias 1970.

64 Instituição 1755.

65 Maxwell 1995; Azevedo 1990; and Serrão 1987.

66 Saraiva 1947; and Santos 1971.

67 Saraiva 1947.

68 Péllissier 1989.

69 Carreira 1983a.

70 Carreira 1983a.

71 Carreira 1983a, 209.

72 Péllissier 1989.

73 Curtin 1975, 238.

74 *Réis* is a common deformation of the plural of 'real', an old Portuguese monetary unit. At least since 1692, the value of a thousand *réis* was represented as 1U000. The symbol U, known as 'delta,' was still being used in Brazil during the 19th century. In Brazil and in Portugal, however, from 1747 on, the $ (money sign) began to be used in the same way as the delta. The conto de *réis* (a million *réis*) was represented by two points, as in 1:000$000. See Fernandes 1856.

75 See Pallaver's chapter in this volume for more on glass beads as currency in East Africa.

76 Andrade 1952, 61–62.

77 For a complete series of prices in Portugal throughout the period see Godinho 1955.

78 Andrade 1952, 65–66.

79 Lovejoy and Richardson 1995, 101.

80 Andrade 1952.

81 Andrade 1952, 120.

82 Fernandes 1856, 12.

83 Gervais 1982; Pond 1941a, 1941b; Curtin 1975, 266, n. 5 and 267, n. 7.

84 Lovejoy and Richardson 1995.

85 Carreira 1983, 212.

86 See Heap's chapter in this volume for more on gin as currency in Southern Nigeria.

87 Brooks 1993a and 1993b.

88 Carreira 1968, 128.

89 Carreira 1983b, 68.

Bibliography

Alpern, S.B., 1995. 'What Africans Got for Their Slaves: A master list of European trade goods', *History in Africa* 22: 5–43.

Andrade, B.A.A. de, 1952. *Planta da Praça de Bissau e suas adjacentes, anno de 1796*. Lisbon.

Azevedo, J.L. de, 1990. *O Marquês de Pombal e a sua época*. Porto.

Barcellos, C.J. de S., 1905. *Subsídios para a história de Cabo Verde e Guiné (III)*. Lisbon.

Boser-Sarivaxévanis, R., 1972. *Les tissus de l'Afrique Occidentale*. Basel.

Brásio, A., 1963. *Monumenta missionária africana: II. África Ocidental, 1500–1569*. 2nd series, Lisbon.

Brooks, G.E., 2003. *Eurafricans in Western Africa: Commerce, social status, gender, and religious observance from the 16th to the 18th century*. Athens, Ohio.

Brooks, G.E., 1993a. 'Historical Perspectives on the Guinea-Bissau Region, 15th to 19th centuries', in Lopes ed.: 25–54.

Brooks, G. E., 1993b. *Landlords and Strangers: Ecology, society, and trade in West Africa, 1000–1630*. Boulder, Colorado.

Brooks, G., 1980a. 'Luso-African commerce and settlement in the Gambia and Guinea Bissau region, 16th–19th centuries', *Boston University African Studies Center Working Paper 24*, Boston.

Brooks, G., 1980b. 'Kola trade and the state-building: Upper Guinea Coast and Senegambia, 15th–17th centuries', *Boston University African Studies Center Working Paper 38*, Boston.

Carreira, A., 1968. *Panaria cabo-verdiano-guineense: Apectos históricos e sócio-econômicos*. Lisbon.

Carreira, A., 1972. *Cabo Verde: Formação e extinção de uma sociedade escravocrata, 1460–1878*. Bissau.

Carreira, A., 1983a. *As Companhias Pombalinas*. 2nd edn, Lisbon.

Carreira, A., 1983b. *Notas sobre o tráfico português de escravos*. 2nd edn, Lisbon.

Carreira, A., 1986. *Ensaio e memórias econômicas sobre as ilhas de Cabo Verde, século XVIII*. Lisbon.

Carreira, A., 1988. *A Companhia Geral do Grão Pará e Maranhão*. 2 vols., São Paulo.

Coelho, F. de L., 1953. *Duas descrições seiscentistas da Guiné*. Lisbon.

Cornevin, R., 1962. *Histoire de l'Afrique: I. des origines au XVIe siècle*. Paris.

Cornevin, R., 1966. *Histoire de l'Afrique: II. L'Afrique précoloniale, 1500–1900*. Paris.

Curtin, Ph. D., 1983. 'Africa and the Wider Monetary World, 1250–1850', in Richards ed.

Curtin, Ph. D., 1975. *Economic Change in Precolonial Africa: Senegambia in the Era of the Slave Trade*. 2 vols. Madison, Wisconsin.

Curto, J.C., 2004. *Enslaving Spirits: The Portuguese-Brazilian alcohol trade at Luanda and its hinterland, c. 1550–1830*. Leiden and Boston.

Dias, M. N., 1970. *Fomento e mercantilismo: A Companhia Geral do Grão Pará e Maranhão, 1755–1778*. 2 vols, Belém.

Fairlie, S., 1965. 'Dyestuffs in the 18th Century', *Economic History Review*, new series 17(3): 488–510.

Feijó, J. da S., [1797]. 'Ensaio político sobre as ilhas de Cabo Verde para servir de plano à história filosófica das mesmas', in Carreira 1986, 1–56.

Fernandes, M.B.L., 1856. *Memória das moedas correntes em Portugal: Desde o tempo dos romanos até o anno de 1856*. Lisbon.

Fernandes, V., 1951. *Description de la côte occidentale d'Afrique, 1506–1508*. Th. Monod, A. Teixeira da Mota, and R. Mauny eds. Bissau.

Fyfe, C., 1980. 'The Cape Verde Islands', *Tarikh* 6(4): 20–30.

Gervais, R., 1982. 'Pre-colonial Currencies: A Note on the Maria Theresa Thaler', *African Economic History* 11: 147–52.

Godinho, V.M., 1956. *Documentos sobre a expansão portuguesa*. 3 vols. Lisbon.

Godinho, V.M., 1955. *Prix et monnaies au Portugal, 1750–1850*. Paris.

Gregory, C.A., 1996. 'Cowries and Conquest: Towards a Subaltern Quality Theory of Money', *Comparative Studies in Society and History* 38(2): 195–217.

Hair, P.E.H., 1974. 'Sources on early Sierra Leone (2): Andrade, 1582; Ruiters, 1623; Carvalho, 1632' *Africana Research Bulletin* 5(1) (October): 47–56.

Hall, G. M., 2005. *Slavery and African Ethnicities in the Americas*. Chapel Hill, North Carolina.

Hawthorne, W., 2003. *Planting Rice, Harvesting Slaves: Transformations along the Guinea-Bissau coast, 1400–1900*.

Portsmouth, New Haven.

Hogendorn, J. and Johnson, M., 1986. *The Shell Money of the Slave Trade*. Cambridge, UK.

Hogendorn, J.S. and Gemery, H.A., 1988. 'Continuity in West African Monetary History? An Outline of Monetary Development', *African Economic History* 17: 127–146.

Hopkins, A.G., 1973, *An Economic History of West Africa*. New York.

Inikori, J.E., 1977, 'The Import of Firearms into West Africa, 1750–1807', *Journal of African History* 18 (3): 339–368.

Instituição da Companhia Geral do Grão Pará e Maranhão, 1755. Lisbon.

Johnson, M., 1980. 'Cloth as money: The cloth strip currencies of Africa', *Textile History* 11: 193–202.

Johnson, M., 1977. 'Cloth strips in history', *West African Journal of Archaeology* 7: 169–178.

Johnson, M., 1974. 'Cotton imperialism in West Africa', *African Affairs* 73: 178–187.

Kriger, C., 2006. *Cloth in West African History*. Lanham.

Lamb, V., 1975. *West African Weaving*. London.

Lereno, A., 1942. *Subsídios para a história da moeda em Cabo Verde, 1460–1940*. Lisbon.

Lopes, C., ed., 1993. *Mansas, escravos, grumetes e gentio: Cacheu na encruzilhada de civilizações*. Bissau.

Lovejoy, P.E. and Richardson, D., 1995. 'British Abolition and Its Impact on Slave Prices Along the Atlantic Coast of Africa, 1783–1850', *Journal of Economic History* 55 (1): 98–119.

Lovejoy, P.E., 1980. 'Kola in the History of West Africa', *Cahiers d'études africaines* 20 (77): 97–134.

Lovejoy, P.E., 1974. 'Interregional Monetary Flows in the Pre-Colonial Trade of Nigeria'; *Journal of African History*, 15 (4): 563–585.

Martin, P.M., 1986. 'Power, Cloth and Currency on the Loango Coast', *African Economic History* 15, 1–12.

Maxwell, K., 1995. *Pombal: Paradox of the Enlightment*. New York.

Meillassoux, C., ed., 1971a. *The Development of Indigenous Trade and Markets in West Africa*. London.

Meillassoux, C. 1971b. 'Le commerce pré-colonial de le développement de l'esclavage à Gûbu du Sahel, Mali', in Meillassoux ed.: 182–195.

Menzel, B., 1972–1973. *Textilien aus West-afrika*. 3 vols., Berlin.

Montandon, G., 1934. *Traité d'ethnologie Culturel*. Paris.

Monteil, C., 1927. *Le Cotton chez les Noirs*. Paris.

National Museum of African Art, 1992. *History, Design, and Craft in West African Strip-Woven Cloth*. Washington, D.C.

Pélissier, R., 1989. *Naissance de la Guiné: Portugais et africains en Sénégambie, 1841–1936*. Orgeval.

Pereira, D.P., 1954. *Esmeraldo de situ orbis*. 3rd edn, Lisbon.

Peres, D., 1948. *Viagens de Cadamosto e de Pedro da Sintra*. Lisbon.

Picton, J.M., 1992. 'Tradition, Technology, and Lurex: Some Comments on Textile History and Design in West Africa', in *National Museum of African Art 1992*, 13–52.

Pond, S., 1941a. 'The Maria Theresa Thaler: A Famous Trade Coin', *Bulletin of the Business Historical Society* 15(1) (April): 26–31.

Pond, S., 1941b. 'The Spanish Dollar: The World's Most Famous Silver Coin', *Bulletin of the Business Historical Society*, 15(1) (Feb.): 12–6.

Pusich, A., [1810]. 'Ensaio físico-político das ilhas de Cabo Verde', in Carreira 1986, 57–82.

Richards, J.F., ed., 1983. *Precious Metals in the Later Medieval and Early Modern Worlds*. Durham, N.C.

Richards, W.A., 1980, 'The Import of Firearms into West Africa in the 18th Century', *Journal of African History* 21(1): 43–59.

Santos, N.V. dos, 1971. 'As fortalezas de Bissau', *Boletim Cultural da Guiné Portuguesa* 26(103): 481–512.

Saraiva, J.M.C., 1947. *A Fortaleza de Bissau e a Companhia do Grão Pará e Maranhão*. Lisbon.

Serrão, J.V., 1987. *O Marquês de Pombal: O Homem, o Diplomata e o Estadista*. Lisbon.

Vogt, J., 1975. 'Notes of the Portuguese Cloth Trade in West Africa, 1480–1540', *International Journal of African Historical Studies* 8(4): 623–651.

Webb Jr., J.L.A., 1982. 'Toward the Comparative Study of Money: Reconsideration of West African currencies and neoclassical monetary concepts', *International Journal of African Historical Studies* 15(3): 455–466.

'A recognized currency in beads'. Glass Beads as Money in 19th-Century East Africa: the Central Caravan Road

Karin Pallaver

After hard fare and long marches, you find yourself suddenly planted down among some hundreds of Arabs and well dressed coast people- in a second Zanguebar, in fact, without the sea, the Hindis and Banyans and other Europeans. You find plenty of fine fruit, abundance of wheat, and milk and meat, a market and a recognized currency in beads.[1]

During the 19th century, glass beads were still seen in Europe as mere imitations of true pearls and gemstones and produced, as it was said, 'pour les Sauvages et les Nègres'.[2] However, in other parts of the world, glass beads had a great value and were widely used as currency, as it was the case of the interior of present-day Tanzania. Starting from the beginning of the 19th century, this region became systematically involved in the commercial world of the western Indian Ocean. New trade patterns spread over the interior, which led to important social, political and economic changes.[3] As in other parts of Africa, one of these changes was the development of a complex monetary system based on the use of different types of currencies. Glass beads of Venetian origin, among others, became one of the main means of payment and exchange along the central caravan road that connected Bagamoyo on the coast, to Tabora, in the Western region of Unyamwezi, to Ujiji, on the Eastern shores of Lake Tanganyika.[4]

As many observers of the time lamented, the types of glass beads requested by the populations living along the caravan roads were subject to frequent fluctuations. As glass beads were widely used as ornaments in the interior of 19th-century Tanzania, European travelers commonly attributed the changes in the glass bead demand to the 'capricious' fashion of the African populations. This explanation, however, reflected their prejudice against the African use of money, which they often considered as primitive and backward. The monetary system of East African caravan trade was, instead, very complex. As we are going to see, the frequent changes in the demand were not only the result of fashion, but rather a response to the needs of the local economy and trade.

The aim of this article is to explore the different currencies in use along the caravan roads in 19th-century East Africa. The main focus will be the role of glass beads, which, I will argue, performed a critical function in the entire monetary system, being the link between long-distance trade and African inter-regional trade. The first part of this article gives a brief overview of the historical context in which glass beads were used as money. The second part will deal in more detail with the different currencies used along the central caravan road and in the surrounding regions. A third part will then investigate the economic functions of glass beads along the caravan roads and show how they performed the role of a recognized currency in the main markets of the interior. A final brief part will then provide some notes on the glass bead production in Venice during the 19th century.

1. The historical background: long-distance trade and Nyamwezi interregional trade

The Indian Ocean is one of the oldest economic and cultural world-systems: thanks to the presence of the monsoon winds, the driving force of the Indian Ocean commerce, India and the Arabian peninsula established close commercial relationships with East Africa.[5] Until the beginning of the 19th century, however, the East African coast remained almost completely separated from its interior and was more part of the commercial world of the western Indian Ocean than of East Africa.[6] The goods requested by Indian and Arab traders could be obtained in the immediate coastal hinterland and therefore there was no need to organize expensive commercial expeditions into the interior. At the same time, the regions of the interior were characterized by the presence of a widespread network of African local and interregional trades, mostly in salt, iron, copper, foodstuffs and forest products.[7] It was only from the first decades of the 19th century that these two separate worlds began to establish a strong connection as a consequence of the huge increase in the international demand for ivory and slaves.[8] East African ivory was very valuable since it was particularly suitable for being carved, being softer than West African and Indian ivory. In the 19th century, East African ivory began to be widely requested in Europe and America to produce luxury goods such as carved figures, parts of instruments, combs, billiard balls, and so on.[9] It was also requested by the Indian market, where it was used to produce jewellery. The increased demand for slaves was due to the establishment of clove plantations in Zanzibar and Pemba and to the sugar-cane production of the Mascarene Islands. There were other East African goods requested by the international markets like gum copal,[10] which was used to produce varnishes for the American furniture industry and hides, which were used in American and European tanneries.

All of these products had growing prices on the international markets during the 19th century and this gave African producers and traders favorable terms of trade. Between 1826 and 1857, for example, the price of ivory in Zanzibar doubled and it doubled again in the next 30 years.[11] The international demand for these products became a great stimulus for Indian, Swahili and Arab traders operating on the coast to expand their commercial activities into the East African interior. At the same time African traders already operating in the interior organized their own caravans to the coast. Nyamwezi traders, in particular, pioneered the commercial routes to the coast and with the development of the long-distance trade they began to enlist as porters in the Arab-Swahili caravans and organized at the same time their own caravans to the coast. The active response of the Nyamwezi came from their long tradition in the interregional trade networks that connected Unyamwezi, their place of origin, with Lake Tanganyika on the west, Lake Victoria on the north and the southern regions of Ufipa and Ruemba.[12] Nyamwezi interregional trade included many types of goods, but was centered around four major products: copper, tobacco, iron and salt.[13] Copper was produced for the most part in the region of Katanga and was used to make jewellery. In around 1860 Nyamwezi traders established themselves in Katanga to deal in copper, and, according to the explorer Thomson, in 1880 they dominated the biggest part of its trade towards the coast.[14] Tobacco was taken by Nyamwezi traders in Usukuma and then sold in Ugogo where it was in great demand.[15] Iron was highly requested in Unyamwezi, as iron forging was one of the main activities of the Nyamwezi, besides porterage and agriculture. It was used to produce tools of everyday use, such as hoes, knives, axes, arrows and spears.[16] Nyamwezi traders also went regularly to Uvinza to buy high quality salt.[17] This long tradition in commercial exchanges allowed the Nyamwezi traders to take part in the coastal trade and to rapidly adapt to the new patterns of trade. They extended their interregional trade networks and put in contact two commercial worlds that until that moment had been almost completely separated.

The monetary system of these trade networks was very complex and involved the use of different types of currencies. On the coast, the most widely accepted currency was the Maria Theresa (MT) thaler or dollar, also known as the 'black dollar', which was used as the main means of payment and as a unit of account in Zanzibar and along the coast.[18] The other currency used on the coast was the Indian rupee and its fractional coins, the *anna* and the *pice*.[19] In the coastal markets the Indian rupee and the MT thaler often coexisted; even if accounts were usually kept in dollars and cents, in market transactions the fractional coins for the dollar were *annas* and *pice* rather than cents. For this reason, in 1845 the British authorities introduced large quantities of *pice* from India in order to mitigate the shortage of small change in Zanzibar.[20] Together with the MT thaler and the Indian Rupee, another coin that was in use on the coast was the Spanish dollar or *piastre*. In 1857, when Richard Burton was on the coast organizing his caravan the Spanish dollar did not have a fixed rate, as it was not a legal tender, contrary to the MT thaler, which was the main unit of account.[21] It seems, however, that towards the end of the 1870s, the Spanish dollar begun to be more popular than before, at least as a unit of account. In fact, the White Fathers, who in that period began to regularly organize their caravans to go into the interior, kept their accounts in Spanish *piastres* and barely mentioned the MT thalers.[22] These currencies were in use on the coast and in Zanzibar, but were not accepted in the interior. The caravans travelling inland had to supply themselves with commodities, which were used as a means of payment and exchange.

2. The monetary system of the caravan roads

The use of commodity currencies in Africa was very widespread during the pre-colonial period. Many scholars have worked on the definition of pre-colonial African money, investigating its main functions in the African economic context. According to Karl Polanyi, an object is called money when used in any one of the following ways: for payment, as a means of indirect exchange, or as a standard. Money can be all-purpose money, answering to all of these uses, and special-purpose money, when the different uses of it are separated from one another.[23] With reference to the case of pre-colonial Senegambia, Philip Curtin has underlined, however, that no currency is all-purpose in any society because no society makes payments for all the purposes that payments can be made for. According to him, a more fruitful approach in the analysis of pre-colonial African currencies is 'to recognize that anything can be money as long as the people who use it accept it as a recognized medium of exchange and standard of value.'[24]

Of the same opinion is Paul Lovejoy, who, dealing with the case of Central Sudan, underlines the need to focus on market integration and economic growth and to understand pre-colonial monetary systems in order to evaluate the extent to which a capital market developed. According to him, the question is not if these currencies were all-purpose money, but the extent to which each currency met these requirements: medium of exchange, common measures of value, stores of value, standards of deferred payment.[25] In the framework of 19th-century East African trade, there were different currencies which met these requirements.

The biggest part of the provisions of a caravan starting from the East African coast for the interior was made up of cloth, glass beads, metal wires; then came other items of trade which could vary from arms to musical boxes, from hats to sugar and so on. Some of these goods were used to make gifts for local chiefs residing along the caravan roads. Other goods, particularly cloth, glass beads and brass wire, were used as a means of exchange and payment during the caravan journeys and in the market centers of the interior and were commonly described by European observers of the time as the 'African money' or 'the African coins'.[26]

Cloth, 'the gold and silver of Equatorial Africa' as a missionary defined it,[27] was highly valued in acquiring the goods of long-distance trade and was also widely requested to pay *hongo,* the tributes imposed by local chiefs on passing caravans. There were three main varieties of common cloth requested along the caravan roads, together with many different types of coloured cloth used for higher unit of exchange. Until the 1860s, the most requested cloth in the interior was a kind of unbleached cotton produced in America, particularly in Salem, Massachusetts, which in East Africa was called *merikani* or *merekani*. A second type was an indigo-dyed cotton from India, called *kaniki*, which was generally acquired at a lesser price than the American one; it was, in fact, totally rejected from some populations of the interior and therefore as currency it was not used as much as the *merikani*.[28] After the 1860s, a thin grey shirting produced in England, called *satini,* also entered the market. In the 1880s it was much in vogue along the caravan roads and because of it lesser quality it was cheaper than the *merikani* and the *kaniki*.[29] American textiles dominated the East African market until the US Civil War when the cotton supplies of Salem were cut off. From this point onwards, the East African market began to be flooded with Indian made cloth produced in Bombay, which from the 1860s onwards took the place of American produced cloth in the East African trade networks.[30]

Glass beads were generally second only to cloth among the most requested goods of 19th-century East African trade and were largely in demand along the main caravan roads and around Lakes Victoria and Tanganyika.[31] Traders who wanted to go from the coast into the interior had to buy beads from Banyan traders who had the monopoly of the bead trade in Zanzibar, where, according to Burton, glass beads were imported yearly 'by the ton'.[32] In some parts of the interior glass beads were accepted as a means of exchange for ivory and slaves and as a means of payment for tributes. During the 19th century, there were many different types of beads in use; among the most requested there were the *same same,* or *sami-sami* beads, made of red coral, the white beads, popularly known as *merikani*,[33] the *gulabi* beads made of pink porcelain, the black beads called *bubu*, the *sungomaji*, white and blue beads produced in Nurmberg, and a variety called *sofi,* Venetian cylindrical beads available in different colours.[34]

Brass and copper wires, finally, were other important articles in the East African trade and were considered by 19th-century observers as troublesome items as their value was influenced by many factors, such as their weight, the length of the coil and their packaging.[35] Along the central caravan road, brass wire was particularly valued in Unyamwezi. There it was used to produce coil-bracelets, which were also in demand in the market of Ujiji, where they were used to buy slaves and ivory.[36] In Ugogo, brass and copper wires were widely requested as *hongo* and then used to make ornaments.[37]

Imported goods were used by the caravans traveling inland from the coast, but not by those going in the opposite direction. Once a commercial caravan had reached the interior and had acquired the ivory, slaves and other goods to be carried to the coastal markets, it was necessary to reorganize a new caravan to travel back to the coast. New porters had to be engaged and new goods had to be acquired in order to pay the caravan personnel, to buy food and to pay taxes along the road. Buying cloth and beads in the interior would not have been economic, as the prices of these commodities increased substantially from the coast towards the interior. The prices between Zanzibar and Tabora could increase from two to five times and from Tabora to Lake Tanganyika or Lake Victoria they increased again.[38] In glass bead costs, for instance, there was generally a 50–100% difference between Zanzibar and Tabora and there was the same variation between Tabora and Ujiji.[39] There was also a significant increase in the cost of cloth: in 1881, for example, the price of *merikani* was 3.25 *piastres* on the coast and 7–8 *piastres* in Ugogo, whereas the English type, *satini,* was valued 2.5 *piastres* on the coast and 6–7 *piastres* in Ugogo.[40]

Because imported goods were so expensive in the interior, the articles carried by the caravans towards the coast were those of the African interregional trade, particularly iron hoes, tobacco, salt and hemp.[41] As we have already seen, Nyamwezi traders played a significant role as intermediaries in these interregional networks. Being very well acquainted with the dynamics of the different networks of trade, they knew exactly which goods were requested along the caravan roads towards the coast. It was a huge and valuable knowledge on which the success or the failure of a commercial expedition could depend. When Father Deniaud of the White Fathers reached Unyamwezi, he discovered that all the iron hoes he had carried with him had no value; the iron hoes in demand in Unyamwezi were those smelted in Ukerewe.[42] Nyamwezi traders, in fact, imported to Tabora iron hoes from Ukerewe and Usukuma, which were used as a means of payment in the regions situated between Unyamwezi and the coast.[43] Tobacco was also in

demand along the caravan roads, particularly in Ugogo; Nyamwezi traders brought it from Usukuma and then exchanged it for food during their travels towards the coast.[44] Salt also had an important role and was brought by Nyamwezi traders to Tabora from Uvinza.[45] Besides being used as a means of payment by caravans traveling towards the coast, the goods of African interregional trade were also used to buy the products requested by the coastal markets. For example, Nyamwezi traders carried salt to Karagwe and used it to buy ivory from Bunyoro, Ankole and Butumbi, which they carried to Tabora and then to the coast. During the 19th century, long-distance and interregional trade became strictly interconnected: the goods coming from African interregional trade were used by caravans as a means of payment from the interior towards the coast, serving as "lubricant" of the long-distance trade.[46]

The coexistence of different currencies along the caravan roads was not incidental, but functional, as they worked in a complementary relationship. As Akinobu Kuroda points out, human history is rich with examples of single markets in which an assortment of money could do what a single currency could not and where the presence of multiple currencies was determined by the needs of the market.[47] The presence of plural currencies was obviously partly determined by the peculiar attributes of every type of money which made one currency preferable to others in specific commercial exchanges.[48] With reference to the case of 19th-century Tanzania, the coexistence of cloth, glass beads and metal wires was partly determined by the need for small change. Cloth was generally the most important medium of exchange for the purchase of high-valued goods like ivory and slaves, whereas glass beads and metal wires were used for smaller transactions. Glass beads, for instance, were particularly requested in exchange for food. Foodstuffs were generally carried to the caravanserais by local women who sold them directly to porters and other caravan personnel during caravan stops. Cloth could be used to buy food, but glass beads were often the more convenient currency. The availability of small change was essential for these small transactions and since beads could be split up in smaller units, they became the most widespread means to buy food during caravan journeys.[49] This does not mean, however, that glass beads were not used to buy ivory and slaves or that cloth was not accepted in exchange for food. Along the caravan roads of 19th-century East Africa there was not a clear distinction between mono-function money and full-function-money. What is important for our analysis is that these currencies circulated side by side and that they were not substitutive but complementary, in the sense that plural monies could do what a single money could not.[50] The presence of plural currencies in the interior was the result of the existence of a multi-layered market, composed by local, interregional and long-distance trade networks. And, as we are going to see, glass beads played the role of an intermediary currency among these different spheres of trade.

3. Glass beads as money along the central caravan road

The history of glass beads in East Africa is a very ancient one, as they had been imported for centuries on the East African coast from South-East Asia. When the first Portuguese arrived on the East African coast, glass beads of European origin were not yet accepted by the local traders, but in the following centuries, beads of Venetian origin became more and more valuable in purchasing the East African goods requested by the international markets.[51] During the 19th century, with the development of strong commercial relationships between the interior and the coast, glass beads became one of the main components of the complex monetary system of the East African caravan trade. We can observe a major difference in the value and the functions of glass beads when they were used along the caravan roads or in the main market centers of the interior. Along the caravan roads, glass beads were not always in demand and the types requested were subject to frequent fluctuations. Instead, in the main towns of the interior glass beads were accepted as a recognized currency in the framework of a composite monetary system generally based on cloth. During caravan journeys glass beads were used to discharge different types of obligations: to pay taxes along the roads, to pay the caravan personnel and to buy different types of goods, such as foodstuffs and, in some regions, the goods of the long-distance trade.

Beads were commonly used for the payment of *hongo*, which were the taxes imposed by local chiefs on passing caravans. *Hongo* were particularly costly in the region of Ugogo, situated between Tabora and the coast, and glass beads together with cloth, were highly requested to settle their payment.[52] The Belgian explorer Jerome Becker, who traveled in the interior during the 1880s, considered it fundamental for an expedition to have a supply of different kinds of beads in order to pay *hongo*. During his expedition, brass wire was requested as *hongo* in Ugogo and Unyamwezi, and glass beads from Unyamwezi onwards.[53] The types of glass beads requested to settle the *hongo* varied significantly over time and glass beads were in some cases even refused by local chiefs, who preferred cloth to beads. During Burton's times, for instance, black beads called *bubu* were highly requested as *hongo* in Ugogo, whereas 20 years later, the White Fathers used only *merikani* white beads and cloth to pay *hongo* there.[54] In 1871 the American explorer Henry Morton Stanley found that beads were of almost no use to pay *hongo* in Ugogo, even if his beads were widely accepted as *hongo* on Lake Tanganyika.[55] In Ugogo, glass beads had also the extremely important function of being a privileged means of payment for water. According to Becker, local people dug a hole in the ground where they put water and sold it to passing caravans. He paid with beads, tobacco, hemp and gunpowder.[56]

Besides being used to pay taxes, glass beads were used to compensate the caravan personnel. In the interior of 19th-century Tanzania the only means of transport were human porters, who carried on their shoulders the goods requested by the international markets from the interior to the coast.[57] Caravans were also always accompanied by armed guards, called *askaris*, who had the task to maintain the order in the caravan ranks and to defend them from the attacks of thieves. Porters and *askaris* were hired by caravan organizers and traders and they received a wage in exchange for their work.[58] The amount was decided before the caravan departure from the coast or from the caravan places in the interior, and the payment was generally settled in cloth or in beads. Cloth and glass beads were often alternated to pay porters and *askaris*. The White Fathers, for example, during their first travel into

the interior in 1878–1879, paid their porters with cloth from the coast until Unyamwezi, and then with beads from Unyamwezi to Lake Victoria.[59] Glass beads were also exchanged for food along the road. They were used in the payment of *posho*, the food rations due to porters and *askaris*. The amount of *posho* was decided when the caravans were organized and was given to porters and *askaris* on a regular basis by the caravan master or guide. It could be directly given in grains, generally millet or sorghum, or in glass beads and cloth. In this case, glass beads and cloth were then exchanged for food along the road and particularly in the caravanserais where the caravans stopped to rest and to replenish their supplies. As glass beads could be split up in small units, they were generally the preferred currency for the purchase of food. We can observe that the cheapest quality of beads could generally buy the cheapest kind of foodstuffs; for example, according to Burton, the cheaper varieties of beads could be exchanged for grain and vegetables, but they could not buy fowl, milk and eggs.[60] Glass beads were also extensively used in larger commercial exchanges and contemporary reports are full of details concerning the use of glass beads in acquiring ivory and slaves. However, the general trend was to use cloth, guns and *piastres* to purchase slaves and ivory and to use glass beads in smaller transactions such as the purchase of food. This system of exchange was in use both in Ujiji and Tabora and also in the Congo region.[61]

Contrary to what happened along the caravan roads, where the types of commodities requested for payment could vary in a significant way, in the main commercial centers of the interior, like Tabora and Ujiji, beads were used as a recognized currency. The existence of a currency in beads was determined by the need to have a recognized exchange rate in the main markets of the interior, where the different types of currencies used along the caravan roads were put in relation to one another. We find a lot of references to the use of a bead currency in the market of Ujiji. The German explorer Hermann von Wissmann reports that in the Ujiji market the smallest coins were represented by red and blue glass beads. Cotton cloth and copper crosses represented silver money, whereas slaves, cattle and ivory represented 'European' gold.[62] The explorer Joseph Thomson tells us that in the market of Ujiji

> they have made the first advance towards the use of money in the adoption of a bead currency, which performs all the functions of our coppers, cloth being the medium for the larger purchases.[63]

According to Beverly Brown, in 1874 at the latest, glass beads were the accepted currency in the market of Ujiji.[64] Being part of a monetary system composed by different types of currencies, the value of glass beads was directly related to that of cloth; the rates of exchange were based on a cloth standard and were set each morning. It was not a true market price, but rather part of a complex set of equivalents.[65] After reaching Ujiji, the missionary Edward C. Hore, reported that:

> Here for the first time we find a regular currency or money in use by the natives; it consists of strings of blue and white cylindrical beads, each string containing 20 beads. Bunches of 10 strings are called "fundo". From 9 to 11 fundo are given in exchange for 4 yards of good heavy American calico; the value varying daily, according to the quantity of cloth in the market.[66]

Owing to the presence of different types of currencies, money-changers operated in the market of Ujiji, who exchanged cloth for beads or a particular type of beads for another one, in this way facilitating market transactions.[67] This offered to them a profitable daily business, as market prices were supplemented with service charges to any buyer not dealing in *sofi*, the white and blue cylindrical beads accepted as currency.[68] According to Brown, glass beads were primarily market currency and their value fluctuated considerably in response to market exchanges. The arrival of a caravan with hundreds of porters and ample stocks of cloth and beads, for example, always generated numerous exchange adjustments.[69]

In the region of Unyamwezi, glass beads were reported to be used as currency. Captain Stairs, stopping at the market of Tabora, found that food was set out in small quantities equivalent to the value of a string of beads. During his stay in Tabora, Stairs noticed that it was possible to buy foodstuffs with one string of beads and with 30 strings a dozen eggs. Beads could then be exchanged for cloth as soon as a seller had collected enough of them and the cloth so obtained was then used to buy goods of higher value than foodstuffs.[70] Also the missionary Dodgshun reports that in the market of Tabora there was a recognized currency in beads.[71] According to Burton, in the market of Msene, in Western Unyamwezi, there was a recognized currency in beads, which were the white and blue glass beads called *sofi*.[72] During the 19th century, glass beads were therefore used not only along the main caravan roads to buy food and to pay taxes, but were also used as currency in the main market towns of the interior. There glass beads could buy different types of market goods, like foodstuffs, tobacco or iron hoes, and could be exchanged for cloth, which was then used to acquire valuable goods.

Tabora and Ujiji were not only the most important inland markets along the caravan road connecting the interior to the coast, they were also the places in which the African interregional caravan trails, coming from neighbouring regions, intersected. In the market of Ujiji traders arrived from Uvinza and Uhha in order to sell salt, from Urundi with palm oil and cattle, from Ukanga and Kaole with fish, from Uvira and Usowa with ivory, and so on.[73] Also in the market of Tabora a great variety of products of the African interregional trade was available; dried fish coming from Lake Tanganyika, salt coming from Uvinza, iron hoes from Ukerewe, cattle from Usukuma, copper from Katanga, etc.[74] The markets of the commercial towns of the interior were therefore also the place where coastal and African traders could acquire the goods of African interregional trade, which were used, as previously noted, as a means of payment during the caravan journeys towards the coast. In the towns of the interior, glass beads, being the recognized currency, played a critical role, as they represented the main medium of exchange to purchase the goods of African interregional trade. In the market of Tabora, for example, tobacco was pressed and then cut in small cubes weighing about 15–20 grams, each one equivalent to one *kete*[75] of glass beads.[76] After being purchased with beads, tobacco was then used to buy foodstuffs and water and to pay *hongo* in Ugogo. Iron hoes, which played a key role as a means of exchange during travels from the interior to the coast, could also be bought in the market of Tabora with glass beads: when William Stairs was there, in 1887, 30 strings could be exchanged for an iron hoe.[77] Since glass beads, as we have noted above, were particularly suitable for small transactions, it is very likely that they were preferred by African traders in

exchange for their salt, iron and tobacco, which were then used as a means of payment during long-distance travels towards the coast. This is confirmed by Stanley, who states that in the market of Ujiji glass beads were the most popular currency among local traders. According to him, cloth, like *merikani* and *kaniki*, could be accepted as a means of payment, but white and black beads, called *sofi*, were 'the *only* current money accepted by *all* the natives attending the market.'[78]

Even if cloth has generally been considered as the main medium of exchange in the market economy of the interior of 19th-century Tanzania, we can observe how glass beads, though less requested than cloth as *hongo* and in exchange for ivory and slaves, were actually the most important means of payment in the inland markets. Beads, in fact, contrary to cloth, could be split up in smaller units, therefore becoming more suitable in acquiring the goods of African interregional trade. As glass beads were widely accepted by African traders in the interior, this commodity facilitated the exchanges among the different spheres of trade and played the role of the intermediary currency that the market needed as a medium of exchange between the currency circuit of the interregional trade network and that of the long-distance trade.[79] Considering the functions of glass beads as money can also help us to better understand why the demand for glass beads along the caravan roads was subject to so many fluctuations, which were not only due to local fashion, as contemporary observers deemed, but depended on the complexity of the East African market.

4. Fashion and inflation: the fluctuations in the demand for glass beads

In Europe, at least until the first half of the 20th century, glass beads were considered as 'minor' trade objects, being used in distant parts of the world to buy far more valuable goods, such as ivory, gold and slaves.[80] Asymmetry of exchanges is, of course, a recurrent theme in the reports of European travelers and missionaries in Africa, but it was not applicable to the case of 19th-century East Africa, where glass beads were used as currency in the long-distance trade with the coast and in local commercial transactions. European travelers of the time were very well acquainted with the fact that East African populations did not accept cheap knickknacks in exchange for their goods. The request for foreign commodities was in fact very detailed and European, Arab and Swahili traders could not easily circumvent the local demand.[81] As an observer of the time wrote,

> In Europe it is generally thought that the savages of Inner Africa accept a string of beads or a yard of cloth as a sufficient recompense for dozens of elephants' teeth, and that the nourishment of a caravan is repaid by the honour of the visit. These happy days are long since passed.[82]

What struck European travelers, and irritated them even more, were the rapid changes that characterized the demand for glass beads in the regions of the interior. As noted by many travelers, each population had its particular preference as to tint, colour and size. In Burton's times, for example, as much as 400 different types of beads were in demand.[83] Later, in 1871, when Stanley was organizing his caravan on the coast to go into the interior in search for Livingstone, it took him a long time to decide which kind of glass beads to bring with him. He decided, at the end, to buy 11 different types of beads among the great number in use.[84] According to contemporary observers, the types of beads requested could, in fact, change every year or every month. Burton, while describing the bead currency of Msene, explained that the information he was giving could be considered valid only for that year, 1858, because currency was liable to perpetual and sudden change, often causing severe losses to merchants, 'who after laying in a large outfit of certain beads, find them suddenly unfashionable and therefore useless'.[85] The demand was therefore not easy to predict, and traders and explorers going into the interior had to pay particular attention to buy the right types of beads to avoid severe losses. Speke and Burton, for instance, were obliged to throw away many beads considered worthless; they had bought the wrong types of glass beads, which had no value and were not accepted even as gifts.[86] Generally they consulted the recently returned caravan leaders, traders or porters about the prevailing kinds of beads requested among the populations living in the interior.[87] In Burton's times, for instance, black glass beads (called *bubu*) were the recognized currency in Uzaramo, but during Stanley's journey into the interior in 1871 the same beads, though currency in Ugogo, were 'worthless with all other tribes'.[88] At the beginning of the 1870s, *merikani* beads were accepted only in Ufipa and some parts of Usagara and Ugogo, but at the end of the decade they were accepted only from Unyamwezi onwards. A particular kind of beads could also remain in demand for a long period: again, during Burton's travels in the 1850s, the most requested beads in Unyamwezi were the red ones, called *sami-sami*, which were still in demand during Stanley's first travel in 1871. In 1878, the White Fathers found that the same beads were still in demand along the central caravan road from Unyamwezi onwards.[89]

Fashion and tastes were depicted by European observers of the time as the main reason for the rapid changes in the demand. Stanley complained that

> The various kind of beads [to be carried into the interior] required great time to learn, for the women of Africa are as fastidious in their tastes for beads as the women of New York are for jewelry.[90]

Père Livinhac of the White Fathers noticed that, as barter goods, glass beads were second in importance only to cloth, but were far more subject to the 'caprice' of the people he met along the road.[91] These references to fashion and even caprice are a clear indication of a European prejudice against the African use of money, which was considered as backward, particularly when the use of glass beads was involved. According to this interpretation, the frequent changes in the types of glass beads requested were related to the vanity of African women, who could abruptly change their tastes according to current fashion.

Fashion undoubtedly influenced the demand, as glass beads were widely used as ornaments among many African societies. As Lidia D. Sciama rightly points out, 'beads, in their different colours, arrangements and styles, are important symbols of collective, as well as individual identity for many social groups'.[92] In the interior of 19th-century Tanzania glass beads were used to decorate beards and hair, to embroider cloths, masks and dolls, and to make jewellery, like necklaces, bracelets, and so on. As they were worn by chiefs, they were also considered important as a sign of aristocratic status. In Unyamwezi, glass beads, together with cloth and iron hoes, were also an important part of the bride price.[93] Glass beads

also had ritual values. Both Cameron and Stanley speak about propitiatory sacrifices in beads made to gods on Lake Tanganyika. Stanley was told by his guide that there was a custom, both among the Arabs and the local people, to throw *merikani* beads into the water to appease the god of the lake, Kabogo. Stanley's guide warned him that,

> those who throw the beads generally get past without trouble, but those who do not throw beads into the lake get lost and are drowned.[94]

Lieutenant Cameron confirms this version, when he reports that at a certain point of his exploration of Lake Tanganyika, near the Machahezi river, two Jiji guides put three *fundo* of beads into the water to appease the god of the lake, Kabogo.[95]

For some travelers, the fluctuations in the demand for beads were not only due to fashion, but also to the inflation that took place when too many beads of the same type were in circulation in a particular region. For example, after discovering that coloured beads were preferred to the white beads he had brought with him, Speke reached the conclusion that

> It is always foolish to travel without an assortment of beads, in consequence of the tastes of the different tribes varying so much; and it is more economical in the long-run to purchase high-priced than low-priced beads when making up the caravan at Zanzibar, for every little trader buys the cheaper sorts, stocks the country with them, and thus makes them common.[96]

Fashion and inflation were obviously important factors in determining the changes in the demand, but that is not the entire story. A more comprehensive explanation of the continuous fluctuations in the bead demand could come from the analysis of the role of glass beads as money. We have noted in the previous section that the circulation of different types of glass beads was strictly related to the presence of a multi-layered market in the interior, in which glass beads played the role of an intermediary currency among different networks of trade. Cloth was also accepted as currency in these trade networks, but glass beads, with their range of colours and their assortment, were more suitable to respond to the variety of the local demands. In the different regions of the interior many types of glass beads were therefore in circulation and were accepted as a means of payment. In the most important markets of the interior not only the diverse trade networks intersected, but also the different types of glass beads used in these networks were put in relation to one another. The presence of a recognized currency in the main markets, like the *sofi* beads used in Ujiji, was exactly determined by the need to have a currency that could mediate among the varieties of beads in use in the interior. This is why money-changers operated in the main markets of the interior, dealing daily with hundreds of varieties of beads.[97]

Even if we do not know exactly which currencies were used outside long-distance and interregional trade circuits, we could infer that in local commercial exchanges, glass beads were accepted as a means of payment. There was therefore a relationship between the changes in the demand for glass beads and the kind of goods put up for sale in the markets or in the caravanserais. African traders who carried their iron hoes, tobacco, salt and agricultural products to the markets or to the caravanserais, obviously exchanged their goods for a commodity that could be used as a means of payment in their place of origin. Since the goods available in the towns of the interior and along the caravan roads came from different areas of production, in which different kinds of glass beads were in demand not only for actual wear, but also used as a means of payment, European travelers found that a particular product could be purchased only with a certain kind of beads. This was due to the kind of beads used as a means of payment in the region where these goods came from. The changes in the bead demand could, for example, be related to the seasonality of the agricultural production or to the temporary availability of certain types of goods. European explorers and missionaries did not have a comprehensive picture of the whole trade network and in a simplistic way attributed the rapid changes to the 'fastidious tastes of African women', as Stanley put it, rather than to the complexity of the East African monetary system.

European travelers were not the only ones convinced that the request for glass beads was subject to local fashion. In Venice, the glass bead producers also believed that the frequent fluctuations in the demand coming from abroad were due to the changeable fashion of the populations living in distant parts of the world. Jeremy Prestholdt has demonstrated how the cloth production of Salem and Bombay was strictly dependent on the demand coming from East Africa.[98] The 19th-century Venetian glass production was also largely dependent on the foreign demand for glass beads, like that coming from the East African market.

5. Some notes on the glass bead production in Venice and its connection to East Africa

The glass bead production in Venice can be traced back to the Middle Ages. From the beginning of the 15th century onwards, Venice obtained its supremacy in world glass-bead production, when Venetian glass beadmakers filled the void left by the decline of western Asian industries.[99] To maintain its supremacy, the government of the Venetian Republic established in 1490 restrictive laws that obliged glass beadmakers, upon penalty of death, not to divulge glass beadmaking secrets and not to export their know-how abroad. Even if in Europe glass beads continued to be largely disregarded until at least the 20th century, Venetian glass bead production and export had a continuous increase from the 15th century until the end of the 19th century. Thanks to their vivid colours and their durability, Venetian glass beads were extensively used in many parts of the world as ornaments and to decorate different kinds of objects.[100]

During the period under examination, the glass production of Venice was hit by a severe crisis, which affected both artistic and ordinary glass production.[101] The glass bead production, however, was not involved and during the 19th century glass beads were the most important article of Venetian export and the only one to survive the general crisis. From 1848 glass bead manufacturing in Venice had been subject to an extensive mechanization, which led to an output growth and definitely contributed to the success of Venetian glass beads. The power of the glass bead industry of Venice and the ability to face foreign competition were also largely due to a peculiarity of its productive system; the work of stringing beads was, in fact, assigned to Venetian women at home. This gave great flexibility to the production, which could be easily increased or diminished according to the fluctuations of the demand.[102]

Glass bead production remained, therefore, during the 19th century, the most trade-oriented of all Venetian glass manufactures, and, as Francesca Trivellato points out, 'during the alternate vicissitudes of the Venetian economy, glass-bead manufacturing represented a major source of work and profit; and seed-beads in particular, became the backbone of industrial development'.[103] The biggest part of the production was exported to satisfy the foreign demand, which, in a period of crisis, largely sustained the Venetian economy.

An important part of the glass bead production of Venice was undoubtedly directed to East Africa, as it is confirmed by many sources and by the glass beads found there.[104] In 1874, for example, the Venetian Chamber of Commerce commissioned statistics on the export of glass beads: India was the main destination, with ITL 1,860,000, followed by England with ITL 1,470,000 and then Zanzibar and East Africa, with ITL 650,000.[105] There were two types of Venetian glass beads which were in high demand in the interior of East Africa during the 19th century: the black ones and the cylindrical beads called *sofi*. Among the beads produced in Venice, black beads were one of the most requested, as it is evident from the many shapes and sizes of black beads available in the sample books of Venetian glass bead firms. These kinds of beads were particularly requested in France, where they were used in clothing and in making funeral wreaths.[106] In East Africa *bubu*, as black beads were called, existed in many different sizes, the small being the most valued, and were much in demand in the interior, particularly in Uzaramo.[107] *Sofi* beads could be of different colours: red and blue, white and blue or white and black. These beads were in great demand in 19th-century East Africa, and, as we have seen, they were used as currency in the market of Ujiji. In the 1850s they were used as currency in Usagara, Unyamwezi and the Western regions. The East African Expedition arrived in the interior lacking this kind of bead and its members were obliged to sell their cloth in exchange for *sofi*.[108]

Being largely dependent on the export to foreign markets, the glass bead production of Venice had to adapt itself to the fluctuations of foreign demand. The frequent and sudden changes in the bead demand, in fact, were not only a problem for the traders, missionaries and explorers operating in East Africa; they were also a problem for the centres of production, situated in distant parts of the world, like Venice. If we take, for example, a survey on the Venetian production ordered by the prefect of Venice in 1879, we find that the author lamented the continuous variations in the Venetian production of glass beads. According to him, the production changed greatly from year to year and even from month to month, in response to the fluctuations of the foreign fashion. This was, indeed, a frequent complaint among the producers of the time.[109]

Much of the research on the specific connection between Venice and the East African market is still to be done, but what is clear is that during the 19th century a strong link was established between these two parts of the world. The huge demand for glass beads coming from the East African market definitely sustained the production in Venice, whereas Venetian glass beads performed the function of a recognized currency in the economy of the regions of the interior.

Conclusions

In 19th-century East Africa different types of trade co-existed together with the use of different types of currencies. Along the many caravan roads that intersected in the interior, goods coming from African interregional trade and those of foreign origin carried from the coast were exchanged in the framework of a complex monetary system, where different types of currencies responded to the needs of trade and where the bargaining was based on the assortment of different types of goods. Multiple monies, in fact, were used as a means of payment and performed different functions, responding to the need of a market-economy mainly based on the export of ivory, slaves and gum copal. In the main markets of the interior these different types of currencies were put in relation to one another and this led to the need of a recognized exchange rate. The most important role in connecting the different currencies used along the caravan roads was played by glass beads. Throughout the 19th century this commodity was highly requested along the caravan roads as a means of payment and exchange, but also in the main markets of the interior, where glass beads were the recognized currency. Even if cloth has generally been considered as the main medium of exchange in the market economy of the interior of 19th-century East Africa, we can observe how glass beads, though less requested than cloth as *hongo* along the caravan roads and as a means of payment to acquire ivory and slaves, were the most important means of payment in the inland markets. The huge request for glass beads coming from the East African market definitely linked this area to the main centres of production of glass beads in Europe, like Venice. There, the production had to adapt itself to the fluctuations of the demand coming from abroad and had to take into account the rapid changes in the demand coming from all over the world. Tracing the paths followed by Venetian glass beads in the 19th century, allow us to link the history of Africa to the history of Europe in a revealing way, studying not only the consequences of European economic expansion and production on marginal economies, but traveling, 'that same road in the opposite direction, to see what light Africa's experience can cast on European history'.[110]

Notes

1 Dodgshun 1879.
2 Montesquieu, as cited in Trivellato 2000, 239.
3 Koponen 1988.
4 Sheriff 1987, 57; the central caravan road was the main commercial road along which ivory was exported from the regions of the interior to the coast.
5 Gilbert 2004, 25.
6 Unomah and Webster 1977, 270.
7 Roberts 1970.
8 Sheriff 1987, 156.
9 Beachey 1967.
10 Sunseri 2007.
11 Nolan 1977, 43.
12 Holmes 1971.
13 See Roberts 1970, for a detailed account of Nyamwezi interregional trade and its connection to long-distance trade.
14 Thomson 1968, 46.
15 Menard 1880–1881.
16 Roberts 1970, 45.
17 Sutton and Roberts 1968.
18 Following Kuroda 2007, 89, the Maria Theresa thaler was first minted in Vienna in 1751 and continued to be minted after the death of the Empress in 1780; in the Red Sea region it was still popular during WWII.
19 According to Sheriff 1987, XIX, the universal rupee was established in 1836, but its value fluctuated until 1899.
20 Sissons.
21 Burton 1859, 422–423. Sissons 1984, 36–37, states that during the period 1860–1890 the Spanish dollar was approximately equal in value to the Maria Theresa thaler, whereas the relation between the Spanish *piastre* and the rupee was 2.10 Spanish *piastre* for 2.18 rupees.
22 See White Fathers Archive, Rome C 11 Caravanes and C 20 Provicariat de l'Unyanyembe
23 Polanyi in Dalton 1971.
24 Curtin 1975, 235.
25 Lovejoy 1974, 564.
26 Burton 1859, 425, for example, said that '…beads in East Africa represent the copper and smaller silver coins of European countries'; J.M. Hildebrandt in Rigby 1877–1878, 422, defines cloth, glass beads, iron, and brass wire as the 'African money'; H.M. Stanley in Bennett 1970, 5–6, says: '…and [I] entrusted to them my bales of cloth, bags of beads and coils of wire, which you must recollect are as gold, silver and copper money in Africa'.
27 Guillet 1881.
28 Sissons 1984, 47.
29 Burdo 1891, vol. I, 170; Schynse, 1891, 29, called *satini* 'bad cloth'.
30 Prestholdt 2004, 773–776; Sheriff 1987, 135, points out how the decline of American textile production, together with a refusal of the African market to fully accept English textiles, led to a great increase of the request for glass beads and brass wire.
31 For a general history of glass beads in East Africa, see Vierke 2006, chapter 12, 263–342.
32 Burton 1859, 454.
33 Even if *merikani* was the name usually given in East Africa to unbleached American cotton, the same name was used to refer to white glass beads, probably because they had a colour resembling that of the American cloth.
34 Burton 1859, 426–427; Deniaud 1878–1879.
35 Sissons 1984, 56–58; Prestholdt 2004, 763.
36 Burton 1859, 428.
37 Becker 1887 vol. I, 415; Nicq 1906, 109.
38 According to Burton 1859, 185, between Zanzibar and Tabora the prices increased five times; according to Jerome Becker,1887, vol. I, 466, the prices between Zanzibar and Tabora only doubled.
39 B.Brown and W.T. Brown 1971, 189–190.
40 P. Blanc 1881.
41 Becker 1887, vol. I, 136.
42 Deniaud 1878–1879
43 Deniaud 1878–1879; according to Sigl 1892, 164–166, still during the first part of the German colonial period iron hoes remained one of the main items of trade in Unyamwezi. In a report of 1892 he states that 150,000 iron hoes had reached Tabora and were then used as currency from Ugogo to the coast, particularly to buy foodstuffs.
44 Coulbois, 1883.
45 Roberts 1970, 51–53; Menard 1880–1881.
46 Smith 1963, 253–296.
47 Kuroda 2008,7.
48 Kuroda 2008, 14.
49 Hobley 1929, 246.
50 Kuroda 2007, 109.
51 Van der Sleen 1958, 211–212.
52 From the 1860s onwards, arms and gun powder begun to be more and more requested as hongo in the interior; for an account of the arms trade in 19th-century East Africa, see Beachey 1962 and Iliffe 1979, 51.
53 Becker 1887, vol. I, 470.
54 Livinhac 1878–1879.
55 Stanley 2006.
56 Becker 1887, vol. I, 155.
57 The literature on porters is rather rich; for a recent work see Rockel 2006.
58 For an account of monthly wage rates for caravan porters, see Rockel 2006, 7.2, 226.
59 Livinhac 1879.
60 Burton 1859, 190.
61 B. Brown 1971, 622.
62 von Wissmann 1890, 235.
63 Thomson 1968, vol. II, 90.

64 B. Brown, 1971.
65 Curtin 1975, 238.
66 Hore 1883, 9.
67 Stanley 2006, 421.
68 B. Brown 1973, 72.
69 B. Brown 1973.
70 Quiggin 1970, 102.
71 Dodgshun 1879; see the opening quotation.
72 Burton 1859, 189.
73 Stanley 2006, 421–422.
74 Roberts 1970.
75 A *kete* (or *khete*) was a unit of measurement for beads, corresponding to the distance from the thumb to the elbow and back; ten *kete* were equivalent to one *fundo*.
76 Becker 1887, vol. II, 24.
77 Quiggin 1970, 102.
78 Stanley, 1879; the evidence is mine.
79 According to Kuroda 2008, 13, a currency circuit is a coupling of a trade zone and a particular currency.
80 Sciama 1998, 14.
81 Prestholdt 2004.
82 Rigby 1877–1878, 452.
83 Burton 1859, 424.
84 Stanley 2006, 33.
85 Burton 1859, 189.
86 Stanley 2006, 32.
87 For example, Stanley 1875, 204, asked to caravan leaders, Becker 1887, vol. I, 470, to porters and Burton 1859, 423 to Arab traders.
88 Burton 1859, 427; Stanley 2006, 31.
89 Livinhac, 1879; Harding 1962, 104; Stanley 2006, 32–33.
90 Bennett 1970, 5.
91 Livinhac, 1879.
92 Sciama 1998, 18.
93 Broyon-Mirambo 1877–1878.
94 Stanley 2006, 347; Harding 1962, 106.
95 Cameron and Markham 1874, 199.
96 Speke 1864.
97 Stanley 2006, 421.
98 Prestholdt 2004.
99 Dubin 1987.
100 Sciama 1998, 27.
101 According to Trivellato 1998, 54, the crisis was contemporary to the abolition of the glass guilds, which were replaced by a free labour market.
102 Bellavitis 1990; Bernardello 2002.
103 Trivellato 1998, 54.
104 Some contemporary sources talk specifically about Venetian beads; see, for example, Cameron and Markham 1874, 256; Burton 1859, 425–427; Stanley 2006, 21; see also van der Sleen 1958.
105 Bertagnolli, Sega and De Gheltof 1993, 80; then followed North America with ITL 570,000, Germany, Denmark and Sweden with ITL 560,000 and West Africa, with ITL 520,000.
106 Trivellato 1998, 70.
107 Burton 1859, 427.
108 Burton 1859, 426.
109 Trivellato 1998, 59.
110 Fenoaltea 1999, 145.

Bibliography

Beachey, R.W. 1962, 'The arms trade in East Africa in the late nineteenth century', *Journal of African History*, 3(3), 451–467.
Beachey, R.W. 1967, 'The East African ivory trade in the nineteenth century', *Journal of African History*, 8(2), 269–290.
Becker, J. 1887, *La vie en Afrique ou trois ans dans l'Afrique Centrale*, Paris and Brussels.
Bellavitis, A., 1990, 'In fabbrica e in casa. Il lavoro femminile nelle 'conterie'a Venezia', in *Perle e Impiraperle. Un lavoro di donne a Venezia tra '800 e '900*, Venice, 9–21.
Bennett, N.R. (ed.) 1970, *Stanley's Despatches to the New York Herald, 1871–72, 1874–77*, Boston.
Bernardello, A. 2002 'Venezia 1830–1866. Iniziative economiche, accumulazione e investimenti di capitale', *Il Risorgimento*, 1, 5–66.
Bertagnolli, E., Sega, M.T. and Urbani de Gheltof, R., 1993, *Perle veneziane*, Venice.
Blanc, P., 1881, White Fathers Archive, Rome, C 20–217 [1].

Brown, B. 1971, 'Muslim influence on trade and politics in the Lake Tanganyika region', *African Historical Studies*, 4(3), 617–629.
Brown, B. 1973, *Ujiji: History of a Lakeside Town*, PhD Thesis, University of Boston.
Brown, W.T. and Brown, B. 1976, 'East African towns: a shared growth', in W. Arens (ed.), *A century of Change in Eastern Africa*, Paris, 183–200.
Broyon-Mirambo, P. 1877–1878, 'Description of Unyamwezi, the territory of King Mirambo, and the best route thither from the coast', *Proceedings of the Royal Geographical Society* 22(1), 28–38.
Burdo, A.M.L. 1886, *Les Belges dans l'Afrique Centrale: Voyages, Aventures et Découvertes d'après les Documents et Journax des Explorateurs*, Brussels.
Burton, R.F. 1859, 'The lake regions of Central Equatorial Africa', *Proceedings of the Royal Geographical Society* 29, 1–454.
Cameron, V.L. and Markham, C.P. 1874, 'Examination of the Southern half of Lake Tanganyika', *Journal of the Royal Geographical Society*, 19(4), 246–263.
Coulbois, P. 1883, Simbawenni, 14/8/1883, White Fathers Archive, Rome, C11–53.
Curtin, P.D. 1975, *Economic Change in Precolonial Africa: Senegambia in the Era of the Slave Trade*, Madison.
Dalton, G. (ed.), 1971, *Primitive, Archaic and Modern Economies: Essays of Karl Polanyi*, Boston.
Deniaud, P. 1878–1879, *Journal de la première caravane*, White Fathers Archive, Rome, C11–18.
Dodgshun, A. 20/01/1879, *Journals. From London to Ujiji, 1877–1879*, Central Africa, Journals 1877–79, Box 1, Council for World Mission, SOAS, London.
Dubin, L.S. 1987, *The History of Beads. From 30,000 BC to the Present*, London.
Fenolatea, S. 1999, 'Europe in the African mirror: the slave trade and the rise of feudalism', *Rivista di Storia Economica* 15(2), 123–65.
Gilbert, E. 2004, *Dhows and the Colonial Economy of Zanzibar, 1860–1970*, Oxford.
Guillet, P. 1881, *Rapport du Père Guillet*, 08/10/1881, White Fathers Archive, Rome, C 20–62.
Harding, J.R. 1962, 'Nineteenth-century trade beads in Tanganyika', *Man* 62, 104–106.
Hobley, R. 1929, *Kenya. From Chartered Company to Crown Colony. Thirty Years of Exploration and Administration in British East Africa*, London.
Holmes, C.F. 1971, 'Zanzibari influence at the Southern End of Lake Victoria: the Lake Route', *African Historical Studies* 4(3), 477–503.
Hore, E.C. 1883, 'On the twelve tribes of Tanganyika', *Journal of the Anthropological Institute of Great Britain and Ireland* 12, 2–21.
Iliffe, J. 1979, *A Modern History of Tanganyika*, Cambridge.
Koponen, J. 1988, *People and Production in late pre-colonial Tanzania. History and Structures*, Helsinki.
Kuroda, A. 2007, 'The Maria Theresa Dollar in the early twentieth-century Red Sea Region: A complementary interface between multiple markets', *Financial History Review* 14(1), 89–110.
Kuroda, A. 2008, 'What is Complementarity among Monies? An Introductory Note', *Financial History Review* 15(1), 7–15.
Livinhac, P. 1879, *Quelques Indications pourrant faciliter le voyage aux missionaires qui se riendront dans l'Ouganda*, S. Marie près de Roubaga, White Fathers Archive, Rome, C 11–12.
Lovejoy, P.E. 1974, 'Interregional monetary flows in the Precolonial trade of Nigeria', *Journal of African History* 15(4), 563–585.
Menard, P. 1880–1881, *Journal de la Troisième Caravane*, White Fathers Archive, Rome, C 11–48.
Nicq, A. 1906, *Le Père Simon Lourdel de la Societé de Pères Blancs*, Algiers.
Nolan, F.P. 1977, *Christianity in Unyamwezi 1878–1928*, PhD Thesis, University of Cambridge.
Prestholdt, J. 2004. 'On the global repercussions of East African consumerism', *American Historical Review* 109(3), 755–781.
Quiggin, M.A. 1970, *A Survey of Primitive Money*, London.
Rigby, C. 1877–1878, 'Mr. J.M. Hildebrandt on his travels in East Africa', *Proceedings of the Royal Geographical Society* 22(6), 446–53.
Roberts, A.D. 1970, 'Nyamwezi trade', in R. Gray and D. Birmingham (eds), *Pre-colonial African Trade: Essays on Trade in Central and Eastern Africa before 1900*, London, 649–701.
Rockel, S.J. 2006, *Carriers of Culture. Labor on the Road in Nineteenth-century East Africa*, Portsmouth.
van der Sleen, W.G.N 1958 'Ancient Glass Beads with Special Reference

to East and Central Africa', *Journal of the Royal Geographical Institute of Great Britain and Ireland* 88(2), 203–216.

Schynse, A. 1891, *Con Stanley ed Emin Pascià attraverso l'Africa Orientale,* Milan (orig. edn Cologne 1890).

Sciama, L.D. 1998, 'Gender in the making, trading and uses of beads: an introductory essay', in L.D. Sciama and J.B. Eicher (eds.), *Beads and Bead Makers: Gender, Material Culture and Meaning,* Oxford and New York, 3–45.

Sheriff, A. 1987, *Slaves, Spices and Ivory in Zanzibar: Integration of an East African Empire into the World Economy, 1770–1883,* London.

Sigl, A. 1892, 'Bericht des Stationchefs von Tabora, Lieutenant Sigl, über den Handelsverkeher von Tabora', *Deutsches Kolonialblatt* 3, 164–166.

Sissons, C.J. 1984, *Economic Prosperity in Ugogo, East Africa, 1860–1890,* PhD Thesis, University of Toronto.

Smith, A. 1963, 'The Southern Section of the Interior, 1840–1884', in P. Oliver and G. Mathew (eds.), *History of East Africa,* Oxford, 253–296.

Speke, J.H. 1864, *What led to the Discovery of the Source of the Nile,* Edinburgh.

Stanley, H.M. 2006, *How I found Livingstone,* Vercelli (orig. edn London 1872).

Stanley, H.M. 1875, 'Explorations in Central Africa', *Journal of the American Geographical Society of New York* 7, 174–282.

Stanley, H.M. 1879, *A travers le continent mistérieux,* Paris (orig. edn London 1878).

Sunseri, T. 2007, 'The Political Ecology of the Copal Trade in the Tanzania Coastal Hinterland, c.1820–1905', *Journal of African History* 48, 201–220.

Sutton, J.E.G. and Roberts 1968, A.D., 'Uvinza and its Salt Industry', *Azania,* 3, 45–86.

Thomson, J. 1968, *To the Central African Lakes and back. The Narrative of the Royal Geographical Society's East Central African Expedition 1878–1880,* (orig. edn London 1881).

Trivellato, F. 1998, 'Out of women's hands: Notes on Venetian glass beads, female labour and international trades', in L.D. Sciama and J.B. Eicher (eds.), *Beads and Bead Makers: Gender, Material Culture and Meaning,* Oxford and New York, 47–82.

Trivellato, F. 2000, *Fondamenta dei vetrai. Lavoro, tecnologia e mercato a Venezia tra Sei e Settecento,* Rome.

Unomah, A.C. and Webster, J.B. 1977, 'East Africa: the Expansion of Commerce', in J.E. Flint (ed.), *Cambridge History of Africa,* vol. 5, Cambridge.

Vierke, U. 2006, *Die Spur der Glasperlen. Akteure, Strukturen und Wandel im europäisch-ostafrikanischen Handel mit Glasperlen,* PhD Thesis, University of Bayreuth.

von Wissmann, H. 1890, *Unter deutscher Flagge quer durch Afrika von West nach Ost von 1880 bis 1883,* Berlin.

'A bottle of gin is dangled before the nose of the natives': Gin Currency in Colonial Southern Nigeria

Simon Heap

Background

The trade in imported liquor rose to prominence during the first half of British colonial rule in Southern Nigeria. Not all was drunk, however. Single bottles or whole cases of liquor went from hand to hand through barter transactions. Imported liquor's economic functions complemented its social role, with the supreme examples being its use as a colonial revenue-earner and as a transitional currency.[1] This paper takes up a challenge by Jane Guyer to fellow historians 'to trace out the implications of sudden aggressive surges in particular imports', by examining the economics of the growth of the trade in imported liquor in Southern Nigeria in the late 19th and early 20th centuries.[2]

Nigerians had for long time fermented low-alcohol drinks. Liquor consumption mixed concerns on personal, communal and ritual levels throughout the life cycle of many Nigerians: from naming ceremonies, entertaining guests at weddings, chieftaincy instalments and funeral obsequies, to pouring libations to the ancestors. Although with a huge variety of indigenous liquors to consume, Nigerians did not know how to brew lager beer or distil spirits. Their expertise was restricted to tapping palm wine or fermenting grain beers. The Atlantic slave trade, which encouraged the purchase of slaves with rum and whisky, fostered the fashion for imported liquor. Imported drinks did not completely displace local beverages, however: they coexisted, complemented and competed with each other. While there were other items of barter, fiery alcohol seemed to have a premium among the local populace above other goods like beads, cloth, guns and gunpowder. When the slave trade ended, the liquor trade continued, reaching large volumes in the second half of the 19th century. The demand for imported liquor in Nigeria grew to a large extent in tandem with the growth and expansion of British control over the territory from the 1860s onwards. Liquor was the most significant import in terms of volume and value in the British colonies of Lagos, Oil Rivers Protectorate, Niger Coast Protectorate and Southern Nigeria, all of which were eventually integrated into the Southern Provinces of Nigeria in 1914.[3] Imported liquor was banned from sale to the general public in the Northern Provinces because of the large Muslim population there.[4]

A trade is the buying and selling of a commodity, sometimes with money, sometimes by barter. Commodities are theoretically defined by reference to their exchange value, that is, the value they realize in the market, but here money is far from being an inanimate, depersonalized instrument: it contains and transmits the moral qualities of those who transact it. This is particularly so when the commodity to be valued and exchanged is alcohol. But the meaning or value attached to it, like other things that define them as commodities, is not consistent or stable but fluctuates over time and within contexts.[5]

Consequently, the Nigerian liquor trade provoked fierce debate: was it advancing development or fashioning an economy based on the economically unproductive consumption of alcohol? The liquor trade was caught between two prevailing colonial perspectives on economic development in Africa: the Darwinian-based notion that Western civilization had a duty to protect Africans from all bad external influences like strong liquor, and the civilize-through-trade concept which sought to modernize Africans by exploiting colonies to their fullest economic potential.

Positive views of the liquor trade claimed its necessity in developing the Nigerian economy. Some admitted that the trade formed a necessary evil, but did not fail to emphasize its role as a transitional currency, promoter of cash-crops-for-export, and a desirable commodity among those with money to spend.[6] On the other hand, critics of the liquor trade used the temperance equation to further their cause: drinking alcohol was bad, abstinence was good. The critics included a wide cross-section of Nigerians concerned for their fellow citizens in the face of the liquor deluge, as well as such foreign bodies as the Native Races and Liquor Traffic United Committee (NRLTUC), the Aborigines' Protection Society and the Church Missionary Society (CMS) led by the vociferous Bishop Herbert Tugwell. They believed the imposition of 'a Rum and Gin Civilization' would be 'a hydra that devours the natives', halting useful commerce and hindering economic development.[7] Nigeria would have a purely zero-sum economy, with merchants' profits gained at the expense of the indigenous population. Critics argued for Prohibition and a restructuring of the economy along alcohol-free lines.

Ironically the one group in Nigeria sure of the economic value of the liquor trade was the British colonial administration. The taxing of the imported liquor trade proved a major source of revenue.[8] Liquor custom duties averaged three-quarters of annual revenues in the Niger Coast Protectorate, two-thirds in Lagos and half in Southern Nigeria. The liquor trade seemed ideally suited to being taxed by the government: given the constraints of smuggling bulky, breakable bottles across land or through ocean surf meant products of the trade landed at a small number of southern coastal ports in standard cases of bottles and demijohns which could be counted quickly. The tapping of Nigerians' desire for imported alcohol proved an ideal, cost-efficient method of revenue generation:

> It is a very easy and cheap way of raising revenue. A vessel comes into Lagos and deposits 10,000 cases on a wharf... All that the Government has to do is to send down a clerk and have the cases counted, and on each case to charge 5 shillings, which practically means realising £2,500.[9]

Critics naturally condemned this: 'Is it creditable to any Government, and particularly a Christian Government, that any portion of its revenue, not to speak of the largest, is raised from such a fearfully destructive source?'.[10] But Mary Kingsley, the famous Victorian lady explorer of West-Central Africa, found no objection 'to living on the proceeds of a grog shop'.[11] While the Colonial Office felt uneasy about liquor revenues, to rid itself of it and the opprobrium that went with it from critics would have resulted in 'a complete dislocation of its finances'.[12]

The liquor-for-produce system

The label of *Fraternity Superior Gin* portrayed a black trader standing on a barrel of palm oil on the left with his glass raised in celebration, and a white maiden standing on a gin case on the right returning the toast. The exchange of Nigerian agricultural produce for European liquor represented one of the central tenets of the liquor trade (**Fig. 1**). The course of the liquor-for-produce system was as follows: from hulks moored to river banks self-styled 'Palm Oil Ruffians' established their presence on the coastal littoral of Nigeria. They exchanged gin, guns and cloth for rubber, palm oil and palm kernels from inland markets. To facilitate smooth relations with the local chiefs, economic rituals developed, such as *comey* (locally-imposed export duty) and *dashes* (gratuities mainly in the form of liquor). In the 1880s, hulks gave way to permanent land-based trading stations or factories, bringing the producer nearer to the coveted imported goods. The European merchant's Nigerian agents or independent local middlemen took considerable quantities of liquor to the so-called 'native export produce markets', where the local farmers brought their agricultural goods. Farmers did not concern themselves with such esoteric forms of value as world market prices; their incomes depended on how their commodities translated into quantities of gin. After bargaining the rate of exchange, the farmers returned home with their liquor to drink or convert it into social value in the ceremonies associated with new born babies, marriages, chieftaincy installations and funerals. Meanwhile the agents or middlemen returned to the European factory with the produce for export.[13]

This same trading pattern repeated itself over and over again across Southern Nigeria; its visible method of commercial exchange in public places can be seen in the south-western town of Abeokuta. One liquor critic saw hundreds of canoes coming down the Ogun river from Abeokuta to Lagos 'laden with ivory tusks, gold, palm oil and the most precious products of the interior, and returning with nothing but filthy spirits'.[14] Of 250 carriers walking the 2 miles (3.2km) between the Titi gate and Aro on the outskirts of Abeokuta, one-third carried corn and yams, about 20 carried salt, and the

remainder cases of gin and demijohns of rum.[15] Thousands of bottles of gin never even reached the town, but found their way to nearby farming villages. Two hundred women head-loading kernels to market in the morning returned in the evening with gin. Thousands of empty gin bottles were scattered around the town itself, visible proof of liquor's significance to the local economy. Even a local church's pews were made out of empty gin cases.[16]

Between one-third and two-fifths of Southern Nigeria's exports went to purchase imported liquor in the early 20th century (**Table 1**). But there were wide variations in the ratios of liquor-to-exports: The port of Warri imported spirits worth 17% of its total exports of £261,025 in 1908; that of Brass exported £72,100 of produce and imported £42,200 of liquor and £41,300 of other goods in 1907; and Burutu paid for 75% of its £30,000 of exports in gin.[17] While some farmers changed up to 90% of their produce into gin, some European factories had an unwritten exchange rule of a-half-and-half split between liquor and other items, such as half the palm products at Oron paid for with liquor in 1908.[18]

Yet merchants made little profit from the sale of the liquor itself, simply using it as a bartering commodity to gain the desired local produce which they sold on to others at a profitable rate. Merchants sold spirits below cost price, so keen were they to get their hands on the agricultural produce. Others used liquor to tempt locals to their factories to buy other goods with higher profit margins which caught their eye.

> Traders will often try to keep the gin in the background, and display the attractions of their other wares to their Negro customers. But it frequently happens that the latter arrive with the fixed determination to have a certain quantity of spirit whatever else they get, and set themselves to drive as hard a bargain as possible, getting what they want in exchange for the smallest quantity of produce or the least amount of money. That satisfactorily settled, they are less keen about the rest, and may give good value for the prints and trinkets and pots they require to take back with them. Thus the part of the trade associated with spirits is usually the least profitable and consequently the least popular with the importer.[19]

On this last point, while liquor might have been unpopular, it seemed necessary as it was the most sought-after commodity in the colony's markets. Trade in many areas relied on spirits; as one British MP stated in 1916: 'it seems to be the accepted doctrine in Nigeria that it is not possible to have a proper output of palm kernels unless a bottle of gin is dangled before the nose of the natives'.[20] Alcohol provided the incentive to farmers to bring their produce to market: 'Spirits give a kind of stimulus to these people to get rubber and palm oil, and without spirits they would not do anything'.[21] In so doing, the

Table 1: Spirit imports and agricultural exports, Southern Nigeria, 1906-13 (in £s)

Year	Spirits volume (gallons)	Spirit declared value	Spirit import duty	Total value of spirit imports	Total agricultural exports (a)	Total spirit imports to agricultural exports (%)
1906	3,321,902	301,738	600,784	902,522	2,292,404	39.37
1907	4,055,204	385,505	806,942	1,192,447	3,089,333	38.60
1908	3,235,669	332,577	691,190	1,023,767	2,709,377	37.79
1909	2,950,111	308,770	639,503	948,273	3,382,930	28.03
1910	4,748,139	456,485	999,823	1,456,308	4,356,460	33.42
1911	4,835,363	440,818	975,557	1,416,375	4,492,494	31.53
1912	4,450,196	440,952	1,013,808	1,454,760	4,667,906	31.17
1913	4,635,273	452,939	1,138,305	1,591,244	5,259,920	30.25

Note: (a) Cocoa, palm products, rubber and timber
Sources: Southern Nigeria Blue Books of Statistics, 1906-13

Figure 1: Representation of the liquor-for-produce system
Source: NRLTUC 1909, Native Races and the Liquor Traffic, London, front cover.

liquor trade became entwined in the general health of the economy in the years before the First World War.

After 1914, however, the wartime economy brought overwhelming pressure on firms to change their stance as regards the necessity of liquor to trade in the country. First, Germany, which previously supplied a lot of the liquor and took most of Nigeria's agricultural exports, became an enemy market closed for business.[22] Second, cash-crop producers bucked at the market trend of rising liquor prices for not adequately rewarding them for their war-time production. The barter terms of trade not only failed to turn favourable but actually declined. A lack of shipping cancelled out rising wholesale prices for Nigerian cocoa and palm products in Europe. Yet Miller Brothers reported at the same time 'trade can be carried on without Spirits'.[23] 1917 recorded the best year

for trade at £16,261,000 in value and a record low for spirit imports, indicating that export production was not dependent on imported liquor.[24]

Gin currency

Although not confined solely to gin, all transactions with liquor were called 'gin currency'.

Trade spirits, especially gin are not used merely for drinking, but are in some parts of the country employed as a substitute for currency and large quantities are stored as accumulated wealth. In the more backward parts of the country British coin is regarded with suspicion by the natives and either does not pass current at all or only passes at a depreciated rate. The people are still in the barter stage, and for various reasons gin furnishes the most convenient standard of value.[25]

What did gin currency look like? While there were small, medium and large demijohns, jars, tins, wooden casks, puncheons, pipes and barrels, bottles came in a multitude of shapes and sizes. In the example of bottles, this could lead to fraud as they gave consumers little clear appreciation of the actual volume of liquor being purchased. Commonplace hazards included false bottoms and thick glass, increasing the weight of a case but not its liquid volume. Other sharp bottle practices included long necks containing nothing more than air or darkly coloured glass to obscure the level of its liquid contents. Extra thick wicker baskets made the volume of the demijohn appear larger than it actually was. Some merchants felt genuinely appalled by the sheer variety of their stock, but others used it as an excuse to defraud their customers.[26] The issue came to a head in 1905 when people in Western Province refused to pay the usual price of 9 pence for a bottle of gin, 'the contents of which they found had been reduced to a Minimum'.[27] But merchants themselves saw the disastrous effect of such practices on their collective reputation and responded to official calls for a prompt and satisfactory solution. After consultation with the Lagos Chamber of Commerce, the Southern Nigeria government passed a comprehensive law listing the size and weight of bottles, small, medium and large demijohns, jars, tins, wooden casks, puncheons, pipes and barrels, and the volume of liquor they were to contain. The contents of every spirit case had to be legibly and indelibly marked on the outside, while every demijohn had to have its contents stamped on a tin tag or lead seal attached to its neck.[28]

Liquor could only be imported into Nigeria under trade marks, a colonial commercial invention requiring traders to register the brands of alcoholic beverages on the market. Trademark owners had sole use, with others banned from copying the original design and wording. Liquor bottle labels reveals sophisticated selling: 'some traders have adopted for their liquor brands tribal names, and attractive labels bearing these names appear on the liquor bottles', inferring that such recognizable features would help the generally illiterate population to distinguish one brand from another.[29] Some illiterate Igbo men went to market with *Peters* tattooed on their arms to get that particular brand of gin in exchange for their goods, while the list of winning medals at international spirit competitions on some labels, which looked like a series of coins to the uninitiated, made it easier for some customers to ask for 'coin gin'.[30] Images of dinosaurs, kangaroos, mermaids, and penguins featured on some labels, but the majority of cases appropriated images and names familiar to customers, including drums and drummers, *Black Prince* and *Canoe* gin as well as *Hyena, Grasshopper* and *Three Matchetes* beer.[31]

To critics, gin currency was 'one of the most important, and one of the most deplorable aspects' of the whole liquor trade, symptomatic of the enormous hold alcohol had on a significant part of the Nigerian population.[32] The Archbishop of Canterbury, Randall Davidson, condemned the 'current coin' of Lagos and Southern Nigeria in 1905: the liquor bottle.[33] His missionaries had trouble adjusting to the need to have the hated gin with them when they went shopping, as Tugwell exaggeratedly described in 1909:

> In some parts of the Delta it is not possible to purchase food unless you are prepared to pay for it in gin. Archdeacon Dennis, when travelling through the country, could not get a fowl because the people insisted on a bottle of gin in payment, and I have been frequently refused in the same way. At Agberi, we opened a station when the Niger Company retired, but we had to withdraw the man there because the people would not sell him food unless he produced gin in exchange.… Again among the canoe-men the very first thing they ask you when you start on a journey is for an instalment of their payment in gin.[34]

Christian missionaries at Atari petitioned their headquarters to allow them to use gin 'otherwise they would starve'.[35] Trade spirits surfaced in all sorts of transactional situations. It was legal to pay wages in spirits throughout the Niger Territories until May 1887; two murderers from Aba were paid for their services with gin, while it was strongly rumoured that the trading firm of Swanzy's would buy its rubber from Ibadan with imported spirits.[36] An Onitsha town crier summoned the waterside people to meet on the following day to elect a chief, proclaiming that non-attendees would be fined one case of gin.[37]

Several reasons account for the use of gin currency as an integral part of the Southern Nigerian economy. First, gin was a useful transitional currency. While liquor bottles were fragile and prone to breakage, they did not deteriorate over time unlike more delicate articles like cloth and tobacco. Its transport was less cumbersome than bulky, heavy cowries and brass rods. Second, every case of liquor could be conveniently divided into smaller units of its 12 constituent bottles for commercial transactions. Even when the British tried to monetize the economy, they found their 12 pence to 1 shilling merely paralleled what was already in place: 12 bottles to one case. Third, and paradoxically, the government's ban on *manilla* imports in 1902, the depreciation of brass rods, and the high degree of local suspicion of sterling notes and coins boosted the use of the alternative currency in gin. Opobo Chief Cookey Gam equated money with gin because of the prohibition on *manillas* and copper wires but not gin.[38]

Fourth, once enough people accepted gin as currency the process led to increased liquor imports, which in turn accentuated the process across the economy: 'the convenience and popularity of gin as a means of exchange with the native races have undoubtedly encouraged the traders to stimulate the gin traffic'.[39] Gin could be kept for economic and social purposes. Because agricultural produce consisted of perishable commodities, it was difficult to store as wealth and so it was converted into forms that could be stored, such as land, slaves, or alcohol. A person's wealth was not reckoned merely by the amount of cash he possessed. 'Stored gin is like banked wealth', said the visiting Liquor Trade Committee, who were handed a photograph of a big stack of gin bottles outside a house; though the bottles were empty, they nevertheless had economic and social value, signifying the abode of a person of high status, 'a big man'.[40] In another example, 1,400 bottles were piled up next to a chief's house – this was a sign of his importance.[41] Also, bottle-covered graves were not an indication of the cause of death, but symbolic of the wealth of the deceased.[42]

Fifth, as the bottles passed from hand to hand, the storage of gin as currency did not completely check consumption because they were frequently opened for drinking a mouthful of the contents and then refilled with water. As liquor import duty rose, merchants faced two alternatives: watering down their stock or hiking prices. Sometimes middlemen diluted, or 'washed', the liquor, sometimes the retailers, and occasionally both.[43]

No matter who carried out the practice the object remained the same: to defraud the customer and make extra profit. Tin foil capsules commonly found on the spout of liquor bottles could be removed, while Abiraba blacksmiths made corkscrews.[44] Sealing wax stoppers proved only slightly more troublesome:

> The bottles are opened by the native trader by means of two nails or two pieces of flat bamboo inserted on each side of the cork, which is thus gently removed. About a gill of spirit is removed and its place supplied with water. The cork is then replaced. It is held in the fire for a moment till the wax is heated and is then dipped in the sawdust, and appears intact.[45]

Dilution led to spirits sold at the coast having a stronger alcoholic content than those sold in the hinterland; the last people in the line of transmission 'simply buy water'.[46] Some gin was as weak as to be unsalable at Onitsha market even when offered at 2 pence a bottle.[47] But it was John Holt's experience that any kind of bottle tampering led to selling difficulties, forcing retailers to accept a much lower price than otherwise or face a fight with customers over adulteration.[48] Yet while dilution took place, and so depreciated the gin currency, this offset its tendency to appreciate in value whenever the government increased the customs duty.

Gin currency was even found at the heart of the colonialist's legal system in the payment of court fines in one area, as a trader told Bishop Tugwell:

> I recently imported £1,000 in sovereigns, hoping thereby to establish a specie basis for trade in place of the gin basis currency.... But at present, the Government accepts fines paid in gin. And thus the Government not only recognizes the principle of a gin currency, but helps to maintain and establish it.[49]

Struck by this statement, Tugwell questioned the local District Commissioner who confirmed that payments of fines came in the form of gin bottles and cases. Given the colonialists' and merchants' mutual need to monetize the economy in the interests of their commercial activity, Tugwell thought the situation financially and morally corrupt. The government categorically denied it as 'absolutely untrue', however, and the *Lagos Weekly Record* newspaper described Tugwell's story as 'dubious and curious... impossible'.[50] But Tugwell handed the Colonial Office a copy of his diary entry for 22 January 1908 confirming his side of the incident.[51]

Unhappy at what they considered a slur on their rule in Southern Nigeria, the colonial government instituted a thorough investigation, but instead found information substantiating Tugwell's story. While the presiding judge did not fine in gin, at six Native Courts in Brass District – Amassoma, Ekow, Nembe, Ogbayan, Sabagreia and Twon – 90% of court fines were paid in gin currency. Litigants deposited gin as security for a court payment, being converted into cash by the court clerk at the rate of 10 shillings per case before being written up in the court's ledger. With the market price of gin a couple of shillings higher, the clerk made a personal profit on the transaction. A modified payment of fines in gin then developed a further twist to court business. Merchants attended courts armed with a supply of cash; when a litigant had to pay a fine he went to one of these traders and converted his gin into cash at the requisite 10 shillings a case.

So instead of the clerk selling the gin to the trader, the litigant sold to the trader directly. On government discovery of the practice of payment of court fines in gin in June 1908 – contrary to Southern Nigeria Rule number two of 1901 – it was stopped.[52] Yet even after the 1908 ban, litigants still paid their fines with money raised from converting their bank account of gin cases into cash.[53]

The unseemly practices of these Native Courts and the events surrounding the discovery of their illegal ways embarrassed the colonial government as the courts were initially the most visible sign of British authority in many rural areas. When these courts were established the people of the area were ignorant of cash currencies so payments in gin had to be accepted otherwise the courts would have had to close:

> Gin is, and has been for the last 50 or 60 years, the native equivalent of money. The case, or bottle, of gin is the recognised unit of value in all commercial transactions between natives, and in cases where gin has been accepted in payment of fines, it has been accepted as the native's only form of cash.... If a native is asked the value of any article he will always reply quoting the amount of gin he values it at... any sudden reversal [of this custom] would dislocate the trade of the entire district, and seriously complicate the administrative work of the district.[54]

All six Native Courts in the Brass District started by receiving fees and fines in gin. Elsewhere in Nigeria, two witnesses from Onitsha and Abeokuta described the identical court process of Brass District's paying in gin.[55] A vicar at Modakeke also revealed that gin and rum were the chief means of paying fines.[56]

The African Association's Brass Agent Donavan, who had spent many years in the port, declared Tugwell's statement given by the unnamed merchant 'all bunkum'. Yet it emerged that Donavan had been associated with a protest against the Native Courts on the grounds that the firms were being undersold by the courts, the latter taking gin at 10 shillings while the factory price was 15 shillings per case in cash. Eventually the mystery of the nameless Brass trader was solved: Acting Agent Maysmore of the Brass Trading Company, whose import of only £750 of specie during his nine month's tenure was treated as collaborative evidence on the matter.[57]

As to the unnamed political officer who confirmed Maysmore's views on the payments of fines in gin, Tugwell had misremembered the place of the conversation. It was Acting District Commissioner Leigh-Lye at Bonny. Back in 1905, Leigh-Lye had even invited a Scottish doctor friend of his to accompany him on his round of the Native Courts, giving him the job of checking that gin bottles collected as fines had not been watered down.[58] Why Leigh-Lye had not enforced the law reveals the weak nature of early colonial rule in this part of Nigeria because of 'the rapid change of officers and the manifold duties, both executive and judicial, imposed on these officers'.[59] Further confirmation came from a prisoner in Calabar jail, John Epe, a former court clerk at Brass, languishing there while he served a five-year sentence for embezzling 50 cases of gin paid as court fines.[60] Surely a colonial official must have been on the bench when sentencing Epe to jail, and so known of the existence of the payment of fines in gin, yet it appears that nobody outside the ranks of missionaries and Nigerians themselves knew the true state of affairs in the native courts.

Monetization and the decline of gin currency

There were growing calls from anti-liquor trade critics to end the 'mischievous practice' of gin currency.[61] Monetizing the Nigerian economy faced enormous problems, however. Colonial coinage faced a deeply suspicious public, farmers unwilling to swap their produce backed by hard work for pieces of paper and circles of metal denoting a certain value backed by alien rule. This was further compounded by the fact that incomes were relatively low and small value purchases commonplace. Coins were too high in value and too scarce in circulation to serve as an extensively functioning currency, 'a form of cash utterly unsuited to the needs, modes of life and habits of the local population.'[62] Unlike gin, cowries or *manillas*, large values of coins and notes did not form big bulks when put together, and therefore were not seen by Nigerians as an impressive form of currency to hold. Others did not imbue the coins with monetary value, regarding them as only suitable raw materials for ornamental jewellery. Coins were all too easily lost or stolen. Paper notes suffered from the heat and humidity of the climate and destruction from fire, insects and rodents. The shilling notes were small and made of thin paper, very inconvenient for locals without purses or pockets. Stories about people being palmed off with telegraph envelopes as they were the same colour as 1 shilling notes made the mainly illiterate population doubly wary of any paper currency. When the West African Currency Board introduced coins with a palm tree motif, locals thought the government was about to nationalize their palm trees (**Fig. 2**).[63]

The colonial government nevertheless pressed ahead with monetization. Nickel-bronze pennies and aluminium ones worth 1/10 of a penny were introduced in the hope of finding favour.[64] Colonial officers explained the advantages of a coin currency to the population, while the government endeavoured to supply an adequate amount of coin to the market to 'win its way by degrees.'[65] For example, along the Cross River, in the face of competition from gin, brass and copper rods, 'British currency is gradually spreading throughout the country.'[66] Even Brass, the heart of the gin currency economy, saw a rise in specie and a decline in imported spirits. On the whole, the first decade of the 20th century witnessed a certain degree of success in the switch away from transitional currencies; several of them began to have their circulation severely circumscribed. This change, however, did not occur at the same time; as late as 1912, 'an astonishing variety of currencies were still in use': *manillas*, cowries, iron rods and wires, salt, copper and brass rods, cloth, tobacco, palm oil and gin.[67] Yet by that time, Southern Nigeria had imported £8 million of specie and as the use of the cash currency extended transitional currencies retreated.

It was the First World War and the consequent dearth of trade spirits imported during those four years that firmly and irrevocably moved the country towards a cash economy: 'in some ports trade spirits have lost their place as a staple'.[68] There was good reason for believing that 'the produce trade in the native markets could be carried on without trade spirits'.[69] Taken together, 1916 and 1917 saw £1,939,844 of more specie imported than exported from Nigeria and cash had taken the place of spirits in the way of a reserve – 'possibly it may also mean that Chiefs are beginning to hoard their wealth in coin instead of in gin!'[70] Just before the war's end, the British Colonial Secretary expressed the wish that,

> the bartering of spirits for Native produce is one of the most objectionable forms of that trade, and it will certainly be a satisfactory result of the war if this should cease and not be revived on the return of peace.[71]

In fact, the combined effects of the war and the 1919 ban on trade spirits made gin difficult to function as a currency in its few remaining enclaves.[72] What happened to it then is not difficult to guess: it was drunk.

However, this was not quite the end of the story of gin currency in Nigeria, as it could be argued that the post-war economic slump was to a certain degree worsened by the loss of this convenient medium of exchange:

> Ninety per cent of Commerce's post-war problems are due to the grandmotherly legislation that would make it a crime for a native to have a bottle of gin inside his house, and to use it for the purchase of a boxful of yams or cassava![73]

Remnants of gin currency remained. Gin was used for the hire of canoes at Ikom in the 1920s.[74] Gin was still used in paying marriage dowries, which one newspaper labelled 'a farce'.[75] Presenting gin as part of the annual present of a tenant to his landlord was common in Oyo in 1936.[76] Nevertheless, such practices (which continue to this day) are isolated relics of the gin currency age.

Conclusions

From the macro-scale of a colony's budgetary finances based on shiploads of liquor to the micro-scale of a farmer exchanging his agricultural wares for a bottle of spirits, imported alcohol had significant economic importance in the colonial economy of Southern Nigeria from 1860 until the First World War.

Situationally defined, but also constantly renegotiated, imported alcohol had innumerable fluid cultural and economic contexts. In terms of the latter, the liquor trade provoked questions over the ultimate goal of colonial economics. Critics of the liquor trade saw it as commercially unsound, socially destructive and morally indefensible: 'It is not the Union Jack which would be regarded as most characteristic of the advance of British rule, but the little green boxes well known as gin cases, and the demijohns of rum'.[77] Yet the swapping of bottles of liquor for items in the market was a common-place occurrence and for many years the fortunes of both the liquor trade and the general economy became increasingly interdependent. It was only during the First World War that the absolute necessity of alcohol as a catalyst for commerce were tested to the full and found to be lacking solid foundations in economics. Business fortunes could be 'achieved without the aid of the trade gin and rum accessory, which is alleged to be

Figure 2 One-shilling and 2-shilling coins, British West Africa, 1916 and 1924

the *sine qua non* of trade in West Africa'.[78]

The discovery of such a malpractice as paying court fines in gin indicated the strong attraction of some Southern Nigerians for their gin currency, even in the face of colonial efforts to get them into a monetary economy. Critics of the liquor trade continued to use the scandal – the most 'glaring abuse of the liquor traffic' – to remind their audience of the colonial government's shame over the practice of exacting fines in gin.[79]

The only acceptable form of currency to the colonialists was the one they were used to in Britain, and so a system of British-backed pounds, shillings and pence became the specie of Nigeria. A huge effort to monetize the economy was made, and eventually overcame all the other currencies previously in circulation in Nigeria. Although continuing in its myriad social roles, gin currency followed previously useful transitional currencies like cowries and *manillas* into liquidation.

Notes

1 This paper is based on: Heap, S., 2005. '"A bottle of gin is dangled before the nose of the natives": The economic uses of imported liquor in Southern Nigeria, 1860–1920', *African Economic History* 33, 69–85. We are happy to acknowledge the permission granted by the editors of that journal to reproduce it here, with major additions and revisions.
2 Guyer 1995, 89.
3 Heap 1995.
4 Heap 1998.
5 Bloch and Parry 1991, 8; Long 1992, 152.
6 Heap 1995.
7 *Lagos Observer* 1886, 2; *Lagos Observer* 1897, 2.
8 Heap 1996; Heap 2002.
9 *Lagos Weekly Record* 1911.
10 *Lagos Echo* 1894.
11 Kingsley 1898, 546.
12 National Archives (NA), London, Colonial Office (CO) 444/3, Minute by R. L. Antrobus, Under-Secretary of State for the Colonies, Britain, 3 November 1899.
13 Heap 1995.
14 Benson 1889.
15 *Niger and Yoruba Notes* 1897, 52.
16 *Lagos Standard* 1895.
17 Colonial Office 1909b, 375.
18 Colonial Office 1909b, 24, 32, 55.
19 *West Africa* 1902.
20 Cavendish-Bentinck 1916.
21 Colonial Office 1909b, 47.
22 Osuntokun 1979.
23 National Archives, Ibadan (NAI), Chief Secretary's Office (CSO) 20/4/NC.169/16, A.A. Cowan, Miller Brothers, Lagos, to Sir F.D. Lugard, Governor-General, Lagos, Nigeria, 7 October 1916.
24 NA, CO 583/67, Lugard, *Address to the Nigerian Council*, 28 December 1917, 5.
25 NA, CO 520/66, D.E. Price, District Commissioner, Brass, *Report*, 4 August 1908, 2–3, in Egerton to Crewe, 26 September 1908.
26 NAI, CSO 1/1/50, Birtwistle, Commercial Intelligence Officer, Lagos, to F.H. Derriman, Acting Colonial Secretary, Lagos, 16 March 1905; *Lagos Weekly Record* 1906.
27 *Lagos Weekly Record* 1905.
28 *Lagos Standard* 1905; Southern Nigeria Ordinance no. 10 of 1906.
29 Blackburn 1921, 26.
30 I am grateful to Dmitri van den Bersselaar of the University of Liverpool for this latter point.
31 Heap 1995.
32 NRLTUC 1910, 34.
33 Davidson 1905.
34 Colonial Office 1909b, 24.
35 Colonial Office 1909b, 386.
36 Royal Niger Company Regulation no. 20 of 1887; Colonial Office 1909b, 224; *Lagos Weekly Record* 1895.
37 Colonial Office 1909a, 16; Colonial Office 1909b, 392.
38 Colonial Office 1909b, 312.
39 MacDonald 1916, 91.
40 Colonial Office 1909a.
41 Colonial Office 1909b, 301.
42 Ambler 1987, 14–15.
43 Waller 1887, 8; Colonial Office 1909b, 57.
44 Colonial Office 1909b, 33, 78, 421.
45 Colonial Office 1909b, 78; Heap 1999.
46 Colonial Office 1909b, 311.
47 Colonial Office 1909b, 410.
48 NA, CO 147/147, John Holt & Co. to J. Chamberlain, Secretary of State for the Colonies, Britain, 20 July 1899.
49 NRLTUC 1908, 5.
50 NA, CO 520/62, Sir W. Egerton, Governor, Southern Nigeria, to Lord Crewe, Secretary of State for the Colonies, Britain, 25 June 1908; *Lagos Weekly Record*, 1908.
51 NA, CO 520/63, Bishop H. Tugwell, CMS Bishop of Western Equatorial Africa Tugwell to Strachey, 25 July 1908.
52 NA, CO 520/66, H.S. Gladstone, Acting District Commissioner, Brass, to J.J. Thorburn, Colonial Secretary, Southern Nigeria, 1 September 1908.
53 Colonial Office 1909b, 75.
54 NA, CO 520/66, Price, *Report*, 4 August 1908, p.1–3, in Egerton to Crewe, 26 September 1908.
55 NA, CO 520/87, Reverend Sidney Smith, in *Humble Memorial of the NRLTUC* to Crewe, 7 April 1909, p.21; PRO, CO 520/87, Reverend J.J. Olumide, in *Humble Memorial*, 30.
56 NA, CO 520/87, Reverend E.A. Kayode, in *Humble Memorial*, p.30.
57 NA, CO 520/66, Gladstone to Thorburn, 1 September 1908.
58 NA, CO 520/77, Thorburn to Crewe, 2 January 1909.
59 Colonial Office 1909a, 8.
60 Papers of Randall Davidson, Archbishop of Canterbury, Lambeth Palace Library, vol. 232, p.84–85, Tugwell to Davidson, 12 March 1909.
61 *Nigerian Daily Times* 1926.
62 NA, CO 657/19, *Governor Clifford's Address*, 26 February 1923, 23.
63 Mwangi 2002, 39.
64 Ekundare 1973, 187–192.
65 NA, CO 520/55, Elgin to L.H. Nott, Secretary, NRLTUC, 15 April 1908.
66 NA, CO 520/62, Egerton to Crewe, 6 July 1908.
67 Johannson 1967, 48.
68 *Nigeria Customs* 1916, 7.
69 *Nigeria Annual Report* 1916, 7.
70 NA, CO 583/67, Lugard, *Address to the Nigerian Council*, 28 December 1917, 4.
71 NA, CO 583/67, W.H. Long, Secretary of State for the Colonies, Britain, to Lugard, Governor-General, Nigeria, 10 October 1918.
72 *Convention relating to the Liquor Traffic in Africa and Protocol* 1919.
73 *Nigerian Daily Times* 1926.
74 National Commission for Museums and Monuments 1996, 59.
75 *West African Star* 1936.
76 NAI, Oyo Provincial Office [OYOPROF] 2/3/C.204, J.M. Simpson, Acting District Officer, Oyo, to H.L. Ward-Price, Senior Resident, Oyo Province, 7 September 1936.
77 *Niger and Yoruba Notes* 1894, 8.
78 *Niger and Yoruba Notes* 1911, 197.
79 MacDonald, 1916, 93.

Bibliography

Ambler, C.H. 1987. 'Alcohol and disorder in precolonial Africa'. *African Studies Center Working Paper Number 126*, Boston University.

Benson, E.W. 1889. Archbishop of Canterbury, House of Lords, London, *Hansard*, 6 May, column 1,208.

Blackburn, A.E. 1921. *Report of an Enquiry on the International Convention Relating to the Liquor Traffic in Africa during His Tour in South and West Africa, 1920–21*. London.

Bloch, M. and Parry, J. 1991. 'Introduction: money and the morality of exchange'. In Parry and Bloch (eds.), *Money and the Morality of Exchange*. Cambridge.

Cavendish-Bentinck, Colonel Lord H. 1916. Member of Parliament, House of Commons, London, *Hansard*, 3 August, column 556.

Colonial Office, 1909a. *Report of the committee of inquiry into the liquor trade in Southern Nigeria, Part I: report*, His Majesty's Stationary Office, London.

Colonial Office, 1909b. *Report of the committee of inquiry into the liquor trade in Southern Nigeria, Part II: minutes of evidence*. His Majesty's Stationary Office, London.

Convention relating to the Liquor Traffic in Africa and Protocol, signed at St-Germain-en-Laye, 10 September 1919, Command Paper 478, 1919.

Davidson, R.T. 1905. Archbishop of Canterbury, House of Lords, London, *Hansard*, 6 June, column 827.

Davidson, R.T. 1909. Papers of Randall Davidson, Archbishop of Canterbury, Lambeth Palace Library, vol. 232, 84–85: 12 March.

Ekundare, R.O. 1973. *An Economic History of Nigeria: 1860–1960*. London.

Guyer, J. 1995. 'Wealth in people, wealth in things – introduction'. *Journal of African History* 36(1), 83–90.

Heap, S. 1995. *The Liquor Trade and the Nigerian Economy, 1880–1939*. Ph.D. University of Ibadan.

Heap, S. 1996. 'Before "Star": The import substitution of western-style alcohol in Nigeria, 1870–1970'. *African Economic History* 24, 69–89.

Heap, S. 1998. '"We think prohibition is a farce": Drinking in the alcohol-prohibited zone of colonial Northern Nigeria'. *International Journal of African Historical Studies* 31(1), 23–51.

Heap, S. 1999. 'The quality of liquor in colonial Nigeria'. *Itinerario: European Journal of Overseas History* 23(2), 29–47.

Heap, S. 2000. 'Transport and liquor in colonial Nigeria'. *Journal of Transport History* 21(1), 28–53.

Heap, S. 2002. 'Living on the proceeds of a grog shop: Liquor revenue in Nigeria. In D.F. Bryceson (ed.), *Alcohol in Africa: Mixing Business, Pleasure and Politics*, Westport, 139–159.

Heap, S. 2005. '"A bottle of gin is dangled before the nose of the natives": The economic uses of imported liquor in Southern Nigeria, 1860–1920'. *African Economic History* 33, 69–85.

Johannson, S.O. 1967. *Nigerian Currencies: Manillas, Cowries and Others*, Norrköping.

Kingsley, M.H. April 1898. 'The liquor traffic with West Africa'. *Fortnightly Review*, 537–560.

Lagos Echo, 1 December 1894. Editorial, 2.

Lagos Observer, 17 April 1886. 'Rum and gin', 2.

Lagos Observer, 7 May 1897. 'The drink traffic and the natives', 2.

Lagos Standard, 18 September 1895. ‚Abeokuta', 2.

Lagos Standard, 15 November 1905. ‚The West African liquor traffic: how British traders cheat the natives', 2.

Lagos Weekly Record, 12 October 1895. 'The Swanzy rubber concession and the liquor traffic', 1.

Lagos Weekly Record, 25 November 1905. 'The spirit trade', 2.

Lagos Weekly Record, 1 September 1906. 'The law for standardizing the receptacles for spirits', 2.

Lagos Weekly Record, 19 September 1908. 'Bishop Tugwell and the liquor traffic', 2.

Lagos Weekly Record, 27 May 1911. 'The liquor traffic', 3.

Long, A. 1992. 'Goods, knowledge and beer'. In N. Long and Long (eds). *Battlefields of Knowledge*. London, 147–170.

MacDonald, A.J. 1916. *Trade, Politics and Christianity in Africa and the East*. London.

Mwangi, W. 2002. 'The lion, the native and the coffee plant: Political imager and the ambiguous area of currency design in colonial Kenya'. *Geopolitics* 7(1), 31–62.

National Commission for Museums and Monuments (NCMM), 1996. *The story of Old Calabar: a guide to the National Museum at The Old Residency, Calabar*. Lagos: NCMM.

Native Races and Liquor Traffic United Committee (NRLTUC), 1908. *Bishop Tugwell's speech, 7th May 1908*, London: NRLTUC.

NRLTUC, 1910. *The liquor traffic in Southern Nigeria as set forth in the report of the government committee of inquiry of 1909: an examination and a reply*. London: NRLTUC.

Niger and Yoruba Notes, 1894. 'Native races and the liquor traffic'. 1(1), 8.

Niger and Yoruba Notes, 1897. 'Spirits and other trade goods'. 3(31), 52.

Niger and Yoruba Notes, 1911. 'Commercial success without the aid of gin and rum'. 16(83), 197.

Nigeria Annual Report, 1916.

Nigeria Customs, 1916.

Nigerian Daily Times, 1926. 'Liquor traffic in West Africa'. 27 August: 1.

Osuntokun, A. 1979. *Nigeria in the First World War*. London.

Royal Niger Company Regulation no. 20 of 1887. The Spirituous Liquors (no. 2) Regulation.

Southern Nigeria Ordinance no. 10 of 1906, *The Trade Spirits (Regulation of Receptacles) Ordinance*.

Waller, H., 1887. *Trafficking in liquor with the natives of Africa*, London: Church of England Temperance Society.

West Africa, 26 April 1902. The liquor trade in West Africa, 449.

West African Star, 20 January 1936. 'Our women problem: who is responsible?', by 'A Nigerian Youth', 11.

Manillas, Money and the Cost of Legitimacy in the mid-20th Century: A Royal Account in Eastern Nigeria

Jane I. Guyer

Introduction

My analysis and discussion here are devoted to the detailed account book of a Nigerian chief that surfaced as I was searching the archive of G.I. Jones, formerly of the British Colonial Service in Eastern Nigeria and then of the Department of Social Anthropology at Cambridge University. It is 89 pages long and purports to cover the ten years between 1944 and 1954. It is not itself dated, but was probably given to Jones during his commissioned study of chieftaincy in Eastern Nigeria in 1956.

The interweaving of value and price, of calculation and record-keeping, and of currencies and their deployment in the legitimation of authority for the African past is such a difficult nexus to enter, and so crucial for any understanding of trade and governance that even the most mysterious and perhaps eccentric of sources demands study for the glimpses it may offer. I have argued elsewhere that monetary transactions appear to have been precise enough, and the sources voluminous enough, to create a model of a cultural system in Atlantic Africa. But on finances and leadership, secrecy prevails. Felix Iroko worked on cowries in Dahomey, looking at counting and hoarding;[1] Law has looked at the dilemmas of financial administration in Dahomey;[2] Karin Barber has recently drawn on oral sources to imagine how equivalences were fixed in Eastern Nigeria.[3] But the place of explicit numeration and accounting seems intermittent, giving way in the sources to symbolic moments of powerful value-configuration. Iroko describes a kind of cowrie longhouse in Dahomey, decorated conspicuously. But the sources offer no sense of what the contents really were, how much and how grouped they were for storage, how they were accessed and deployed, and so on. Law extrapolates from the logic of cowry values to the dilemmas of attempting to control a cowry economy in a multiple-currency region. But the argument remains an extrapolation: very important, but supported by limited enough direct evidence that Law expresses his conclusions cautiously. Barber's imaginative leap to the value-anchoring of sacrificial actions in Eastern Nigeria is based on linking the literary and religious sources to clues in the political and historical sources. But it takes that leap, and powerful circumstantial contextualization, to fix her inspired inference in our minds. Possibly all accounting reverts to symbolic frames, as Carruthers and Espeland argue for the 'purism' of Western double-entry book-keeping, with its focus on the moral, as well as economic, value-anchor of 'the bottom line'.[4] But the capacity of the account and the symbolic value configuration to be mutually translatable is centrally at issue, especially in economies where accounts were not kept in written form. People surely shifted back and forth in highly skillful ways that created both the pragmatic and symbolic workability of power.

As far as I know there is no systematic study of African mnemonics with respect to monetary transactions and accumulations over time and in place, even though exchanges were mediated by currencies for centuries and precise calendars did exist.[5] Praise poetry focuses on wealth accumulation as a process and a performance,[6] but not as a calculation or a record. Shipton has argued that money was never indexed to time in Africa, in the manner assumed by concepts of credit, interest and account.[7] And yet there are presumably written accounts in Arabic, Amharic and possibly other written languages, with respect to affairs of state and religious institutions and there are tantalizing indications of numerical systems in non-literate traditions that applied to money alone.[8] Possibly there have been oral poetic forms that acted as monetary mnemonics, analogous to the plastic forms that Roberts and Roberts have shown for Luba historical memory.[9]

The dilemma for scholarship is enormous: to have to assume and infer some mode of accounting in order to posit ordered monetary processes, or else to face an ignorance with respect to direct evidence that may be very difficult to mitigate. If the latter, we may imply – by simply leaving a large gap here – that in much of Africa the 'function' of money as 'unit of account' (in the strict sense of account, relative to a temporal rhythm of some sort) was not practised or recognized. If not, we need a way of teasing something out of the evidence that we are still able to generate. If so, then we might give some concentrated attention to whether, and in what sense, such a situation would encourage critique of the very concept of account, in general and in other places.

So glimpses need to be opened up further, not only for insights into monetary practices themselves but also into the methods scholars might use to do justice to the full cultural complexity of African monies. We cannot assume, by default of any alternatives, that frameworks of monetary management are 'rational' or 'administrative' in a narrow western sense, even in the west itself. African philosopher Paulin Hountondji's recent collection *Rationality: Singular or Plural?*[10] is a challenge to those of us working on monies, number, mnemonics and records, just as it is to philosophers of causation, agency, language and the public sphere. Do we expect equivalence in transactions, stability in payments, balance in summations and regular temporal benchmarks in accounting? If we cannot be confident of any of these conceptual foundations, should analysis just assume them? Is impersonality a defining characteristic of monetary transactions, and if so, what do we do with an account that personalizes, rather than typifies, every transaction, as my source here does?

My paper is only a foray into such questions. The topic is vast, whereas my source here is a single document. If accounting frames constitute a general technique, their rubrics should be shared and general, whereas the longer I have studied the case presented here the more eccentric it seems. After the original presentation of the paper I was able to read the Stephen Jaja and Opobo files in the Nigerian National Archives at Ibadan and to incorporate these contextual sources into my understanding. Difficult and partial though my discussion must be of the larger issues of accounting, grappling with this one source from the colonial period has confirmed my conviction of the importance of monetary record-recording in African history, even if the sources are so limited. This account straddles the modernization of tradition, so it indicates the African dilemma of defining what such a modern tradition of public finance should be: the categories it should comprise, the detail of the reporting, the summation in a balance. It is clearly patterned after colonial practice, in the lay-out of the pages, the punctiliousness of the record (down to the last penny) and the categories of income and expenditure. But the itemization reveals a massive network of 'traditional' and personalized commitments. The way in which it constitutes an argument for a certain kind of modern African rule has become the main theme of the paper.

The paper has four parts. First is a description of the document itself, as a simple historiographical exercise. The following two parts concern high profile historical events of colonial rule related to money and value, and trace their path through the document but are not centre-stage in it. One is the topic I had initially hoped could be addressed from it, namely the co-existence of *manillas* and colonial money in Eastern Nigerian communities over the era of the famous *manilla* withdrawal of 1948.[11] The other is the payments made in the famous reparation/compensation case and the subsidy case won by the Opobo against the British government in the 1940s on the basis of documents they – but not their British co-signers – had preserved from 1890, before the imposition of colonial rule.[12] Finally, I discuss the analysis of such locally organized records for the study of the history of money in Africa, and particularly of modes, purposes and standards of accounting in the legitimation of rule.

I. The document

In the autumn of 2000, while working on the personal papers of former colonial officer and then Cambridge anthropologist G.I. Jones in the archives of the Department of Social Anthropology at Cambridge, for the chapter on Igbo and Ibibio ranking and money for my book, *Marginal Gains*,[13] I came across an 89-page, single spaced, carbon-copy typescript, stamped with the royal seal of Opobo and signed longhand by Chief Stephen U. Jaja. It is entitled as follows, in an exactly constructed inverted pyramidal style that I discovered later he used for many of his formal letters and petitions:

GENERAL ACCOUNT OF INCOME AND EXPENDITURE

OF OPOBO ROYAL HOUSE (1944–1954) BY

CHIEF STEPHEN UGBORGU JAJA,

HEAD OF OPOBO ROYAL

HOUSE, AND THE PRE

JAJA III OF

OPOBO.

The years of Jaja's accounts covered the years of the *manilla* campaign in the Igbo and Ibibio areas of Eastern Nigeria, which was the last and most organized effort by a colonial government to withdraw 'indigenous currencies' from circulation and replace them with colonial money. It was a massive, original and controversial undertaking, so I hoped that any and all sources would illuminate one aspect or another of the monetary dynamics. The Opobo tradition did emphasize the place of chieftaincy in control of the *manilla* supply. For example, in 1946 S.U. Jaja claimed that the *Atorni manilla* had been commissioned by the original King Jaja, founder of Opobo, from the firm of S. Alfred and Co. of 5 Huntly Road, Elms Park, Liverpool, that he held a patent to it, and that it should be held in consideration if indeed its status as legal tender would be abolished. 'The Atorni manilla is the last vestige of Opobo's greatness…'.[14]

To my surprise, the campaign did not figure in Jaja's accounts. *Manillas* and colonial pounds do both figure, but not any of the mechanics of the withdrawal and replacement. The chiefship did not seem, by this time and in this account, to be at the anchoring apex of a money-*manilla* and social rank valuation system, nor of a centralized money management organization. Even if *manillas* had still figured in general social life at the beginning of the period he covers, S.U. Jaja's interest in preserving their history in this document seems entirely tied up with their role in the status of chieftaincy rather than the mediation of daily purchases (see below).

The entries include rather, dozens of ceremonial expenses: the cost of doing such things as making an inventory of the royal house's firearms, repairing boat docks, providing send-offs to British officials, receiving visitors such as Dr Nnamdi Azikiwe (a leader of the independence movement) and ferrying witnesses to court for land cases; and the purchase of publications (the *Nigerian Gazette*, the *Manchester Weekly Guardian*, *Time Magazine* and various handbooks from the CMS bookshop in Lagos). Many outlays are also explained at length, from the sums paid to named laborers to clear up rubbish to the itemized cost of festivals, oracular divinations and court cases.

These entries and their organization are all in the nature of what might be considered affairs of state, under a sovereignty model of chiefs and people. They are denominated in the pounds, shillings and pence of the British colonial economy, except for a few entries recorded in *manillas* (of which more below). The following summary constitutes the introduction to the detailed breakdown of the expenditures. Reporting it in complete form conveys the total amounts at issue and the large difference that is presented between income and expenditure, for potential comparative purposes with other administrative accounts. We can already suspect that one point of the account was to convey the structural deficit situation of chiefs, when faced with the kinds of expenditures that supported their claims to legitimate rule.

Summary of Income (p. 2):

A. Egwanga New Market Rental (3 yrs)	£66-0-0
B. War Canoe Compensation	£369-5-5
C. Account deposited in U.A.C. Ltd.	£518-0-0
D. Arrears of Subsidy	£512-10-0
E. Bonus from Subsidy Houses	£115-0-0
Total £1,580-15-5	

Expenditure (22 categories re-compiled for brevity):

A. Rituals of State	£806-7-11
B. Running a royal household	£780-0-0
C. House debts	£257-17-9
D. Repairs and Demolitions	£54-9-8
E. Councils and Conferences	£154-16-6
F. Disputes and Lawsuits	£514-11-4
G. Funerals, care of Jaja's sepulcher	£53-16-0
H. Deposit in UAC	£229-4-0
H. Receptions (for colonial officers)	£80-12-5
I. Miscellaneous	£208-5-7
Total	£3,120-2-1

The functioning of an indirect rule kind of governance model was explicitly at stake at the time the account was written. Faced with the question of how to bring chieftaincy into a national state and local government system of governance the British commissioned a study in 1956 whose terms of references were:

> to enquire into the position, status and influence of chiefs and Natural Rulers in the Eastern Region, and to make recommendation as to the necessity or otherwise of legislation regulating their appointment, recognition and deposition.[15]

The study was undertaken by G.I. Jones, in whose papers we find the Jaja accounts. Jones's final report notes that, in fact, no-one was interested in any of the topics defined by the terms of reference, so:

> the enquiry therefore was directed primarily to determining the part played by chiefs and Natural Rulers in their traditional systems of government and the part which people wished them to play in the contemporary system.[16]

Nothing could illustrate everything a chief does, and justify it better, than an account … if such records existed. S.U. Jaja may have been attempting to supply such an inventory of responsibilities and their financial implications.

The oddest circumstance of the account however – which is not explicitly referred to in it – is that its author, Chief Stephen Ugborgu Jaja, was not the head of King Jaja's House at the time he wrote the accounts, as the title and signature imply. He was deposed by his own House in 1949, half way through the period covered by the account. After a long drawn out process of appeal, the British upheld a dispensation that the Opobo chiefs were chosen by their Houses and not in any way, or at any stage, by the government. And in fact, when we look closely at the entries, most of the records only refer to 1944 to 1948, when he certainly held the position of Chief of King Jaja House. In financial terms, this would double any inference of *per annum* costs of chieftaincy we might be tempted to make by dividing the summaries by ten. He appears to be validating his account by claiming it to be current at the time of writing, even at the cost of under-estimating the total monetary costs. Why? Having read his deposition file in the Nigerian National Archives,[17] I am now inclined to see this chieftaincy account as a kind of pretension or policy document, whose argument – the way that legitimacy and money become mutually referential – I elaborate in the final section. The topics I originally hoped to document as 'history' are better seen in light of the account as a rhetorical device, as indeed Carruthers and Espeland have argued all accounts to be.[18] So Parts 2 and 3 use history to identify enduring principles of money and legitimacy, rather than to establish the past *per se*.

2. Traces of the *manilla* economy

I had hoped to find evidence of the famous transition from *manillas* to pounds that was mandated and managed by the British in 1948. While these Opobo accounts do show a pervasively monetized imagination about social and ritual life, as Latham argues for the Cross River in the 19th century,[19] this particular record gives only glimpses into the domains where two currencies – 'traditional' and 'modern', *manillas* and pounds sterling – were options as means of payment. *Manillas* figure primarily in ritual contexts, which may validate legitimacy claims, but we can still search there for modes of calculation from the past that might still be operative.

There are nine entries where *manillas* were either mandated or could substitute for colonial money in transactions, but equally there are many places where one might have expected 'traditional' payments where none are mentioned. The main category I expected as the destination for *manillas* was funerals. Chief Jaja had to contribute substantially to the funerals of close or indigent royal family members over an undated period. There were 53 cases (pp. 77–79), each named and Jaja's gifts are itemized, for a total cost of £44-2-4. All the payments are enumerated in colonial money. I quote some entries because they also give a flavour of the style of the document as a whole. The basis for the obligation is described; the components of the transactions are precise in type, quality and amount; and the recipients and their locations are denoted by name. From fieldwork elsewhere in Nigeria, I suggest that these entries are close to the particularism by which memories are retained in oral mnemonics. As formal records, written in English, they have a performative quality, as if to announce an age-old indigenous capacity for accounts that surpassed British expectations of Nigerians and even British projections of their own form of rule. We cannot know for sure, so the reader is presented with evidence that they may reinterpret.

By far the most expensive funeral contribution, at £6-11-0, was for the death of Queen Shuba Jaja:

> 2. Queen Shuba Jaja (p. 77):
>
> (a) Part payment for the cost of a coffin bought for the burial of this Queen ((£3-10-0); Drink to coffin makers (3/-); (b) Funeral gifts: Cash (£1); one fathom white baft (4/-); one fathom Real India (7/-); drink (12/-); provisions to paddlers, Chiefs and Elders who went with the Head of the Royal House to Ozu-efre Ville for the interment (15/-)… £6-11-0

Other funeral entries suggest many directions that the sociological imagination could go, but again, no *manillas*:

> 3. Oto Jaja (indigent but serviceable)… £2-8-0
>
> 11. The murder of Godfrey Bibama:
>
> Fares to and from Egwanga-Opobo in respect of this murder and cost of provisions given to the following Police Constables and others whenever they came to Opobo Town in connection with the murder: (a) Corporal Jonas Ebozue: (b) P.C. Franklin Ikwujieagu; (c) Joseph Onyeanum; (d) P.C. Caleb Umunna; (e) P.C. Godfrey Onodi; (f) P.C. Asuquuo Essien; (g) L.C. Nathan Motianya; (h) P.C. Chukwuemeka Okafor; (i) P.C. Jospeh Igwu and others assessed at … £5-10-0
>
> 30. Four men and three women of Opukalama. £1-8-0

The occasions when *manillas* are mentioned are few and interesting enough to quote all the entries.

A. At the installation of the King (Opooboo) of Opobo:

(a) The accession gift to the Dappa-na-Amakris. (p. 16):

As ordained by the divinities through the oracles, that Opooboo should 'first of all give an offering in kind to the manes of his maternal ancestors before ascending the throne. That the said gift should consist of (1) one white cock; (2) one piece white baft; (3) one piece Real India; (4) one bottle of strong drink; (5) one bottle of sweet drink; (6) a saucer of bitter kola; (7) a small piece of edible chalk; (8) seven times seven *manillas* – all in a wicker tray (an 'egele').

(b) The gala dinner (p. 22):

Custom further ordains that, whereas, the gala vigil ('sodi') with the gala dinner is sacred to God Almighty, it should willy-nilly be kept at the expense of every newly created chief, every successor, and every new ruler; and that if any chief prefer to give the equivalent of the state banquet in money, forty-eight thousand manillas (48,000) which is at present £600, must invariably be paid to Asimini – a legal name under which the national assembly can sue and be sued.

(c) The concluding ceremony (p. 25):

Cost of the concluding ceremony – the ceremony of elevating ekre – on the evening of the 8th day: one cock (6/-); yams, plantains [*sic*], oil, pepper, salt, wood, drinkables, etc. (9/4); four times four manillas (2/8)… £0-18-0

(d) *Ekre* name (p. 26) [paraphrased]:

In accordance with native custom and tradition, every traditional ruler and every chief must have an *ekre* name… dubbed by the Ancient Order of Ekre Players … When Pre was dubbed with this *ekre* name on 31 December 1944, the following traditional expenses were defrayed (itemized in price): One bottle Dry Gin, Two jars of Tombo, One bottle of lemonade, Three eggs, Bitter Kolas, Cayenne pepper, One cock, a small piece of edible chalk, seven times seven *manillas* (0- 8-2)

B. Other festivals

(a) Fongu (1944) (p. 29):

For the concluding ceremony – the ceremony of elevating Owu-akwa, when no pantomimes are produced, four times four *manillas* £0-2-8

(b) New Year (p. 30):

For the ceremony of bringing down the Owu Drum (Owu-akwa) and Masks, seven times seven *manillas* £0-8-2

C. Leopard killed at Umu-ogo in 1945. Over a page of history is given here to thank the inhabitants of a distant area (pp. 58–59) for:

their patriotism and loyalty to the Opobo House; [for disposing of] the carcass of the leopard according to custom; [bringing the head and claws] to Opuwariku in state, [the chiefs were to receive]: 16 *manillas* (£0-2-8), one fathom Real India Madrass (£0-9-0), and One Bottle of White Horse Whisky (£0-9-8) £1-9-8

D. Sweeping of King Jaja's sepulchre (p. 80). This had to be done half-yearly. It included:

Traditional gift to the caregiver and the keepers of the royal sepulchre (seven times seven *manillas*) £0-8-2

E. Childbed gifts (p. 86):

In order to legitimize the birth of a child, as a lawful member of a House of Chiefdom, it is an invariable custom of the Royal House to give each woman who comes to childbed of either a male or a female child, 20 *manillas* and some yams. Spent in respect of this custom £3-10-0

The sum total of *manilla* expenditures for all these purposes would be very low. The gesture is obviously token by this time, and equally obviously indexed to arts and life founded in tradition and continuity with practices of the past.

The number a man was allowed to keep after 1948 was 200, so the level of use indicated here is far below what could have been sustained with all remaining *manillas* in circulation. Only one entry –the gala dinner – truly presents *manillas* as an alternative mode of payment but perhaps because this event happened before the withdrawal campaign of 1948. After it, nothing of this magnitude could have been supported easily by the remnants of the great collections. So if *manillas* had specific uses by this time, they were already acting as tokens and only in one case – care of the sepulchre – were they the only form of payment mentioned. Jones himself suggests that Opobo was more an entrepot for *manillas* than a *manilla* economy, so the practices retained may already have been symbolic for a long time, along with the symbols of royal authority photographed for S.O. Jaja's book (photographs of *Short Manilla Tree and Long Manilla Tree*).[20] The deposition papers in the Nigerian National archives would strengthen this interpretation. The *manilla* and its insignia were claims to sovereignty in Opobo, and no longer a working monetary system by this time.

More intriguing for monetary history is the mode of calculation in S.U. Jaja's accounts. In all but the childbirth case, *manillas* are counted in multiples: 4 x 4 and 7 x 7. It is known from Jones that every river in the Delta had its own mode of reckoning,[21] and from many other sources that higher numbers in monetary calculation might go in multiples rather than additions. In *Marginal Gains* (chapt. 3), I suggested that a mathematics of multiples rather than incremental additions offered a logic of flexibility in the face of fluctuation. Each unit (or composite) of four or seven can be slightly augmented or diminished in specific instances, while maintaining the name that pronounces and announces itself as a stable value: four or seven as a concept rather than a number. Standard western numeration practice of Incremental addition and subtraction cannot perform the feat of

providing more rather than fewer tropic points [that] allow greater room for recomposition of the material transaction without changing the nominal agreement.[22]

It is confirmatory for me to see multiplication around tropic numbers appear in this much later context, where *manillas* have really become tokens rather than currency. G.I Jones's account of *comey* – a form of customs paid by European merchants to the Delta chiefs – also implies the primacy of composites over its units, in that calculation was by capacity per boat rather than the units of the cargo added incrementally, as defined according to western accounting techniques and market orientations. It was not the actual number of slaves or puncheons of oil transported in a particular vessel that was calculated to get at the *comey*, but the boat itself as a unit of account.[23] The unit of value was already both a unit and a composite. Verran's study of Yoruba number makes a similar point.[24] Numerical techniques would seem to be one of the most neglected topics in the study of West African trade, but if evidence of such apparently minor and 'quaint' usages could be assembled and combined with field research it is perhaps not too late to bring into larger comparative view what was surely one of the great skills of Eastern Nigerian commerce and governance. In the case of Opobo, in what sense was the 'control' of *manillas* a control of origins (as in the patent in Liverpool, referred to above), a control of distribution (as in the payments indicated in the account), and/or a control of calculation modes? The specific points at which Africa's legitimate rulers exercised their control on value and circulation, a distinct form other sources of power such as the right to control life and death, cannot simply be assumed from a comparative record from elsewhere. We have a small step here in the knowledge that a) the King of Opobo commissioned the minting of *manillas* in England, b) the *manilla* was a symbol of power, c) key rituals had to be mediated in *manillas;* and d) there were calculative formulae. About the deployment of calculation, prices and circulation, taxation, market control and other daily functions of money, we learn much less.

3. Of subsidies and reparations

Taken together, the sources may also provide a 'reverse side' of the history of the tradition/modernity picture, namely a window into the long-term acumen in 'modern' techniques of power that underwrite Opobo history, back to the career of the original King Jaja: 'The African Merchant Prince', whose photograph in high white collar and tie appears as the frontispiece to the book of documents compiled by S.O. Jaja.[25] And also of his successors: the chiefs who insisted on rights *vis-a-vis* Britain that had been committed to written agreements at several dates in the 19th century, which in all likelihood the British had never intended to keep. Even in the depth of World War II, they were forced, or persuaded, to honour this age-old debt. This section of the paper highlights the fact that Opobo was diligently inserted into merchant and colonial systems throughout its history, and shows the traces of their early seizing of western political and economic contractual negotiation.

The most important and contentious itemized payment in money that appears in the S.U. Jaja account as £369-5-5, or about 25% of total income, was for the value of war canoes, guns and munitions that had been confiscated in 1892. The entire history and documentation of the case has been compiled by historian S.O. Jaja. At the time of confiscation, there was a clause in the agreements that promised a given cash equivalent if the items were not returned, no sooner than 30 and no later than 50 years from the signing. In 1939, 47 years later, the Opobo chiefs brought a formal case against the British government for compensation. After four years searching for documents, and long correspondences between Opobo, Lagos and Whitehall, the compensation was paid to the Opobo chiefs in 1944 and 1945. Stephen U. Jaja of King Jaja House is recorded in S.O Jaja's account to have received exactly the same amount, £369.5.5, as is recorded in S.U Jaja's account on 27 January 1945. His share was approximately 1/28 of the £11,420 paid to the 28 chiefly houses. The chiefs of three other houses pursued another small element of the claim – a money deposit as security in 1889 – until 1952. The documentary history put together by Dr. S.O. Jaja is an astonishingly detailed source in itself, and it also provides testimony to the Opobo diligence and determination to pursue their case in full legal form, and sometimes in archaic English language, by a strict preservation of sources over more than 50 years.[26]

'Subsidy', as another category of Jaja's income, was the term used for payments to chiefs, originally – in this area at any rate – as replacement for the customs duty (*comey*) they had earned under the trade system of the pre-colonial years, when they

were independent political entities with the power of taxation. According to Jones, Opobo's subsidy started out at £500, which was later reduced to £399.[27] But the subsidy was 'distributed between various chiefs at the whim of the colonial government'.[28] It never sufficed for the kind of expense that S.U. Jaja itemizes. One might see here, then, the origin of Jaja's huge deficit and unsustainable sources of income. The deficit would be even higher if all 10 years of 'Emoluments and Domestic Expenses' were included. In fact, the costs of personal householding – at £120 p.a. for 1944 and 1945, and £180 for 1946 through 1948 – are only summarized for those five years: the five years when S.U. Jaja was head of his house. If counted for the whole period, £180 p.a. they would have added another £900 to the shortfall of just over £1,500 (50%). (Of course we do not have accounts from his personal sources, so we must assume that Jaja considers this to be separate from official commitments.)

Clearly the Opobo had benefited enormously from adopting diligence in colonial-style record-keeping, letter writing and recourse to western lawyers, which I think may partly account for the style and substance of S.U. Jaja's accounts and his extraordinarily detailed formal letters to colonial officials. By the time the British finally confirmed his deposition by the family, S.U. Jaja had driven them distraction by his legalistic letters to them. Modern legalism, however, came as easily to the Opobo as reference to 'time immemorial' and the *manilla* economy. Indeed, they are historically intertwined.

We turn now to an interpretation of the nature of these accounts.

4. An account of the cost of sovereign powers

To indicate the style of the account, the following are some examples of where narratives of legitimacy and finance are brought together. The reader's attention is drawn to the mix of a) detailed explanation and naming of traditions, or allusion to them, b) emphatic statement of the compulsory nature and level of payments to ensure various kinds of action, and c) the connection of these customary transactions to the efficacy, not only of tradition, but of colonial law and administration themselves.

Extract 1: The Installation of the *Pre,* (or king) (p. 22)

> Custom further ordains that, whereas, the gala vigil ('sodi') with its gala dinner is sacred to God Almighty, it should willy-nilly be kept at the expense of every newly created chief, every successor and every new ruler; and that if any chief prefer to give the equivalent of the state banquet in money, forty-eight thousand manillas (48,000) which is at present £600, must invariably be paid to Asimini - a legal name under which the national assembly can sue and be sued.

Extract 2: The Harvest Festivals (*Bru-ama-iwo*) for 1945 through 1948 (pp. 44–47). After two and a half pages of description of the performances, and naming of the participants, the following are exemplary of the nine items listed:

> 3. When the bringing of the yams and corn was delayed, Matthew Tatari Jaja and Frank Egecha Jaja were also delegated to go to Chief Yobe in order to hasten him to dispatch the yams and corns. Tobacco (10/-) and another sum of one Pound (£1/3/0) were once more sent to him to defray the initial expenses, if the first sum was not sufficient.   £1-13-0
>
> 4. Paid Benedict for the hire of his small canoe.   £0-2-0

Extract 3: On the Subsidy Suit (p. 75)

Item viii under expenditure heading P, Disputes and Law Cases. Opobo Comey Subsidy Case: Suit nos. MO/52/46, c/17/48, C/32/48,P/7/49. It includes 15 numbered elements, of which the following are exemplary:

> 9. Travelling expenses to and fro Ikot Ekpene for the Hearing of Subsidy Suit No. MO/52/46 which was struck off on 3 May 1948, and for the Hearing of Egwanga Land Case: Suit no. C/12/45, on Tuesday, 14 May 1948, have been stated in Head P, Item vii, paragraph 8... (cost from para 8)   £4-17-6
>
> 10. When Chief Effiom John Eyamba and other Chiefs of Calabar who were subpoenaed by the Subsidised Chiefs of Opobo as their witnesses in the Subsidy Suit paid official visit to the Royal Palace, their entertainment was assessed at   £3-17-1

The style differs little from his letters appealing his deposition as chief of the House of Jaja, which depend on a similar mastery of the technologies of record-keeping and the rhetoric of appeal, which are also similar to the correspondence over reparations.[29] For example, a closely argued and precedent-documented two-page, single-spaced letter from 4 November 1946 starts: 'May it please your Worship, The humble petition of your most obedient servant most respectfully sheweth that... ', and signs off: 'And your humble petitioner, as in duty bound, will ever pray to remain, Sir, Your Worship's Most Obedient Servant.' S.U. Jaja knew perfectly well how to produce British-style documents. He recorded every detail, indulged in legalistic hair-splitting and flowery obsequiousness, using to the full the administrative style of numbering points and prefacing arguments with a page of 'whereas' clauses, and constantly referring to the British 'high sense of justice, refined nature, and acts of humanity',[30] in a manner that bordered on parody and ultimately maddened the British authorities.

Such a royal financial account was not required by the authorities. Chiefs were not paid an official state salary during the period covered, and so were not accountable to the government for their use of funds. Indeed the British moved away from a Warrant Chief system in 1929 towards a Native Authority system of local government and finance over the decades from 1931 to 1954.[31] Clearly, however, the document follows the logic of western accounting in many ways, as if it were a financial report to a validating power. There are categories of expenditure, itemized entries, columns of monetary amounts, subtotals and totals. A negative balance is strongly implicit, showing that the responsibilities of chieftaincy surpassed income by a very large margin.

Unless this account is a kind of 'folly' produced by an obsessive and very gifted mind, its purpose tends towards clearly defining the otherwise ambiguous intersection of the personal and the official in a manner that preserves the claims of 'tradition' to sovereign powers of self-determination, such as those that prevailed in the reparations case. S.U. Jaja's personal income, for example from plantations, is not mentioned at all. The cost of running a royal household is simply summarized as £780: exactly 25% of total expenditure. It appears as 'Estimate for 1944 (and each year to 1948) with the strictest economy', shifting only from £120 p.a. to £180 p.a. in 1946 (p. 81). Very little appears with respect to public social investments, such as education and health, which would come under the evolving Native Authority system.[32] A massive amount of the expenditure is about the self-legitimation and reproduction of

the position, the House and legal frameworks for resource control and self-validation.

Eastern Nigerians of the time would be aware of shifting colonial ideas and practices with respect to all the powers and functions of differing governance structures at the local level, so the public or popular functions of chiefs would be in question. The old modernism based on sovereignty claims and indirect rule were giving way to a new modernism of representative bodies financing education and local financial management. In fact, the younger generation in Opobo was very angry when their chiefs won reparations in 1944 then wasted them on their own interests rather than building a secondary school.[33] In both the account and his appeal against deposition, S.U. Jaja was using legal and administrative expertise that had succeeded so dramatically in the reparations case. He consistently supported the consolidation of tradition in a manner that ended up being extremely annoying to all other parties – political opposition within his House, the educated youth of Opobo and the colonial government – at least in part by virtue of its surpassing sophistication in the mastery of procedure and profound conviction about rituals of office. By 1954 his vision would seem delusional or obsessive. Even so, we learn something about money and records that I have not seen elsewhere: an itemized cost-accounting of the maintenance of a kind of traditional authority that is endorsed by the historian S.O Jaja as an 'experiment' in independence that is simultaneously African and modern.

Throughout the account there is striking reference to customs handed down from 'time immemorial', even though the Opobo polity was only founded in 1870, by a former slave turned king, who struck off with his followers from their original polity of Bonny. In keeping with their notion of an African economy and sovereignty,[34] Opobo leaders co-constructed a tradition and a modernity that one sees materialized in the activities and expenditures described in these accounts. The repetition of terms implying obligation to tradition – 'willy-nilly', 'from time immemorial' – punctuates the minutely retailed list of 'pounds, shillings and pence' like a choral refrain.

Conclusions

As in many 'inventions of tradition', S.U. Jaja brought book-keeping to chieftaincy: as a voluntary contribution and persuasive argument. His system contains only traces of old calculative modes, and then for apparently strategic reasons. Its originality lies in the punctilious instantiation of categories invented quite recently, brought forward and probably also elaborated in the present. His account belongs with the record of the reparations suit as an example of a localized African effort to appropriate and develop a modernity after its own model, combining – perfectly logically if idiosyncratically – techniques that neither he nor others could ever bring into balance. In fact, by this time the cost of chieftaincy may have been a quantity that no-one else wanted even to know about, especially in terms that suggested the technical possibility of its assimilability into a colonial accounting mode. So we remain with questions: Was S.U. Jaja making a plea for recognition of the cost of legitimate chiefly rule? Or was he exemplifying a capacity for African modernity? Or perhaps he was parodying colonial accounting, producing (for example) a precise account of how much it cost him to organize ceremonial receptions and send-offs for colonial officers – (£80 sterling, not a mean amount)? I suspect that he was showing, in excruciating detail, the absolute unworkability of British colonial aspirations to create mixed forms of rule by applying colonial accounting methods to the cost of an African legitimacy. Perhaps his relentless persistence, beyond his time in office, in pursuit of Weberian-style bureaucratic rationality, is what persuaded the final colonial commentator on his deposition appeal case to define him as 'off his head'. This still leaves me with my original question of how a *manilla* accounting of chieftaincy might have worked in the past, but by way of a trajectory through the creative confrontations that have occurred along the way to the systems we now choose to define as 'modern'.

Notes

1   Iroko 1987.
2   Law 1995.
3   Barber 2007.
4   Carruthers and Espeland 1991.
5   See McCaskie 1980.
6   See Barber 1995.
7   Shipton 1991.
8   See Guyer 2004, ch. 4.
9   Roberts and Roberts 1996.
10 Hountondji 2007, title translated by the author.
11 The reasons for demonetization of manillas and cowries were partly to do with the disruptive effects of a seasonally fluctuating exchange rate between colonial and local currencies, and especially in the food economy, which could severely affect the purchasing power of civil servants' salaries (Naanen 1993). Not all European merchants were in favour however, and there was an entire system of local expertise in money management that stood to lose mightily (see Ofonagoro 1976; Gregory 1996), not to mention the losses of those holding caches of wealth in cowries which, unlike *manillas*, were not redeemed in colonial currency (Guyer 2004). Another interest in the retention of 'indigenous currencies' was the ritual complex, whose importance was acknowledged by permission being given for each manilla holder to retain 200 for use in funerals and other celebrations. Over 32 million *manillas* were collected and redeemed, from a population in the Calabar Provinces of about one-and-a-half million people, at something close to the going exchange rate of four to the shilling (United African Company 1949; Amogu 1952).
12 S.O. Jaja 1991
13 Guyer 2004.
14 Letter of S.U. Jaja to the Senior District Officer, 4 November 1946. NNA: V/8A, V/9A no. 38322/s.467.
15 Jones Papers, Box A3.
16 Jones Papers, Box A3.
17 Nigerian National Archives V/8A, V/9A No 38322/s.467
18 Carruthers and Espeland 1991.
19 Latham 1971.
20 Jaja 1991.
21 Jones 1958, 51.
22 Guyer 2004, 58.
23 Jones 1962, 94.
24 Verran 2001.
25 S.O. Jaja 1991.
26 S.O. Jaja 1991.
27 Jones 1962, 95.
28 Jones 1962, 187.
29 See S.O. Jaja 1991.
30 Letter of 5 July 1947.
31 Noah 1987.
32 See Noah 1987.
33 See S.O. Jaja 1991, quoting articles in the *Eastern Nigerian Guardian*.
34 See S.O. Jaja 1991.

Bibliography

Amogu, O.O. 1952. 'The introduction into and withdrawal of manillas from the "Oil Rivers" as seen in the Ndoki district', *Nigeria Magazine* 38: 134–139.

Barber, K. 1995. 'Money, self realisation and the person in Yoruba texts'. In J.I. Guyer (ed.), *Money Matters: Instability, values and social payments in the modern history of West African communities.* 20515–20524. Portsmouth, N.H.

Barber, K. 2007. 'When People Cross Thresholds'. *African Studies Review* 50(2): 11115–11123.

Carruthers, B. and W. Espeland 1991. 'Accounting for Rationality: Double Entry Bookkeeping and the Rhetoric of Economic Rationality'. *American Journal of Sociology* 97(1): 31–69.

Gregory, C. 1996. 'Cowries and conquest: Towards a subalternate quality theory of money'. *Comparative Studies in Society and History* 38(2): 195–217.

Guyer, J.I. 2004. *Marginal Gains. Monetary Transactions in Atlantic Africa.* Chicago.

Hountondji, P. 2007. *La Rationalite: Une ou Plurielle?* CODESRIA: Dakar.

Iroko, A.F. 1987. *Les cauris en Afrique Occidentale, du Xème au XXème siècle.* Sorbonne, Paris.

Jaja, S.U. n.d. 'General Account of Income and Expenditure of Opobo Royal House (1944–1954) by Chief Stephen Igborgu Jaja, Head of Opobo Royal House and the Pre Jaja III of Opobo'. Department of Social Anthropology, Cambridge University. G.I. Jones Papers, Box A5.

Jaja, S.O. 1991. *Opobo Since 1870. A Documentary Record.* Ibadan University Press, Ibadan.

Jones, G.I. n.d. 'Report of the Position, Status, and Influence of Chiefs and Natural Rulers in the Eastern Region of Nigeria'. Department of Social Anthropology, Cambridge University. G.I. Jones Papers, Box A3

— 1958. 'Native and trade currencies in Southern Nigeria during the eighteenth and nineteenth centuries'. *Africa* 28(1): 43–54.

— 1962. *The Trading States of the Oil Rivers. A study of political development in Eastern Nigeria.* Oxford University Press for the International African Institute, Oxford.

Latham, A.J.H. 1871. 'Currency, credit and capitalism on the Cross River in the pre-colonial era'. *Journal of African History* 12(4): 599–605.

McCaskie, T. 1980. 'Time and the Calendar in nineteenth century Asante: An exploratory essay'. *History in Africa* 7: 179–200.

Naanen, Ben. 1993. 'Economy within an Economy: The Manilla Currency, Exchange Rate Instability, and Social Conditions on South-Eastern Nigeria, 1900–1948'. *Journal of African History* 34(3): 425–46.

Noah, M.E. 1987. 'After the Warrant Chiefs: Native Authority Rule in Ibibioland 1931–1951'. *Phylom* 48(1): 77–90.

Ofonagoro, W. 1976. *The Currency Revolution in Southern Nigeria, 1880–1948.* Occasional Paper no. 14, University of California at Los Angeles African Studies Center.

Roberts, M.N. and A.F. Roberts 1996. *Memory. Luba Art and the Making of History.* New York.

Shipton, P. 1991. 'Time and money in the western Sahel: A clash of cultures in Gambian local rural finance'. In M. Roemer and C. Jones (eds), *Markets in developing countries: Parallel, fragmented and black,* 113–176. Portsmouth N.H.

United Africa Company. 1949. The manilla problem. Statistical and *Economic Review,* March, 44–56.

Verran, H. 2001. *Science and an African Logic.* Chicago, Ill.

Money and Mercantilism in Nigerian Historical Plays: A Womanist Reading

Foluke Ogunleye

Drama and money in Nigeria: an abiding relationship

The geographical space known as Nigeria has used diverse types of monetary systems over a long period of time. Spanish dollars were used until 11 May, 1880 when they were demonetized, and British coins, and a few foreign gold and silver coins, were made legal tender. In 1958, MacGregor Laird issued token coins in Nigeria. Throughout the period when Nigeria remained a British colony, the British pound sterling (GBP) was used in Nigeria. When preparations for Nigerian independence began in 1959, the Nigerian pound (NGP) was issued. It continued in circulation until January 1, 1973, when the *naira* was introduced, and notes were issued for 50 *kobo*, 1, 5 and 10 *naira*.

However, before 1973 there had been an earlier change of currency during the 6 July, 1967–13 January, 1970 civil war. This was done in order to ensure that Biafran supplies of pre-war Nigerian currency were rendered useless. This forced Biafra to introduce its own currency and coins, the Biafran pound (BIAP), designed to be at par with the Nigerian pound. It became worthless after Biafra was reincorporated into Nigeria. In 1984, the Buhari/Idiagbon administration withdrew all the *naira* notes in circulation and reissued them in new colours. This was because it was felt that too much *naira* was circulating within and outside the country and it was impossible for the Central Bank to really monitor the circulation. The withdrawal and re-issue were therefore designed to instil sanity into the monetary system. Many other denominations of the *naira* notes have been issued since 1973: 20 *naira* notes were issued in 1976, 50 *naira* in 1991, 100 naira in 1999, 200 *naira* in 2000, 500 *naira* in 2001 and 1,000 *naira* in 2005. In 2007, new versions of the 5 to 50 *naira* banknotes were issued.[1]

Over the years the relationship between drama and 'money' in Nigeria has been consolidated through frequent interaction. For instance, every time the currency is changed dramatists would be called upon to take part in the sensitization and acclimatization process. Many Nigerians are illiterates and it would be necessary to explain the new currency to them so that they could understand and be able to use it without being cheated by fraudsters and counterfeiters. Dramatists would produce short skits to be performed through different media – radio, television, stage, 'guerrilla' theatre etc. One of the veterans of the Nigerian theatre, Oyin Adejobi has this to say:

> For one thing, I regard actors as practical journalists because there may be some issues of public importance which the government wants to publicise but which people may not care to read about. And of course many people cannot read in our society. Through special plays we can publicize such issues and interest the people in them …[2]

In 1973, another seasoned dramatist, Moses Olaiya Adejumo designed a series of plays to introduce the *naira* notes to people. The plays would generally end with a refrain which served as a mnemonic device for the mastery of the *naira*:

> *Hafu kobo eepini, kobo kan ni kobo kan, ogorun kobo naira kan, naira meji, poun kan.*[3]

Translation: Half a *kobo* is equivalent to halfpenny, 1 *kobo* is equal to 1 penny, 100 *kobo* is equal to 1 *naira*, 2 *naira* is the equivalent of 1 pound.[4]

Similar dramatizations to promote the new Ghana *cedi* also took place in the Ghanaian media in 2007. The Bank of Ghana provided information to the Ghanaian populace through radio, television, print and internet about notes, coins and security features, assurances that people would not lose their money and that the value of the old currency and the new was the same.[5] Adejumo's plays and the refrain helped the Nigerian masses to master the intricacies of the new *naira* currency. This kind of drama has continued in Nigeria. The latest currency change has also spawned some short skits; the following is a paraphrase of a television skit,[6] which endeavors to help the re-introduction of coins into the monetary system:

> (A motorcyclist has just bought petrol and is being given change by the petrol attendant. The attendant gives the change in notes and turns away.)
>
> Motorcyclist: Please give me my change
>
> Petrol Attendant: I don't have change
>
> Motorcyclist: I know coins have been introduced into the system now, so give me my change.
>
> Petrol Attendant: My brother, what do you want to do with coins? They will be too heavy for your pocket.
>
> Motorcyclist: The new coins are very light and convenient to carry, so give me my change sharp sharp.
>
> (The petrol attendant gives him his change)

The examples given above fall within the contemporary period, but we shall also look at examples from historical plays. Historical drama is an invaluable vehicle of documentation; it serves as a mirror of the society or the age in which the drama is set. Historical drama can be described as a form of drama which reflects or re-presents historical proceedings. Since time immemorial writers have combined fiction and history in creative works. We can describe the history play as:

> that which reconstructs a personage, a series of events, a movement, or the spirit of a past age and pays the debt of serious scholarship to the facts of the age being re-created.[7]

When a dramatist makes conscientious use of historical facts, displaying real comprehension of history and historic periods, the dramatist can then be described as a historian.

Akinwunmi Isola's plays, *Efunsetan Aniwura* and *Madam Tinubu,* fall into the category of historical drama, treating as they do the stories of the eponymous heroines. Efunsetan Aniwura was the second Iyalode (queen of women) of Ibadan and she died on 30 June, 1874. Efunroye Tinubu was the first Iyalode of Egbaland and she died in 1887. These two plays have as subjects two rich women of their era. These women became rich as a result of their mercantile activities. This paper examines how they became rich, what positions in society their riches obtained for them, what they used their money for, what opportunities they had as a result of their riches and finally, how society reacted to their riches.

In concluding this paper, we will provide an insight into the attitude of 19th-century Yoruba people to money. We must admit that these plays are not verbatim historical documents. Scholars have noted two major approaches to history by theatre artists and scholars. These approaches are: the nationalistic approach, which explores the past for the purpose of displaying its grandeur, glory and richness of its cultural heritage, and the critical approach, which probes into the past for the purpose of making our historical experience and cultural heritage positively relevant to the present and future.[8]

Akinwunmi Isola admits taking artistic liberty with historical facts in writing his historical plays. According to Ogundeji, he skillfully selects and modifies historical materials, retaining some, leaving some out, reshaping others and also adding new ones.[9] Akinwunmi Isola himself states:

> … some playwrights of historical drama are not loyal to strict historical details. … [the playwright,] like his counterparts in other literatures, is not a historian. He is an interpreter of history. His interpretation may be subjective and the reasons of the subjective stand vary from writer to writer.[10]

There are many reasons necessitating an alternative source of documenting history. Today, in Nigeria, most people who know about the eponymous heroines of the plays, *Efunsetan Aniwura* (1962) and *Madam Tinubu* (1998), obtained their knowledge either from Akinwunmi Isola's plays or the films made from them. Over 14,000 people watched the stage performance of *Efunsetan Aniwura* in 1981 at the Liberty Stadium in Ibadan when it was staged. Also, the play has been produced on television, film, long-playing record, and as photoplay magazine. These make the play available to a very large audience. *Madam Tinubu* has also been performed on stage on many occasions. It has been performed twice as the convocation play at the Obafemi Awolowo University.

Efunsetan Aniwura

Understanding of Efunsetan's riches and influence can be garnered from her praise chant:

> Efunsetan, Iyalode
> One who has horses and rides them not.
> The child who walks in a graceful fashion.
> Adekemi Ogunrin!
> The great hefty woman who adorns her legs with beads
> Whose possessions surpass those of the Aare
> Owner of several puny slaves in the farm.
> Owner of many giant slaves in the market.
> One who has bullets and gunpowder,
> Who has gunpowder as well as guns.
> And spends money like a conjurer.
> The Iyalode who instills fear into her equals.
> The rich never give their money to the poor.
> The Iyalode never gives her wrappers to the lazy.[11]

It ought to be noted that Efunsetan was a product of her socio-political milieu. She grew up in times of wars. Automatically, she began and centered her trade on war supplies and slave trafficking. In traditional Yoruba society, the administrative structure encompasses the system of chiefdom, among others. At the head is the paramount ruler, supported by various chiefs who are in touch with people at the grassroots.

In Ibadan, the largest city in West Africa, the interests of women are protected by the existence and activities of the office of the Iyalode.[12] This office, according to Johnson:

> is a title bestowed upon the most distinguished lady in the town. She has also her lieutenants Otun, Osi, Ekerin, etc., as any of the other principal chiefs of the town. Some of these Iyalodes command a force of powerful warriors, and have a voice in the council of the chiefs. Through the Iyalode, the women of the town can make their voices heard in municipal and other affairs.[13]

This is a rarity in the patriarchal Yoruba society, but this phenomenon shows that the womenfolk are not entirely muzzled, as one would believe. Women in Yoruba land from time immemorial have always had an important role to play and a strong voice in the affairs of the Yoruba society.

Efunsetan Aniwura became the second Iyalode (leader of all the women) of Ibadan around the 1860s. She was very rich – she had 'hundreds of slaves on her farms, with many others at home'.[14] She was involved in trading with Europeans – taking goods from the hinterland to the coast and bringing imported goods, especially arms and ammunition back to the hinterland. Consequently, she was a force to be reckoned with both economically and politically. According to Bolanle Awe:

> she was noted for extending credit facilities to the warriors whom she gave guns and ammunition when they were going on military expedition.[15]

On their return, she would receive payment in slaves brought from the war, which she would in turn take to the coast for sale. Another way in which she contributed to the political consolidation of the state was through fielding her band of warriors in any expedition embarked upon by the paramount ruler, Aare Latosa. These warriors, about 100 in number, were mainly her slaves, and like other warrior chiefs, she supplied them with guns and ammunition, food, clothing, etc. Latosa was a troublemaker, and he soon became jealous of Efunsetan's riches and political clout. Efunsetan's political woes arose from her participation in the war effort. Aare Latosa and his chiefs were becoming tardy in the payment of debts owed Efunsetan. She therefore stopped extending credit facilities to them. When Aare Latosa set out for another war in 1874, she refused to give her usual support. After returning from the battlefield, Latosa brought three trumped-up charges against Efunsetan:

1. that she did not accompany him to war;
2. that she never sent him supplies during the campaign;
3. that she did not come in person to meet him outside the town wall to congratulate him on his safe return.

Based on these flimsy charges, he deposed Efunsetan on 1 May 1874, replacing her with her Otun (First Lieutenant). Her Otun was blackmailed into taking the title with the threat that refusal to do so would earn her expulsion from the town and that she would only be allowed to take just one suit of apparel. Being a woman of very great means, she had to oblige. Despite the fact that Efunsetan paid all the fines imposed upon her, and through costly gifts sought the goodwill of prominent chiefs seeking to use them as emissaries to request forgiveness from the Aare, these were all in vain.[16]

Madam Tinubu

The playwright, Akinwunmi Isola wrote in the preface:

> My concern here is to interpret those facts of history in a way to draw relevant economic and political conclusions for contemporary education.[17]

Indeed, Efunroye Tinibu left her imprint on the economic and political sands of her time. According to Samuel Johnson, Efunroye Tinubu was an active adversary of the British colonial government, who was banished by the government from Lagos to her native Abeokuta in the 19th century. She was a former slave trader who, once she realized the differences between domestic slaving and the inhumane treatment of slaves in Europe and the Americas, became an active opponent to all slave trade. Madam Tinubu became the first Iyalode or 'the queen of the ladies' of Egbaland. The Iyalode is a member of the traditional council and she protects the interest of womenfolk in the city. She was able to build a small financial empire through trading in arms and salt. She is currently considered an important figure in Nigerian history due to her political significance as a strong female leader.[18]

Indices of Efunroye Tinubu's riches and consequent influence as presented in the play

In the play, we see the character of Madam Tinubu as very influential. Her servants are shown to move freely between towns and villages, buying up agricultural and other products for her without fear of molestation.[19] On a particular shopping expedition her servants returned with 250 tins of red palm oil and 501 bags of cotton, and this was one of their bad days.[20] At one point she had over £500 in deposits from foreign merchants who were doing business with her.[21] One of her foreign associates Mr Birdlake describes her thus: 'she is the most effective trade middleman along the western coast of Africa'.[22]

As a result of her riches and political influence, some people became jealous of her and began to look for ways to bring her business down. For example, a white man, Mr. Sandman, sponsored some Lagosians to become Tinubu's adversaries in trade. Her political weight ensured that King Dosumu relied heavily on her wise advice. In order to stop this, Consul Campbell had to surreptitiously cause a crack to develop in the relationship between the two, so that he would be able to manipulate King Dosumu to cede Lagos to the British.[23] She had powerful friends, both black and white. For example, one of her servants reports:

> At Ibadan, but for the help of your good friend, Madam Efunsetan, the Iyalode, we would not have got much to buy. When she heard of our trouble with our rivals, she sent her servants to buy all the oil and cotton available in every market around.[24]

Also, the foreign merchants were ready to support her with the full force of their influence and military might and were ready to put at her disposal their ships, fighting men, etc. in her fight with King Dosumu and his cronies. It was not possible for King Dosumu to cede Lagos to the British until she was exiled to Abeokuta. She died in 1887.[25]

Relevance of Akinwumi Isola's plays to the contemporary period

Akinwumi Isola reflects his 'fictional' freedom in his plays, Efunsetan Aniwura (1962) and Madam Tinubu (1998). He does this by going beyond mere historical documentation, accomplishing a reconstruction of historical facts with his own artistic interpretation. The plays are not verbatim factual narrations, but they provide insights into the period within which they are situated and the periods within which they were written. The plays reflect contemporaneity through an engraftment of salient socio-political and socio-economic issues within their thematic construct. Efunsetan Aniwura reflects the pre-independence economic terrain in Nigeria and how it affected early post-colonial economy. During the period in question, Nigeria was heavily dependent on agriculture. Slaves were also used as cheap labour to obtain agricultural produce. The British, like other newcomers to the slave trade, formed national trading companies. The first such effective English enterprise was the Company of the Royal Adventurers, chartered in 1660 and succeeded in 1672 by the Royal African Company. These companies built and maintained the forts considered essential to hold stocks of slaves and trade goods. The slave trade was one of the major causes of the devastating internecine strife in southern Nigeria during the three centuries to the mid-1800s (Country Studies Program). These wars and their effects have been documented in Isola's Efunsetan Aniwura. Madam Tinubu also reflects the activities of the trading companies as well as Britain's usurpation of the power of coastal chiefs, gradually paving the way for colonialism.

More importantly, a study of Nigeria's economic history reveals that whereas Nigeria was an agricultural force to be reckoned with during its early post-colonial days, in the decade up to 1983, her agricultural output declined 1.9% and exports fell 7.9%. Nigeria's economy from the 1970s became dependent on petroleum, which accounted for 87% of export receipts and 77% of the federal government's current revenue in 1988. After the short-lived oil boom, GNP per capita per year decreased 4.8% from 1980 to 1987, which led in 1989 to Nigeria's classification by the World Bank as a low-income country (based on 1987 data) for the first time since the annual World Development Report was instituted in 1978. In 1989 the World Bank also declared Nigeria poor enough to be eligible (along with countries such as Bangladesh, Ethiopia, Chad, and Mali) for concessional aid from an affiliate, the International Development Association (IDA) (Country Studies Program).

The two plays under study show the general lopsidedness in the wealth distribution in the Nigerian society. There are slave owners who have more than enough money, and slaves who live in abject penury and are totally at the mercy of their owners. We also see a 'middle-class' that curry the favour of the upper class in order to make ends meet. The plays thereby effectively reveal the economic stratification inherent in capitalistic societies. The end of the oil boom also resulted in endemic corruption within the Nigerian nation. Isola's Madam Tinubu was written and published during this period. It is therefore not surprising that intrigues within the play are structured around money and political influences.

The changing attitude in the issue of gender sensitivity is also revealed in the two plays. The earlier play, Efunsetan Aniwura reveals the male reluctance to ascribe positive value to womenfolk. The play downplays the positive attributes of the heroine, Efunsetan, such as hard work, her ability to build a thriving financial empire, her possession of an army that provided military support for the internecine wars fought by the Ibadan people. Disproportionately, her negative attributes are exaggerated. She is presented as a wicked slave mistress, arrogant and insubordinate to constituted authority. This is because during this period it was an aberration to have a woman towering above the males in the Yoruba society.

However, by the late 1970s and early 1980s, gender equality became the norm in Yoruba society. It is therefore not surprising to note that Isola presents his Madam Tinubu as an empowered heroine, who is able to make an indelible impact upon her society.

Despite Isola's 'fictional' freedom in writing the plays, he still maintains an historical consciousness, which guides him in writing the plays. For instance, he never undermines the greatness of the Yoruba race; rather, he glorifies its heroes and exalts mythical and historical achievements of the Yoruba in both plays. He never lost sight of the fact that the Yoruba culture must be upheld at all times.

Conclusion

The two women of our discourse lived within the same timeframe. They were distinguished women traders whose business acumen had given them undisputed influence not only in the world of commerce, but also in the political and social life of the country. In agreement with these two sayings: 'Money answereth all things' and 'Money speaks', success in business and commitment to a sense of nationhood enabled them to take an active part in the defense and expansion of Ibadan and Lagos. In Ibadan today, a statue erected at one of the ring roads in Ibadan has been named after Efunsetan, the second Iyalode of Ibadan. Tinubu Square on Lagos Island (previously Independence Square) is named after Madam Tinubu.

These two women today serve as beacons of hope to African women, encouraging them to strive to become successful in business. They also serve as proof that women can excel in all areas of endeavor, given the right opportunities. However, the patriarchal system that destroyed these two heroines show that the goodwill of men is not usually extended to women who are richer and more powerful than them. This is a negative attitude that needs to be dealt with through resocialization.

From the two plays we learn that there were a lot of trading activities going on between Europeans and Africans during the historical period covered by the plays. We also have a record of the kinds of trade goods that were in existence in the 19th century. We see Madam Tinubu trading in palm oil and cotton. We also see samples of the currency that was in circulation. For instance, pennies and pounds are mentioned.[26] Efunsetan Aniwura's praise chant is also illuminating. Trade materials mentioned in the chant include horses, beads, slaves, bullets, gunpowder, guns and wrappers. Trading in these goods made her so rich that her 'possessions surpass those of the Aare'[27], the paramount ruler who was supposed to be the richest and most influential person in the society. This implies that her mercantile activities were more profitable than the Aare's war-mongering activities.

Apparently 19th-century Yoruba people revered money, and they felt that it could open all doors. However, they were not ready to tolerate excessive wealth in the hands of women. It is however obvious that in the contemporary period, within which the plays were written, women are no longer vilified for daring to be rich. Efunsetan Aniwura is forgiven for being rich, but she had to be branded as a wicked woman in order to be killed off. Madam Tinubu on the other hand is presented as a positive role model – rich, politically conscious, kind and an activist; the tone of the play about her is laudatory. This reveals

the changing times – society is becoming gender conscious and the sky is the limit for women that possess the right qualities. The plays have succeeded in displaying the grandeur, glory and richness of the Yoruba heritage. At the same time they have stimulated deep thoughts about attitudes, both historical and contemporary, and they have also encouraged formation of positive attitudes towards possession and administration of wealth. Hopefully the messages of these plays will serve as ammunition in the battle for moral rearmament, which is currently being fought to turn Nigeria around from a self-destructive voyage propelled by corruption and an inordinate quest for wealth.

Notes

1   Central Bank of Nigeria Website.
2   As cited in Jeyifo 1984, 116.
3   As relayed on Western Nigeria Television, Ibadan.
4   Translation by the author.
5   Bank of Ghana Website.
6   As relayed on Nigerian television Authority Network.
7   Langner 1960, 238.
8   Rotimi 2003, 90.
9   Ogundeji, nd., 3–4.
10 Akinwunmi Isola 1981, 403.
11 Awe 2001, 65.
12 Johnson 1921, 77.
13 Johnson 1921, 77.
14 Awe 2001, 65.
15 Awe 2001, 74.
16 Johnson 1921, 391.
17 Isola 1998, vii.
18 Johnson 1921, 391.
19 Isola 1998, 3.
20 Isola 1998, 4.
21 Isola 1998, 69.
22 Isola 1998, 69.
23 Isola 1998, vii) and Falola, 33.
24 Isola 1998, 5.
25 Isola 1998, vii and Falola, 33.
26 Isola 1998, 5, 69.
27 Awe 2001, 65.

Bibliography

Awe, B. 2001, 'Iyalode Efunsetan Aniwura (Owner of Gold)', in B. Awe (ed.), *Nigerian Women: A Historical Perspective*. 2nd edn, Ibadan.

Bank of Ghana Website, 2007, http://www.ghanacedi.gov.gh/ (accessed 10 October 2007).

Central Bank of Nigeria, 2007, http://www.cenbank.org/currency/gallery.asp (accessed 10 October 2007).

Falola, Toyin, 1995, Gender, 'Business and Space Control: Yoruba Market Women and Power', in B. House-Midamba and F.K. Ekechi (eds), *African Market Women and Economic Power: The Role of Women in African Economic Development*, Westport and London, 23–40.

Isola, A. 1970, *Efunsetan Aniwura*, Ibadan.

— 1981, 'Modern Yoruba drama', in Y. Ogunbiyi (ed.), *Drama and Theatre in Nigeria: A Critical Source Book*, Lagos, 399–410.

— 1998, *Madam Tinubu: The Terror in Lagos*, Ibadan.

Jeyifo, B. 1984, *The Yoruba Popular Travelling Theatre of Nigeria*, Lagos.

Johnson, S. 1921 (reprinted 1997), *The History of the Yorubas*, Lagos.

Langner, L. 1960, *The Play's the Thing*, Boston.

Ogundeji P. A., n.d., 'Trends in the drama of Akinwunmi Isola', unpublished manuscript (obtained from the author).

Ogunleye, F. 2004, 'A malecentric modification of history: Efunsetan Aniwura revisited', *History in Africa: A Journal of Method* 31, 303–318.

Rotimi, O., interviewed by Coker, A. 2003, 'A Director's vision for theatre in Africa: Adeniyi Coker interviews Ola Rotimi – One of Nigeria's foremost playwrights and directors', *Black Renaissance* 5(2) Summer, 77.

Banks and the West African Currency Board*

Chibuike U. Uche

Banks and the West African Currency Board

During the period in which the four British West African territories[1] were under colonial rule the West African Currency Board (WACB) was the colonial monetary authority. The WACB was set up in 1912 with headquarters in London. The constitution of the WACB charged it 'to provide for and to control the supply of currency to the British West African Colonies, Protectorates and Trust Territories.'[2] In practice, however, the board was no more than a Bureau de Change issuing as much local currency as the banks wanted to buy for sterling and vice versa. Such a system satisfied the Bank of England monetary policy objective of achieving price stability in the colonies.[3] The price stability policy was also compatible with British commercial interests in the colony as it helped facilitate trade with London. The colonial banks that oiled the trade mechanism also benefited from the system.

Given the fact that the Board remained in operation until the early 1960s, it is not surprising that researchers have paid a lot of attention to its origins, operations, defects[4] and subsequent replacement with central banks as the colonies approached independence.[5] Very little attention has however been paid to the relationship between the commercial banks in existence then and the WACB system. The study of such a relationship is important given the fact that banks are an integral part of any monetary system. The level of development of a banking system impacts on the effectiveness of a monetary authority. Actions by a monetary authority could also affect the well-being of financial institutions. Such a relationship has made financial institutions interested in influencing the monetary structures and policies. Also, monetary authorities are interested in shaping financial institutions in order to help them achieve whatever monetary goals they may have. This relationship becomes more complex when the big banks in any territory are foreign banks, which have strong ties with their head offices. The conflicting interests are perhaps best brought out in an era of political change when foreign and indigenous banks viewed the monetary system that was in place differently. Unlike the indigenous banks, the foreign banks were happy with the currency board system, which ensured price stability and did not interfere with their operations. The indigenous banks however favoured the establishment of a central bank with the hope that such a bank could act as lender of last resort to poorly capitalized and poorly staffed indigenous banks. Complications also arise when parties that benefit from the barter system go out of their way to oppose monetization, which would destroy their profitable barter trade. In one particular case a bank was set up specifically to help achieve this aim. This paper examines the origins of the WACB system, and the role, if any, banks played in the establishment process. It then discusses the relationship of banks and the currency board and the role of banks in the demise of the currency board system.

1. Origins of WACB system

With the emergence of colonial rule in British West Africa the British soon put in place an economic and political system for the smooth functioning of this territory. The colonial government, in an attempt to make British coins more prominent, then went on to de-monetize certain coins that were in circulation. By 1880, for instance, formal legislation had been put in place in the Lagos colony which provided for the demonetization of certain coins. The new regulation recognized only British gold and silver coins and a few foreign gold coins as legal tender.[6]

The resultant rise in the use of British coins was, however, not without its problems: Such coins had to be transported from London to the West African coast and then carried inland. The cost of this transfer was not only the transport costs; there were also interest charges building up in London even while the coins were in transit and also during slack trading periods when the coins were stored locally in safes. The predilection of the Africans for silver coins did not help matters either as this necessitated the regular reordering of the coin stock for the colony.[7] The above situation, coupled with the need to service the British commercial interests then in existence, created the opportunity for the establishment of a bank.[8]

This opportunity was first identified in 1871 when the Bank of West Africa was incorporated in London under the Joint Stock Companies Act of 1862 and 1867.[9] The bank, whose head office was located in London, was to have its first two branches located in Sierra Leone and Lagos. There is, however, no evidence that this bank ever opened for business. It was not until 1891 that another party – the African Banking Corporation (ABC) – capitalized on this opportunity by opening a branch in Lagos. This marked the advent of both commercial banking and foreign banks into British West Africa. The ABC, which at the time was headquartered in London and had operations in South Africa, came to Nigeria at the instance of the Elder Dempster Company, which was in control of the shipping business on the West African coast and therefore heavily involved in the importation of British coins into the colony.[10]

The Bank immediately took advantage of the disorderly system of currency supply to the West African territories. By 28 January 1892, it signed an agreement with the Crown Agents by which the Bank was given the right to import new silver coins from the mint into Lagos colony – free of charges for packing, freight and insurance.[11] By May 1892 the Bank further consolidated its position by becoming banker to the colonial government in Lagos.[12] The close relationship between the bank and the Elder Dempster Company soon became the subject of protests by other European merchants in the territory. Such protests, among other factors, caused ABC to develop second thoughts about its Nigerian investment.

In 1893 the Bank invited the Elder Dempster Company to take over its Lagos operations; the Elder Dempster Company obliged and instantly lost its preferential treatment over the importation of silver and the Governor of Lagos was soon instructed to close the official account with the bank. The reason given was that the colonial government wanted such functions to be carried out by a public bank and not a trading company like Elder Dempster. Perhaps because of the initial protests received, the colonial government also required that such an institution should be absolutely independent and restricted from engaging in any business other than that of banking.[13]

To get around this problem, a 'public' bank named Bank of British West Africa, with Alfred Jones as majority shareholder, was established in May 1894. It subsequently established offices in Accra (1898), Freetown (1898) and Bathurst (1902). Soon after, the 'new' bank entered into an agreement with the Crown Agents of the Colonies under which the duties and responsibilities of controlling and regulating the silver currency in Lagos were transferred from the government to the bank. This new agreement was slightly different from the one which the government had with the African Banking Corporation in that it conferred on the bank the sole right of silver importation. The bank swiftly consolidated its hold on the British West African territories by entering into similar agreements with the governments of the Gold Coast Colony in 1896, Sierra Leone in 1898 and The Gambia in 1902.[14]

The bank enjoyed the privilege of being the sole agents for the importation of silver until 1912 when a special silver currency was introduced for the West African colony. This, in itself, was mainly a consequence of the disagreements between the colonial governors and Her Majesty's Treasury over the control, sharing and nature of the seigniorage arising from the importation of silver into the British West African Colonies. The BBWA had no influence in the establishment of a special silver currency for the colony. If anything, it opposed such a currency.[15]

2. Role of banks in the establishment process

An expanding volume of trade ensured the continued absorption of British silver into the British West African colonies. These imports, coupled with the prospects of further future increases, soon enticed some colonial Governors to suggest that their colonies be allowed to share in the profits accruing to the Imperial Treasury from the issue of such silver coins in the colonies. The Treasury, however, did not approve of the above proposal, partly because there was the danger that such coins could be returned to the United Kingdom. Despite this, the Treasury concluded that it had no serious objections to the Colonies adopting a token coinage of their own; though it warned that great care should be exercised to restrain the several governments from the temptation to over-issue, with its consequent dangers in their commerce and to their finances.[16]

It was under the above circumstances that Mr Joseph Chamberlain, the Secretary of State for the Colonies at the time, in 1899 appointed a Committee under the headship of Sir David Barbour to collect information and report on the currency of the British West African possessions.[17] The Bank of British West Africa followed the proceedings of the Barbour Commission closely. In fact, Sir Alfred Jones gave evidence in favour of maintaining the existing *status quo*. He also convinced the Liverpool Chamber of Commerce to submit to the Colonial Office that the introduction of a special colonial currency would harm trade.[18] Any change in the existing currency *status quo* in the colony, it was believed, would adversely affect the BBWA. Any decision in favour of a special colonial silver currency would indeed have involved the appointment of a supervisory board. This, it was presumed, would have ended the bank's silver import advantage.[19]

This opposition ensured that Barbour did not recommend the introduction of a special currency for the West African Colonies. Instead, he advised that the Treasury should release half of the profits accruing from the issue of silver to the colonies.[20] As efforts were being made to reconcile the views of the Treasury with those of the Colonies, silver imports, which were £360,220 in 1900, dropped to £154,730 in 1901.[21] This dramatic drop questioned the colonies argument that there was no likelihood of a relapse in the demand for these currencies. This was perhaps one of the main reasons why the government decided to shelve the Barbour Report. It neither introduced a new silver coinage nor allowed the colonies to share from the seigniorage. The BBWA, therefore, continued to enjoy its monopoly of silver importation into the territories.

The matter was not, however, put to rest as the silver imports into the West African colonies continued to expand rapidly despite occasional fluctuations. In 1906, for instance, £506,600 worth of silver was imported into the British West African territories, while £669,600 worth was imported in 1909.[22] Apart from the pressures from the government in the colonies for the issue to be opened up again, the Treasury was sufficiently worried about the increasing dangers of the system to monetary control in Britain.[23] The increase in the silver exported to the colony was not just rising in absolute terms. It was also rising relative to the total amount of sterling silver in circulation in the United Kingdom. For instance, in the five years ending in 1890, the sterling silver imported into British West Africa was equal, on the average, to about 2.7% of the sterling silver placed in circulation in the United Kingdom. In the period 1906–1910, this proportion had risen to about 85%. Further increase in this proportion was anticipated by the colonial government based at the time on the continued substitution of barter by cash transactions, the opening up of vast tracts of country still underdeveloped and its attendant increase in trade.

These factors subsequently led to the appointment of another commission, headed by Lord Emmott, to re-examine the matter in 1912. Despite the continued preference of the commercial community for the silver import system, the Treasury had their way and the Emmott Commission recommended the establishment of a special silver currency for the West African colonies, with a caution on the use of seigniorage.[24] A West African Currency Board was subsequently set up bringing to an end the BBWA's monopoly over silver imports into the territory. The WACB was headquartered in London and required agents for its operations within the West African colonies; the BBWA became its obvious ally. The bank secured the agency of the currency board in West Africa. In this capacity, it continued to deal with the movement of British money in West Africa, though relieved of control over the supply of it from the mint.[25] The BBWA thus continued to be relevant under the new dispensation. As already mentioned, in 1899 the Bank of British West Africa lost its monopoly on operating in the Nigerian Colony with the advent of the Bank of Nigeria.[26] However, it retained its monopoly in the Gold Coast, Sierra Leone and the Gambia.

3. Relationship between banks and the currency board

By the time the Niger Coast Protectorate came into existence in 1891, there was already in place a community of powerful European traders in the territory. At the time these European traders had put in place a working agreement for the purpose of stifling competition, cutting down their costs, maximizing profits and reducing to a uniform amount the prices paid for their commodities.[27] To forestall the BBWA from gaining a foothold in their territory they set up the Anglo African Bank[28] in 1899 and made a strong bid for the job of importing silver into the colony and for the banking business of the government. The Colonial Office obviously knew that this bank would be of little assistance in the task of establishing the British currency in the colony; this was due to the fact that the companies behind the Anglo African Bank believed that the maintenance of the barter system best served their interest.[29] Such an attitude was against the interest of the colonial government, which was pro-monetization. Monetization, it was believed, would make both governance and the lives of government employees easier.[30]

The colonial government therefore decided to invite the BBWA, which was the only established bank in the territory at the time to set up a branch in Southern Nigeria. The bank was, however, not very keen to accept this offer. Officially Alfred Jones, who for practical purposes was synonymous with the Bank of British West Africa, argued that it was not possible to open a branch of his bank in Southern Nigeria except at an initial loss which he was not prepared to face. Though his main fear may have been the possible repercussions that would befall both the bank and the other interests of Elder Dempster should they cross the path of the powerful European traders then operating in Southern Nigeria.[31] These traders practically had the whole of the trade of Southern Nigeria in their hands and were apparently resolved to prevent, by every means in their power, the establishment of a bank there for the fear that the banking facilities would, in the course of time, liberate the African traders from the barter system under which the firms believed they benefited immensely. In fact, the expected line of action dreaded most by Elder Dempster, should they set up their bank in Southern Nigeria, was the possibility that these European firms would retaliate by establishing an independent line of steamers to West Africa, which would have the effect of breaking the monopoly enjoyed by the Elder Dempster & Company's line of steamers.[32]

The territorial Governor however realized that the monetization of Southern Nigeria could not effectively take place without the co-operation of the powerful merchants.[33] He thus urged Alfred Jones to come to an agreement with the commercial community.[34] This was not to be, at least not immediately, as the two banks had different agendas. It was not until 1903 that the BBWA accepted an invitation to become bankers to the colonial government and to have the sole right of importing silver into Southern Nigeria.[35] This was done, perhaps, with some form of guarantee by the colonial government against possible reprisals from the powerful

European merchants in the territory.

Subsequent to the signing of the contract between the government of Southern Nigeria and the BBWA, the Bank of Nigeria launched an offensive in an attempt to reverse the policy. The Shipping Rings Commission in 1907, for instance, provided the Bank of Nigeria an avenue to protest against the activities of the BBWA and its associated companies.[36] Also in May 1908, many of the West African merchants petitioned the new Secretary of State for the Colonies, the Earl of Crewe, urging him to end the monopoly of the BBWA over the importation of silver.[37] Concurrent with the protests were also moves to merge the two competing banks. From 1906, for instance, Alfred Jones had become very interested in a merger. He tried several times without success. In 1907 Lord Elgin, then the Colonial Secretary, also recommended that the two banks should amalgamate.[38] It was not until 1912, three years after the death of Alfred Jones, that the Bank of Nigeria was finally absorbed by the BBWA.

The opposition of the colonial government to the Bank of Nigeria shows that the interest of the colonial government did not always coincide with those of the colonial banks. The colonial government was at the time interested in using the commercial banks as a tool for advancing the monetization of the economy. The British trading interests that set up the Bank of Nigeria, however, perceived this as being against their interest. Each party subsequently adopted its own strategy in order to achieve its aim. In other words, the relationship between the banks and the monetary authority was such that each tried to influence the other. The opposition of the BBWA to a special silver currency for the region is yet another example of the divergent interests between the Colonial Office and the colonial banks.

It is of course possible for some to argue that the interests of the BBWA and the WACB were similar. This was true only to the extent that monetization and the currency distribution agency suited both parties. Cracks in their relationship would have emerged had the WACB pursued policies that upset the stable macro-economic environment under which the bank operated. The colonial government would also have reacted had the BBWA adopted policies that infringed on their interests. In fact, the BBWA did not always agree with the colonial government and its monetary authorities. In 1916, for instance, the monopoly the BBWA enjoyed in the region was again broken with the advent of the Colonial Bank. By 1919, the colonial government had decided on an equal division of its silver currency distribution agency among the two banks. This was endorsed by the Colonial Office despite protests by the BBWA. Stiff competition soon gave way to an agreement between the two banks. The first such agreement occurred in May 1924. This grew in comprehension over the years.[39] It was therefore not surprising that, as the collusion among foreign banks grew, the idea of indigenous banks to service the needs of Africans emerged.

4. Role of banks in the demise of the currency board system

Nigeria was the only country among the pre-independence British West African territories that established an indigenous banking system alongside the colonial banking system.[40] The first indigenous bank in Nigeria – The Industrial and Commercial Bank (1929–1930) – failed mainly due to mismanagement, accounting incompetence, embezzlement and the non-co-operative attitude and denigration of colonial banks.[41] Despite this set back, further attempts were made and by 1947, six additional indigenous banks had been established out of which two had failed.[42] The colonial government, sensing that further bank failures were imminent, moved to regulate the industry. In 1948 G.D. Paton of the Bank of England was invited to enquire into the business of banking in Nigeria, with the view of regulation. Mr Paton submitted his report in October 1948. This culminated in the 1952 Nigerian Banking Ordinance. An attempt by the Colonial Office to encourage the promulgation of a similar regulation in other colonies met with little success.[43]

Preceding the enactment of the 1952 law, Africans, fearing the imminent clampdown on the establishment of commercial banks following the setting up of the Paton inquiry, had rushed to establish more banks before the advent of regulation. The result was that by 1952 at least 24 local banks had been established thus precipitating a crisis in the Nigerian banking system. It was evident that the majority of these indigenous banks were bound to fail, especially with the advent of regulation. It was against this background that a motion was moved in the Federal House of Representatives for the immediate establishment of a central bank, one of its main aims being to strengthen the existing African banks. In other words, the Africans saw a central bank as a vehicle for assisting their beleaguered commercial banks. Also entwined with this event was the belief by the Africans that a central bank would make it easier for them to access credit, which would help power the much needed development. Such views sometimes stemmed from a misconception of central banking.[44] Also, the WACB was generally seen as the 'financial hallmark of colonialism.'[45] Dismantling it was therefore a legitimate part of the de-colonization process. Foreign banks were uncomfortable with such views. Such banks were registered in London, headquartered in London and therefore fell under the regulatory jurisdiction of London. Policies that involved taking orders from indigenous African governments, with respect to their operations, could not be accepted with joy. The WACB system, which exerted little influence on their operations, therefore suited their interests best. Also, the monopoly of the two chief banks of the distribution of the government's silver currency was bound to be lost with the introduction of a central bank. Furthermore, the Bank of England was against allowing the establishment of central banks in underdeveloped economies. The Bank believed that without developed political structures, political interference with the activities of such central banks was inevitable. It was also believed that such central banks would be of little use in territories with undeveloped money markets. Furthermore, developmental functions were at the time considered, at least in colonial government circles, to be outside the scope of central banking.[46]

As already mentioned, foreign banks were not the only beneficiaries of the WACB system. The colonial government also earned seigniorage profits from the system. The motion for a central bank with lender of last resort functions, not surprisingly, did not please the Financial Secretary appointed by the colonial government, who argued that Nigeria at 'its stage of development' was better served by a currency board than a central bank. He was nevertheless prepared, perhaps

due to the immense support the motion received from the African Parliamentarians, 'to reconsider the matter'. This culminated in the revision of the motion to exclude assistance to indigenous banks.[47] In essence, the colonial government did not consider it important that such a central bank, if established, should concern itself with developmental functions like assisting in the strengthening of the existing African banks. J. L. Fisher of the Bank of England was subsequently invited to examine the matter. He advised against the establishment of a central bank in the colony.[48] A 1953 report of the International Bank for Reconstruction and Development (IBRD), however, disagreed with the Bank of England position on central banking in Nigeria. This helped resuscitate the central banking idea in the colony and culminated in the establishment of the Central Bank of Nigeria in 1958.[49] The IBRD's report on Nigeria also helped influence the establishment, in 1957, of a central bank in Ghana.[50] Central banks were subsequently introduced in Sierra Leone (1963) and the Gambia (1971).

5. Conclusion

The maintenance of price stability was one of the main advantages of the WACB system; this also suited the interests of the major foreign banks then in existence. The foreign banks also benefited from its role as a currency distribution agency for the WACB. The rise of nationalist movements and the change in the political climate culminated in the establishment of central banks in the Gold Coast (Ghana), Nigeria, Sierra Leone and the Gambia. All the above central banks were midwifed by the Bank of England and their pioneering enabling statutes put price stability as their main objectives and limited their ability to expand money supply. Such central banks also had little control over foreign banks. Such a relationship has since changed. Governments have since interfered in both the operations and ownership of foreign banks. Government policies, in this respect, have included the placement of restrictions on profit repatriation, stipulations on sectoral allocation of credits and indigenization of ownership, among others.[51] All these policies were aimed at aiding indigenous development. What such policies, however, succeeded in doing was to weaken the foreign banks in the territories, thus weakening the reinforcing relationship between these banks and the monetary authorities. The emergent government dominated and controlled banks are no more than political institutions unable to pressure the government in order to defend the banking system when the government adopts policies that go contrary to the interest of such banks. In other words, the need for independence of financial institutions from the monetary authorities is very important for the overall development of the financial system of any country. This is even more so in developing economies without developed political structures where pressures are bound to be put on the monetary authorities to expand its money supply sometimes with the aim of aiding development. Such loopholes did not exist under the colonial monetary system in British West Africa. Further understanding of the relationships between the monetary authorities and the banks in the countries of the former British West African colonies will be beneficial to the current efforts to develop a virile monetary and financial system in these countries.

Acknowledgements

* An earlier version of this paper was presented at the London School of Economics seminar on Comparative Economic History of Africa, Asia and Latin America (London, 16 June 1998). I am grateful to participants for their comments. The views expressed in this paper and its attendant errors however remain mine.

Notes

1   The Gambia, the Gold Coast (Ghana), Nigeria and Sierra Leone. Note that in Nigeria, the colony of Lagos first came under British rule (1861) followed by the Niger Coast Protectorate (1891). The Niger Coast Protectorate was subsequently made part of the Protectorate of Southern Nigeria (1900). Lagos was later made part of the Protectorate of Southern Nigeria (1906). In 1914, the Protectorates of Northern and Southern Nigeria were amalgamated to become the Colony and Protectorate of Nigeria.
2   Section one of the regulation of 1949 defining the constitution, duties and powers of the WACB – reproduced in Loynes 1974.
3   The currency board system, no doubt, satisfied other objectives. For instance, the colonial government earned enormous seigniorage profits from the system.
4   Cf. Newlyn and Rowan 1954; Olakanpo 1965 and Fry 1976.
5   Cf. Uche 1995; 1996 and 1997.
6   Note however that some of the demonetized coins continued in circulation long after the 1880 law. One such currency was the *manilla*, which was finally redeemed by the government in 1948/49. See Ekundare 1973, 84, 313.
7   It was not unusual, at the time, for such coins to be melted for use as jewellery. See Newlyn and Rowan, 1954, 27.
8   Fry 1976, 10.
9   There appears to be no connection between this bank and the Bank of British West Africa which was established later on. To the best of my knowledge, this attempt, in 1871, to establish a bank in the West African colony has remained undocumented in Nigerian banking history.
10 Uche 1999, 672.
11 Under this agreement, other interested parties were still free to order new coins from the mint with the Crown Agents approval but they had to pay a premium of 1%.
12 Fry 1976, 20.
13 Evidence of Leslie Couper, 'Report on the Royal Commission on Shipping Rings with Minutes of Evidence and Appendices' (1909), volume III, Cd. 1670, q.9117.
14 'Report of the Royal Commission on Shipping Rings', 1909, q.9117.
15 Cf. Uche 1999, 674-6.
16 Newlyn and Rowan 1954, 27, 29.
17 Fry 1976, 39
18 Ibid.
19 Opposition to the special silver currency at the time also came from the powerful European merchants in the British West African colonies, especially in the Nigerian colony. This will be discussed later.
20 Though this report was never published, its contents and recommendations were at the time widely known. Cf. Newlyn and Rowan 1954, 30, and 'Report of the Departmental Committee Appointed to Inquire into Matters affecting the Currency of the British West African Colonies and Protectorates' (Emmott Report) 1912, 5.
21 Emmott Report, appendix III, table 1.
22 Ibid.
23 Emmott Report 1912, q195.
24 Emmott Report 1912. 6–9.
25 Milne 1914, 48.
26 Named Anglo-African Bank when it was established. The name was subsequently changed to Bank of Nigeria in 1905.
27 Public Records Office/ Colonial Office [PRO CO] 520/15, Moor to Colonial Office, 26 September 1902.
28 Ofonagoro 1976, 376.
29 PRO CO/520/8, The Butler Memorandum, 9 September 1901, Part A.
30 PRO CO/520/1. Sir Ralph Moor to Alfred Jones, 30 January 1901.
31 PRO CO/520/8, 280.
32 PRO CO 520/10, 521.
33 PRO CO/520/1, Sir Ralph Moor to Alfred Jones, 30 January 1901.
34 PRO CO 520/1, Moor to C.O., 31 January, 1900.
35 Ofonagoro 1976, 389.
36 'Report of the Royal Commission on Shipping Rings', Minutes of Evidence (Q4823, 30 April 1907).
37 PRO CO/ 520/73/3502, Petition dated 26 May 1908.
38 Fry 1976, 67.
39 Cf. Austin and Uche 2007, 8–7.
40 In the Gold Coast (Ghana) for instance, the Companies Act of 1906 prevented the establishment of any local company to carry out any form of banking operation and it was not until 1950 that it was repealed *via* Ordinance no. 36. The Bank of the Gold Coast, which was 100% owned by the government, was subsequently established in 1952.
41 Newlyn and Rowan 1954, 98 and Azikiwe 1956, 3.
42 Central Bank of Nigeria 1986, 64.
43 Bank of England Archives London *Country Files (BEAF)* OV/70/1, folio 62. Memo, 'Sierra Leone- Banking Law', 6 January 1956.
44 Uche 1997, 221, 224.
45 Gold Coast Legislative Assembly Debates, 13 February 1957, Col. 852.
46 Sayers 1957, 112–113.
47 Nigerian Government House of Representatives Debate, 9 April, 1952, Col 1181.
48 Cf. Fisher 1953.
49 Uche 1997, 231.
50 Cf. Uche 1995.
51 Cf. Uche 1998.

Bibliography

Austin, G. and Uche, C.U., 2007, 'Collusion and Competition in Colonial Economies: Banking in British West Africa, 1916–1960', *Business History Review* 81, 1–26.

Azikiwe, N., 1989, *Banking Monopoly in Nigeria: Statement made by the Hon. Premier in the Eastern House of Assembly on 8th August,* Government Printer, Enugu,

Bank of England Archives London, Various Years, *Country Files* (BEAF)

Central Bank of Nigeria, 1986, 'The Growth of Commercial Bank Activities 1959–1966', in Oyejide, O. and Soyode, A. (eds), *Commercial Banking in Nigeria*, Unibadan Publishing Consultants: Ibadan.

Ekundare, R.O., 1973, *An Economic History of Nigeria 1860–1960,* London, 84, 313.

Fisher, J.L., 1953, *Report on the Practicability and Desirability of Establishing a Central Bank in Nigeria as an Instrument for Promoting Economic Development of the Country,* Government Printers: Lagos.

Fry, R., 1976, *Bankers in West Africa,* London.

Gold Coast Government, 1957, *Legislative Assembly Debates,* Government Printers: Accra.

Loynes, J.B., 1974, *A History of the West African Currency Board*, The West African Currency Board, London.

Milne, A.H., 1914, *Sir Alfred Lewis Jones,* Liverpool.

Newlyn, W.T. and Rowan, D.C., 1954, *Money and Banking in British Colonial Africa,* Oxford.

Nigerian Government, Various Years, *House of Representatives Debates,* Government Printers: Lagos.

Ofonagoro, W.I., 1976, *Trade and Imperialism in Southern Nigeria,* New York.

Olakanpo, O., 1965, *Central Banking in the Commonwealth,* Calcutta

Public Records Office London, various years, *Colonial Office Files,* PRO/CO.

Report of the Departmental Committee Appointed to Inquire into Matters Affecting the Currency of the British West African Colonies and Protectorates [Emmott Report], 1912, HMSO: London, Cd. 6427.

Report on the Royal Commission on Shipping Rings with Minutes of Evidence and Appendices, 1909, HMSO, London, vol. III.

Sayers, R.S., 1957, *Central Banking After Bagehot,* Oxford.

Uche, C.U., 1995, 'From currency board to central banking: The Gold Coast experience'. *South African Journal of Economic History* 10(2), 80–94.

Uche, C.U., 1996, 'From currency board to central banking: The politics of change in Sierra Leone', *Africa Economic History* 24, 147–158

Uche, C.U., 1997, 'Bank of England vs. The IBRD: Did the Nigerian Colony deserve a central bank?', *Explorations in Economic History* 34, 220–241.

Uche, C.U., 1998, 'The Community Banking Experiment in Nigeria', *International Journal of Development Banking* 16, 37–45.

Uche, C.U., 1999, 'Foreign Banks, Africans and Credit in Colonial Nigeria, *c.* 1890-1912', *The Economic History Review* 52, 669–691.

From Cowries to Coins: Money and Colonialism in the Gold Coast and British West Africa in the Early 20th Century

Harcourt Fuller

Introduction

This paper explores the validity of the arguments articulated by the British colonial administration and business interests in favour of the institution of a colonial common currency system in British West Africa in 1912 (see **Fig. 1**). It also aims to provide an analysis of the extent to which the native populations accepted or challenged the new colonial monetary order. Given its centrality to Britain's colonial project in West Africa, the Gold Coast (which was renamed Ghana in 1957 after gaining independence) will be used as a case study (see **Fig. 2**). The chapter explores how the loss of politico-monetary sovereignty in the Gold Coast was occasioned by the coming of colonialism, and the establishment of a colonial monetary system in the form of the West African Currency Board (WACB). The WACB managed the production and design of a common currency for the British possessions in West Africa, namely, The Gambia, Sierra Leone, The Gold Coast, Northern and Southern Nigeria (see **Fig. 1**).[1] However, the Board faced numerous challenges in maintaining its monetary monopoly on West Africa before and after the First World War. Analysing the history of the WACB is significant because it provides insights into the manner in which early 20th century British colonial policy was formulated in London and executed in the colonies. As A.G. Hopkins attests:

> There was an imperial monetary policy… and the solution propounded with respect to West Africa was fully consistent with that policy.[2]

This examination also enables us to gauge the effectiveness of the African responses to monetary colonization.

The introduction of colonial coinage to West Africa

Before the formal introduction of colonial coins and paper money in British West Africa in the first quarter of the 20th century, Africans had their own currencies. African societies and kingdoms used monies such as cowry shells, gold nuggets and dust, iron rods, *manillas* and cloth currency. In the Gold Coast as well as the other British territories in West Africa, the indigenous currencies and United Kingdom silver coinage were largely replaced by the West African Currency Board currencies (see **Table I**), which were issued after 1912 when the WACB was established. This colonial currency became the sole legal tender for British West Africa in 1912 and was to cover a total area of 451,000 square miles (116,808,464ha) and a combined population of over 18 million people.[3]

Eric Helleiner argues that during the age of imperialism, currency boards were created by European powers in their respective colonies for economic ends, including the reduction of international and intra-colony transaction costs, and to promote imperial political identities.[4] The creation of the West African Currency Board confirms his argument. Its establishment was due to the recommendations of the Report of the West African Currency Committee (WACC), a body commissioned by the Rt. Hon. Lewis Harcourt, M.P., Secretary of State for the Colonies. The mandate of the Committee was:

> To inquire and report as to the desirability of introducing into West Africa a special silver coinage common to the five British West African administrations, and also as to the desirability of establishing a joint issue of currency notes in the same territories, and to advise upon the measures necessary for the regulation of the special coinage if introduced or for the better regulation of the existing currency in the event of a special coinage not being adopted.[5]

While economic considerations were central to the establishment of the Board in West Africa, it also had political ramifications for the local populations. It deprived Africans of the ability to develop and control an indigenous monetary system that would give their leaders greater political autonomy

Table 1: Legal tender coins in the five West African administrations, 1912

Administration	Legal tender without limit			Limited legal tender		
	British gold	**Foreign gold**	**Foreign silver**	**British**	**Local**	**Foreign**
1. Sierra Leone and 2. Gambia	All gold and silver coins legally current in the UK	Certain French, Spanish and American gold coins	5-franc pieces of the Latin Union	All bronze coins legally current in the UK	nil	nil
3. Gold Coast and Dependencies	ditto	nil	nil	ditto	Nickel-bronze 1/10 of a penny, half-penny and 1-penny pieces	nil
4. Southern Nigeria (Western Province)	ditto	Certain French, spanish and american gold coins	nil	ditto	ditto	nil
5. Northern Nigeria and Southern Nigeria (Eastern and Central Provinces)	ditto	nil	nil	ditto	ditto	nil

Source: NA: CO 984/2, WACC Report, 'Statement of the coins which are now legal tender in the five West African administrations', 2

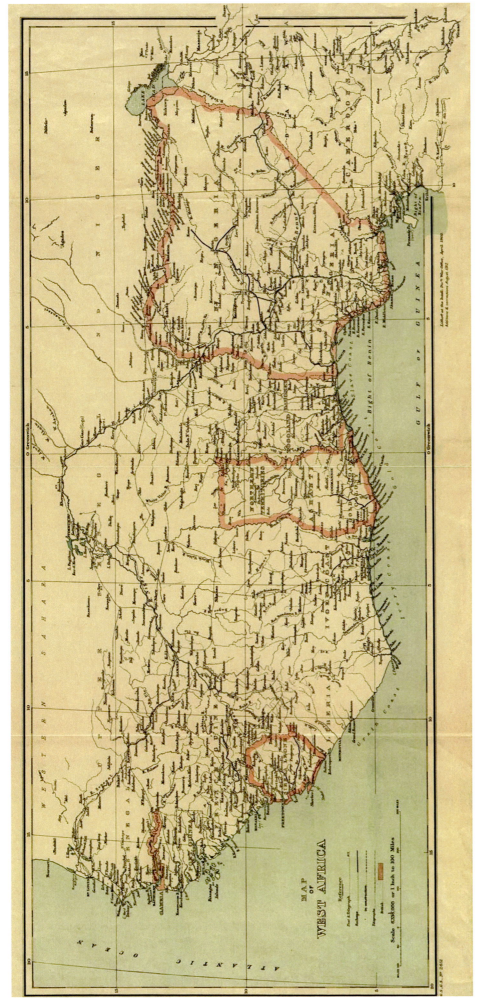

Figure 1 Colonial West Africa (1903/1912), with British colonies highlighted. Scale 1/6,336,000 or 1 inch to 100 miles. Source: NA: CO 984/2, April 1903 and August 1912, 'Map of West Africa'

from the colonial administration. Prior to the publication of the Report, the WACC consulted with 22 of what the Report termed 'witnesses', including the five colonial governments and business interests, such as the major banking and maritime establishments operating in British West Africa.[6] None of the people consulted regarding the new currency system were African however.[7] What does this exclusion of indigenous economic and political interests tell us about the aims of the incoming monetary regime? It appears that the British colonial authority was not aiming to empower Africans to take the reigns of a modern economic and monetary system as top-level administrators. Rather, it is evident that the aim was to replace an existing, albeit less modern economic system across the colonies, with a modern British system. It also appears that Africans were not thought to be capable of, or desired to be, active stakeholders in the ensuing monetary order. This evaluation on the part of the colonial and business officials, that Africans lacked the experience to participate in the new system, as we shall see below, was not completely accurate or justified.

Factors for change

Before 1912, colonial officials and their business counterparts contended that the most widely-circulating medium of exchange in British West Africa was United Kingdom silver coinage. Moreover, a variety of legal tender foreign currencies were also in circulation in the region at the time the WACC Report was published, as **Table 1** shows. At the same time barter trade and traditional African currencies constituted the major aspect of trade in many rural areas.[8] For example, in the Gold Coast Colony, while coin transactions dominated the urban areas, cowry shells enjoyed widespread usage mainly in more remote areas. Gold dust, the Akan all-purpose money, was also used as currency for larger transactions in rural parts.[9] The presumed negative situation in the Colony of Ashanti and the Protectorate of the Northern Territories (see **Fig. 2**) also contributed to the complexity and urgency of implementing a new colonial currency order. Overall, the WACC found that the Gold Coast and Dependencies were:

> In a backward state as regards the employment of metallic currency. In Ashanti, however, the use of British silver is stated to be making rapid progress, and gold is said to be considerably in demand by cattle traders in Coomassie [Kumasi], mainly for the purpose of trade with French territory. In the Northern Territories the natives still employ cowries for the small transactions of the market, but silver is gradually coming into use, and five-franc pieces are in demand by traders from French territory, and stand at a premium in relation to British money.[10]

The characterization of metallic money in the British territories as being in a 'backward state' was not an entirely accurate assessment of the monetary reality in British West Africa. This is evident if we take the case of an important Dependency of the Gold Coast Colony, namely, Asante. The success of the British forces in the Yaa Asantewaa War of 1900-01 resulted in the political annexation of Asante and its incorporation into the Gold Coast Colony. While the use of British metallic money was not common there at the time, Asante metallic currency, namely gold dust, was the currency of choice for official and commercial trade and transactions. Furthermore, gold dust currency was not only important in cattle trading with French territories, but in a variety of

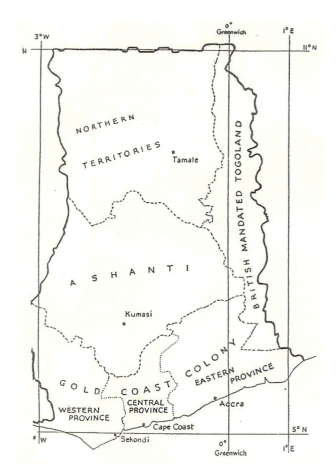

Figure 2 The Gold Coast and Dependencies. Source: Wrangham 1999

commercial transactions beyond the confines of British authority. T.C. McCaskie, in his two-part article, 'Accumulation, wealth and belief in Asante history', reveals the extent to which the Asante state and its commercial sector was economically developed with regard to money and trade. In the late 19th century, the Asante state had a fiscally functioning and effective system of accountancy, taxation and even a 'national' treasury. The latter was a kind of state bank called the 'Great Chest of the Treasury', which was located in the palace of the Asantehene in Kumasi, where gold dust (metallic money) was deposited.[11] In the 20th century, moreover, successful Asante entrepreneurs and traders operating between Asante and the Gold Coast Colony used gold dust currency to trade in commodities including gold, rubber, cocoa and timber. They also provided services as moneylenders, gold dealers, investors, retailers, transportation suppliers and urban developers. Asante businessmen were also involved in the import-export trade.[12] Therefore, for at least one major segment of the Gold Coast Colony and Dependencies, there was a complex economic and political system, with a central administrative authority, banking infrastructure and money that enabled trade to take place. However, McCaskie acknowledges that the advent of British '*laissez-faire* capitalism and the colonial cash economy' ushered in a new economic regime that would eventually replace the local monetary order.[13]

The need to eliminate the competing foreign and native currencies in Britain's West African territories through monetization was also seen as being more crucial given the need to collect taxes. Helleiner explains:

a particularly important colonial objective was that of bringing peasants in colonial societies into a monetized economy as taxpayers, wage labourers in colonial enterprise, and producers of cash crops for export.[14]

For example, by mandating that poll taxes be paid in the colonial currency, the state forced its subjects into the export-oriented cash crop economy and other colonial ventures, where they were paid with said currency. This situation contributed to resistance and resentment of that system by colonial subjects.[15] Secondly, British coins were imported into the colonies by two private banks, namely the African Banking Corporation (ABC, which was established in Lagos in 1892) and the Bank of British West Africa, Ltd (BBWA).[16] These banks had 'special arrangements' which amounted to an exclusive contract with the imperial government to supply currency to the colonies.[17] Britain paid for freight and other miscellaneous expenses for supplying silver coins to the colonies, 'in return for prepayment in the United Kingdom of its nominal value'.[18] After the ABC ceased operations in 1893, the BBWA, which had opened up in Lagos in 1894, took over these functions from the former by securing an exclusive agreement with the Lagos government on 4 May 1894. The BBWA subsequently set up operations for the supply of British coins in the Gold Coast and the other British West African colonies; it had one branch in the Gambia, two in Sierra Leone, eight in the Gold Coast, five in Southern Nigeria, and one branch in Northern Nigeria.[19] Therefore, Britain effectively privatized the importation and repatriation of silver coins in the colonies by contracting it out to big banking interests. These Banks operated by charging merchants and traders a 1% premium for supplying them with British coinage. However, merchants, traders and other stakeholders in the colonies had contested the preferential treatment afforded the ABC and demanded a more egalitarian system. Merchants complained of the Bank's monopoly of the currency supply, the 1% premium that they had to pay for coinage and that other banks in the colonies were 'prejudiced by these arrangements'.[20] This contestation would bring about the cancellation of the contract that the ABC (and later the BBWA) had with the government and usher in a new monetary regime under the auspices of the WACB in 1912.[21]

It is clear from the foregoing reports of squabbling between the British colonial officials and the expatriate merchants, and the jostling for power and influence between the latter themselves, that the monetary and banking debates and the reforms enacted during this period took place above the heads of the local African populations. Helleiner's argument, that the cash-poor in the colonies were only important in terms of the need to incorporate them into the cash economy as taxpayers and not as important decision makers and stakeholders in the

new monetary order, is therefore a plausible one. Moreover, the colonial banks, businesses and officials were also insensitive to the monetary needs of African entrepreneurs, often asserting that Africans were not credit-worthy. The British banks (namely Barclays Bank (DCO) and BBWA) operating in the colony catered mainly to the government, expatriate and non-African interests, and failed to extend adequate credit (or any at all, in some cases) to Gold Coasters.[22] Moreover, as Uche explains, the colonial authorities had outlawed locally chartered banks in 1906, which removed a valuable source of credit for Africans and essentially paved the way for the establishment of the colonial common currency system.[23]

Another major factor, which the WACC pointed out in its Report in support of monetary change, was the increasing demand for British currency in the colonies, particularly in British West Africa. It noted that there was 'a direct inducement to over-issue, because new silver has, in some places, a special value for the purposes of native trade'.[24] From 1886–1911, British West Africa had had a significant increase in the circulation of British currency, at times surpassing the coin circulation in the British Isles itself (see **Table 2**). The Committee speculated that, the potential for British coins to return into circulation in London, was more likely during an economic depression, and the possibility that this could destabilize the imperial economy, made the issue of West Africa having its own independent currency more urgent. The Committee found that:

> the continued issue of the silver coins of the United Kingdom to the West African Colonies is [in]compatible with the successful control of its token coinage by the Home Government without the introduction of radical changes into its financial system… the use of sterling silver in West Africa without limit of tender has now become so considerable as to contain elements of danger, which are intensified by the steady increase of the circulation, and which affect the interests both of the United Kingdom and of British West Africa.[25]

Ironically, the demand for British currency in West Africa was attributed to expanding merchant activities, greater colonial penetration and opening up of the territories, and the replacement of indigenous trading practices such as barter with modern British currency, which now jeopardized the metropolis, monetarily.[26]

The profitability of a new system of currency to the colonial governments and mercantile classes was also a significant factor in the establishment of the WACB regime. As the Committee put it:

> there will, of course, be a very large 'profit' representing the difference between the bullion and face value of [special] silver currency supplied to British West Africa. That country [sic] has absorbed over 6 ½ million pounds (face value) in silver coin during the past 26 years, and the absorption may be expected to continue, even if not at the same rate.[27]

Table 2: Circulation of British sterling silver in the UK, West Africa & other territories

Period		West Africa	United Kingdom	Other territories
		£	£	£
Average for the period	1886–1890	24,426	920,088	255,939
	1891–1895	116,323	761,039	124,461
	1896–1900	257,090	796,425	367,233
	1901–1905	262,786	234,150	231,504
	1906–1910	666,190	781,073	325,347
	1911	874,850	1,219,766	286,575

Source: NA: CO 984/2, WACC Report, 'Analysis of British sterling silver issued for circulation in West Africa in the United Kingdom and in other sterling-using Territories', 6.

The Committee continued that the new currency 'should be a source of considerable ultimate profit to the colonial governments concerned'.[28] The admission that the issuance of a special colonial currency would be a profit-making venture within itself undermines the previous assertions that it was just fear that the continued circulation of British coinage in Africa posed a direct risk to the home government. Profit, in addition to the risk of loss, therefore were the main driving forces behind the establishment of the WACB. Therefore, colonial officials and British merchants in West Africa worked together to advance their own interests, which overlapped for the most part. While officials in London and their colonial counterparts in West Africa sought to protect the political and monetary interests of the home government, expatriate merchants worked to protect their commercial interests and profit-base. The latter lobbied heavily for a new monetary system in the colonies mainly because it represented direct control of the machinery of money making to augment their coffers.

After outlining all the factors affecting the currency situation in the territories, the WACC concluded that:

> the introduction of a distinctive silver currency… is therefore… the only practicable measure that we are in a position to suggest for removing the defects of the present monetary conditions of West Africa.[29]

This recommendation resulted in the creation of the West African Currency Board in 1912 and the establishment of a common colonial currency for Britain's five possessions in the sub-region. For a small service charge, the WACB coins and banknotes were made convertible into British sterling when presented at any of the currency centres in Accra, Bathurst, Freetown or Lagos. The equivalent amount in pound sterling would be paid into the customer's account in London.[30] The establishment of this colonial currency system in 1912 signalled the emergence of a new era in West African history. Whereas the pre-1912 period was characterized by the political consolidation of the colonial state at the expense of the vast majority of the peoples, the post-1912 era proved to be a major monetary victory for Britain. However, this monetary advancement would be tempered by several challenges, most notably the resilience of traditional currencies and the coming of a World War two years later.

Colonial currency designs

The WACB authorities confronted several challenges to their new monopoly on money. Firstly, they had the daunting task of making the new currency popular with and acceptable to Africans. In this regard, the WACC Report had highlighted 'the importance of not giving the natives any ground for discriminating between the new coins and those with which they have been familiar in the past'.[31] The Committee found that:

> the native is suspicious of change, and that it might take a long time to overcome any prejudice on his part against the new silver… if the new coins bear the King's head on the obverse and are of the customary denomination, size, and weight, very little difficulty need be anticipated on this score. When it is remembered that the coins now in common circulation in West Africa include five florins, five shillings, and five sixpences bearing five different effigies of three different monarchs on the obverse… the justification for this view becomes obvious.[32]

As Cusack has argued with respect to stamp designs, the

Figure 3 1-shilling coin 1916 (palm tree, King George V)

empire was 'to be represented by the alternating heads of Kings and Queens'.[33] Therefore, minting the head of King George IV on the WACB coinage was not only meant to ensure consistency with previous designs, but also to symbolize the absolute, centralizing power around which the colonized territories and peoples would be consolidated. Similarly, Mwangi has found that, in the case of the East African Currency Board (EACB), the colonial authorities were adamant about keeping the coin and note designs consistent (by minting the effigy of the reigning British Monarch on the face of EACB coinage) so as to maintain public confidence in the money's value.[34] In addition to the British sovereign's head, the other prominent image of the WACB coinage was of the geographical terrain mostly in the form of a palm tree (see **Fig. 3**). These images subtly reinforced the monarch's lordship over the people and colonial landscape; there were no images of Africans. It was only after the 1948 Accra Riots, which resulted in greater agitations by nationalists for political and monetary independence, that the WACB began to include imagery of Africans on their banknotes. Nonetheless, the natives were mainly portrayed as happily engaged in export-designated cash-crop (groundnuts, cocoa and palm oil) production, reinforcing notions of colonial hegemony and the civilizing mission.[35] There are several assumptions that the WACB made about the nature of 'natives' that warrant analysis. Describing them as being 'suspicious of change' and therefore needing some convincing signals, a certain colonial mindset that Africans (perhaps unlike Europeans) were resistant to change, that is, traditional and averse to modernity. Secondly, the Committee overestimated the familiarity and popularity of colonial coinage among locals. While the circulation of British currency increased over time, the majority of peasants would not have frequently used, or had access to, this currency. Moreover, the use of cowrie, gold dust and other forms of traditional currencies showed a resilience to being eradicated that undermined the rapidity with which the colonial administration wanted its coinage to circulate.

Coins, paper money and World War I

As the previous section demonstrated, the 'native question' was always one of the principal considerations and challenges for the success of the new monetary regime. On the issue of the Africans' acceptance of the new coinage, the Committee had been quite confident; 'There is little reason to doubt that coins of the proposed new currency would be well received by the native population, if certain precautions were taken'.[36] Unfortunately, the new coinage issued in 1913 went into circulation just before the beginning of the First World War. During WWI, the WACB and the Clifford colonial government

Figure 4 5-pound banknote 1954 (palm trees, river, natives harvesting palm nuts)

faced even more difficulties in currency administration in the Gold Coast. Silver was scarce worldwide, creating a shortage of silver coinage, which severely affected trade of farm produce, cocoa, mining and other essential commodities. The shortage of coinage was also created by the high expense of sending the Gold Coast Regiment expedition to fight on Britain's behalf in East Africa.[37] However, silver shortage wasn't the only problem. The nickel-bronze coinage introduced by the WACB in 1912 were being used in the marketplace for everything from making small change to ornaments, gambling counters and washers for galvanized iron roofing. The hole in the nickel-bronze coins also made them usable as jewellery.[38] The shortage of currency was further complicated by London's inability to supply the colonies with adequate coinage on the one hand. On the other, locals also tended to melt down coins for jewellery-making, hoard coins and were reluctant to put their money in the banks. Fluctuating cocoa prices also put further strains on the limited supply of coinage in the Gold Coast. Furthermore, London officials remained indifferent to the locals' disdain for, and culturally related reluctance to use, paper money.[39]

If convincing the locals that the coins issued by the WACB after 1912 were just as good as the previous British coins in circulation, then the issuance of paper money was even more difficult, especially during World War I. Coin or metallic money had intrinsic value and therefore was thought to be more 'tangible' than banknotes, which depended on 'real' money (gold or silver) to guarantee its value. The Committee duly recognized this challenge. 'It is clear that the success of a note [paper money] issue in British West Africa must depend on the willingness of an appreciable part of the native population to use this form of currency, which is at present unknown to them'.[40] But how would the WACB try to ensure this loyalty and 'willingness' of the native population to use the new form of currency? There was always the option to use force, but the Committee discounted the suggestions by some witnesses to resort to force, as 'the prospect of ultimate success would be prejudiced if at any early stage notes were forced on natives who preferred coin'.[41] Given these challenges, Governor Clifford found himself in a diplomatic dilemma. On the one hand, he tried to pressure the WACB and the Colonial Office to supply more silver coinage and hold back on issuing paper money too soon in the Gold Coast. On the other, he tried to temper the wartime instability and anxieties in the colony and implored the native population to have more confidence in paper money. The Governor even initially rejected London's advice to issue paper currency to ease the coin shortage, given

the locals' resistance to paper money.[42]

Given the special circumstances and hardships of the War, why were ordinary Africans so picky about paper? As Wrangham shows, there were practical and cultural causes for their resoluteness.[43] The tropical climate made paper easy to deteriorate, susceptible to fire and to consummation by white ants. Furthermore, the typical 'pocketless' cloth attire of the native population made it hard to carry around paper money; it was easier for them to tie their silver coins into knots on their cloth.[44] Despite these problems, the WACB decided to introduce non-legal tender paper currency in late 1916, but this was met with unsubstantiated success.[45] However, by the end of the war, a combination of the shortage and high price of silver and nickel-bronze currency forced the Clifford government to confer legal tender status on the WACB banknotes (**Figs 4, 5**).

Notwithstanding, the WACB banknotes were met with resistance. For example, some market places from the Northern Territories to the Coast, and even some workers in the formal sectors refused to accept paper currency as payment since many did not regard it as real money. Some farmers, for instance, preferred to sell their cocoa on credit than accept paper money. Ashanti Goldfields mine-workers in Obuasi were initially paid only 15% of their salary in banknotes after the introduction of bills, and some workers for the West African Rubber Plantations company were adamant about not being paid in paper.[46] Given the currency shortages during World War I, the use of barter and cowry shells still continued, especially in the Northern Territories, Eastern Province, Ashanti and other rural zones.[47] Moreover, in the post-1918 period, paper money continued to be unpopular with the locals. In some cases, if paper money were accepted for transactions, its value would be discounted.[48] However, in September 1920 the

Figure 5 1-shilling banknote 1918 (with image of 1 shilling coin)

introduction of a new mixed-metal coinage contributed to a more stable currency environment, coinciding with the fluctuations of the post-war economy.[49] Consequently, the British colonial authorities formulated a massive marketing campaign to ensure the success of the new currency both within as much as outside of their colonial borders.

Conclusion

The coming of coinage to British West Africa in the first quarter of the 20th century, was occasioned by several coinciding factors. There were economic considerations, including: the reduction of monetary transaction costs, between Britain and its colonies and within its colonies; better macro-economic management, and the extraction of seigniorage profits by the colonial governments.[50] These reasons were especially fuelled by the increasing circulation of British currency in West Africa and the fear that unfavourable economic conditions there would cause the repatriation of coins to Britain, which could destabilize the home economy.[51] Hopkins also rightly claims that the WACB was established 'to settle expatriate commercial rivalries in West Africa', among the banking, shipping and other trading interests competing for the spoils of the 'Scramble for Africa'.[52] London officials and their administrators in the colonies, on the one hand, sought to protect the monetary system of the home government from the negative effects of oversupply of British currency in the colonies. On the other hand, colonial administrators on the ground and their expatriate commercial allies viewed the establishment of a colonial currency system as a way to make a profit from seigniorage.

Ideological and politically, monetization represented the last two projects of what missionary and explorer David Livingstone identified as the three C's of British imperialism in Africa, namely, Christianity, Civilization and Commerce. Colonial authorities demonetized a variety of local monies (*manillas*, cowry shells, gold dust, etc.) and foreign colonial currencies (French, American, Latin Union, etc.) that circulated concurrently with the pound sterling. Colonial money was thought to be superior to African currency, and the incorporation of Africans into the world of taxation and waged labour was vital to the success of the colonial machinery.[53] Moreover, the images of the reigning British monarchs and the territorial landscape that were minted on colonial coinage and paper money were symbolic of Great Britain's lordship over the colonized.

The convergence of British colonialism and the WACB's monopolization of currency in the Gold Coast in 1912 signalled the loss of political and monetary sovereignty for the indigenous population. The demonetization of pre-colonial currencies

> produced significant losses for Africans, especially those who held much of their fortune in these forms of money. Without a formal monetary role, cowry shells could only now be sold for their lime content at very low values.[54]

It also forced Africans into colonial enterprises such as the production of cash crops, much of the proceeds of which went into paying taxes and other expenses that were only accepted in colonial currency.

Notwithstanding this loss of politico-monetary autonomy, Gold Coasters, through passive and active strategies resisted the colonial monetary regime throughout the entire period. These subversive measures included the continued use of indigenous and foreign currencies, counterfeiting colonial coins and banknotes,[55] defacing currency, melting down money to make jewellery, and refusing to use bank notes. According to Mwangi,

> through the medium of conflicting currencies… the Africans… without resorting to heroic political action, defied and resisted through their daily lives the ambitions of the [colonial] state.[56]

Political action came in 1957 when Ghana achieved independence from Britian. As I argue in another article, Prime Minister Kwame Nkrumah sought to establish Ghana's status as an independent nation-state by breaking from the WACB colonial common currency and establishing the Ghana pound in 1958 and *cedi* and *pesewa* currency in 1965 – embellished with nationalistic symbols and iconography.[57]

Notes

1   Loynes 1962.
2   Hopkins 1990, 129.
3   NA-CO 984/2, 1.12.11, 19.
4   Helleiner 2002a and Helleiner 2002b, 5–6 for a comparison. See also Hopkins 1990, 103.
5   NA-CO 984/2, 05.06.12, Report of the West African Currency Committee, 2.
6   NA-CO 984/2, 05.06.12, WACC Report, 2.
7   Hopkins 1990, 130.
8   NA-CO 984/2, 05.06.12, WACC Report, 3.
9   NA-CO 984/2, 05.06.12, WACC Report, 3.
10 NA-CO 984/2, 05.06.12, WACC Report, 3.
11 McCaskie 1986, 4.
12 McCaskie 1986, 4, 7.
13 McCaskie 1986, 7.
14 Helleiner 2002b, 12.
15 Helleiner 2002b, 12.
16 See also Uche in this volume.
17 Hopkins 1990, 108–110.
18 NA-CO 984/2, 05.06.12, WACC Report, 3, 15.
19 NA-CO 984/2, 05.06.12, WACC Report, 16.
20 NA-CO 984/2, 05.06.12, WACC Report, 5, 15.
21 Hopkins 1990, 109–111.
22 Uche 2003, 75-90; Helleiner 2002b, 18.
23 Uche 2003; 2008, and this volume.
24 NA-CO 984/2, 05.06.12, WACC Report, 15.
25 NA-CO 984/2, 05.06.12, WACC Report, 6–7; see also Hopkins 1990, 105–106. **Table 2** illustrates the circulation of British sterling silver in the UK, West Africa and other territories.
26 NA-CO 984/2, 05.06.12, WACC Report, 7.
27 NA-CO 984/2, 05.06.12, WACC Report, 9.
28 NA-CO 984/2, 05.06.12, WACC Report, 18.
29 NA-CO 984/2, 05.06.12, WACC Report, 8.
30 Newlyn and Rowan 1954, 46–47; Loynes 1962, 20.
31 NA-CO 984/2, 05.06.12, WACC Report, 10. This wish, however, would prove to be more difficult than anticipated.
32 NA-CO 984/2, 05.06.12, WACC Report, 11.
33 Cusack 2005, 592.
34 Mwangi 2002, 33.
35 See **Figs 3–5** and Helleiner 2002b, 23-24; Mwangi 2002.
36 NA-CO 984/2, 05.06.12, WACC Report, 18.
37 Wrangham 1999, 149.
38 Wrangham 1999, 150–151.
39 Wrangham 1999, 144–155.
40 NA-CO 984/2, 05.06.12, WACC Report, 12.
41 NA-CO 984/2, 05.06.12, WACC Report, 13.
42 Wrangham 1999, 144–155.
43 Wrangham 1999.
44 Wrangham 1999, 148–149.
45 Wrangham 1999, 148.
46 Wrangham 1999, 147–148.
47 Wrangham 1999, 151–152.
48 Wrangham 1999, 153.

49 Wrangham 1999, 154.
50 Helleiner 2002a, 2; Helleiner 2002b, 5–6.
51 Helleiner 2002b, 10; Hopkins 1990, 129.
52 Hopkins 1990, 130; see also NA-CO 984/2, 05.06.12, WACC Report, 9.
53 Helleiner 2002b, 22.
54 Helleiner 2002b, 21.
55 See Olukoju in this volume.
56 Mwangi 2003, 224.
57 The graphical elements of Ghanaian money during the Nkrumah regime featured nationalistic symbolism such as Independence Square (with the inscription 'Freedom and Justice'), Parliament House, the Ghanaian landscape, and national development schemes including logging, cargo shipping, and the harvesting of cocoa. See Fuller 2008.

Bibliography

Cusack, I. 2005, 'Tiny transmitters of nationalist and colonial ideology: The postage stamps of Portugal and its empire', *Nations and Nationalism* 11(4), 591–612.

Fuller, H. 2008, '*Civitatis Ghaniensis Conditor*: Kwame Nkrumah, symbolic nationalism and the iconography of Ghanaian money, 1957–the Golden Jubilee', *Nations and Nationalism* 14(3), 520–541.

Helleiner, E. 2002a, 'Introduction to special section on "the geopolitics of North-South currency blocs"', *Geopolitics* 7(1), 1–4.

Helleiner, E. 2002b, 'The monetary dimensions of colonialism: Why did imperial powers create currency blocs?' *Geopolitics* 7(1), 5–30.

Hopkins, A.G. 1990, 'The creation of a colonial monetary system: the origins of the West African Currency Board', *African Historical Studies* 3(1), 101–132.

Loynes, J.B. 1962, *The West African Currency Board, 1912–1962*, London.

McCaskie, T.C. 1986, 'Accumulation, wealth and belief in Asante history. Part II: the twentieth century', *Africa* 56(1), 3–23.

Mwangi, W. 2002, 'The lion, the native and the coffee plant: Political imagery and the ambiguous art of currency design in colonial Kenya', *Geopolitics* 7(1), 31–62.

Mwangi, W. 2003, *The Order of Money: Colonialism and the East African Currency Board*, Ph.D. Thesis, University of Pennsylvania.

National Archives/ Colonial Office [NA: CO] 984/2 April 1903, 'Map of West Africa', lithographed at the Intell: Division, War Office. Additions and corrections August 1912. Scale 1/6,336,000 or 1 inch to 100 miles.

National Archives/ Colonial Office 984/2, 01.12.11, 'Report of the West African Currency Committee: Appendix I. The area, population, and trade of the West African dependencies'.

National Archives/ Colonial Office 984/2, 05.06.12, 'Report of the West African Currency Committee: Analysis of British sterling silver issued for circulation in West Africa in the United Kingdom and in other sterling-using Territories'.

National Archives/ Colonial Office 984/2, 05.06.12, 'Report of the West African Currency Committee: Statement of the coins which are now legal tender in the five West African administrations'.

Newlyn, W.T., and Rowan, D.C. 1954, *Money and Banking in British Colonial Africa: A Study of the Monetary and Banking Systems of Eight British African Territories*, Oxford.

Uche, C.U. April 2003, 'Credit for Africans: The Demand for a 'National Bank' in the Gold Coast Colony', *Financial History Review* 10(1), 75–90.

Wrangham, E. 1999, *The Gold Coast and the First World War: The Colonial Economy and Clifford's Administration*, (Ph.D. Thesis, SOAS/University of London).

The Currency Revolution in British West Africa: An Analysis of Some Early Problems

Adebayo A. Lawal

Introduction

Notwithstanding a plethora of publications[1] on the introduction of European currency to displace the pre-existing African media of exchange, this modest attempt aims at analyzing some socio-cultural problems that arose among the various rural ethnic groups in the remotest parts of the British colonies in West Africa during and after the First World War. This essay concentrates on the problems of inadequate distribution of coins and notes to some inaccessible communities in Sierra Leone, Nigeria and the Cameroon. The newly-established colonial administrative and judicial structures jointly managed by the African Chiefs and British officials, failed to function effectively in transforming the outlook of the local populace because they lacked frequent supervision and correction. However, this negligence was necessitated by the overwhelming demands of the First World War for recruitment of soldiers, diversion of administrative personnel and suspension of on-going road construction works. There was also the post-war burden of administering the mandated territory of the Cameroons, which Britain had to bear in alliance with the colonial government in Nigeria.[2] The issues raised in this paper include the perception and misperception of the new coins and notes, the new banking system, the misinterpretations of the embossed symbols, the changing socio-economic values and attitudes, the problems of currency devaluation across the borderlands between the French and British colonies, the unresolved exchange rates, harmonization of import and export duties, the circulation of the German mark and prevalent Germanophilism in the Cameroons.

Theoretical framework

Embedded in the crusading spirit of British colonialism was the civilizing mission, which was to be vigorously executed through the medium of a wholesale modernization of African political economic and social institutions and relationships. Colonialism would be seen as a broad road to consistent modernization by virtue of the military conquest of Africans by European powers, albeit with some challenges.[3] Notwithstanding the several strands of modernization theory, which have attracted positive and negative reactions from several disciplinary perspectives, its substance will be appropriate to this endeavour.

Contact between advanced and undeveloped countries inaugurated an era of mutual understanding between an inferior and a superior race. After the dust of conflict settled, and the defeated inferior race accepted the hegemonic status of the superior race, the latter dictated and imposed its values and institutions to replace those of the former. By propaganda, persuasion and military expeditions, the traditional institutions, social systems and social relations must be revamped and modernity must replace traditionalism. The traditional society was seen as stagnant, lacking in innovation, progress, science, technology and European industrialization. To break the jinx of stagnation therefore, undeveloped societies must adopt capitalism, which was the engine of growth from the West.[4] Hence social changes must be predicated on the eradication of the perceived ills of traditional beliefs and practices and the introduction and imposition of a European educational system, which emphasizes and promotes modern science and rationality. African societies were compelled to accept an efficient bureaucracy and modern state apparatus which groomed the educated elite within them for the eventual emergence of the Western-styled liberal democracy. To guarantee their expectations, advanced countries are always prepared to render the necessary assistance in terms of funds, personnel, advice, science, technology and markets to transform the undeveloped countries from tradition to modernity and to avoid the pitfalls experienced by the West.[5]

The general impact of the British currency

Many studies have described the socio-economic and cultural impacts of the new currency and the resistance and opposition of the West African communities to the use of some modern currencies until 1956.[6] But in the coastal towns where trade with Europeans was firmly established, it was easy for African traders to adjust to the change by patronizing the new banks. However from the colonial perspective, the consequences of the currency revolution were stimulating and supportive of the British trade and colonial exploitation. The colonial economy was integrated into the capitalist world market. Henceforth the pre-existing African economic institutions and relations of production in the domestic economy were either adjusted or overhauled. All British colonies in West Africa – the Gambia, Sierra Leone the Gold Coast (now Ghana) and Nigeria embraced the market economy and used a common currency for exchange purposes. It was then easy to subsume the colonies under the British policy of money supply, regulation of market prices, inflation, trade, banking, taxation, wages and salaries; public finance and development projects. Slavery was abolished and was replaced with wage labour, hence the new trend of migrant farmers in towns and rural areas for the cultivation of such export produce as cocoa, cotton, palm oil, palm kernels, groundnuts or rubber. The rapid rate of diffusion of these elements of modernization was relative to the speed of introduction of transportation infrastructure in each colony. Thus where roads, the railways and water transport facilities were provided, the supply of the new currency was easy and the expansion and growth of European trade was implemented.[7]

The monetization of the indigenous economy created new values, tastes and status symbols mostly in towns at first and later in the rural areas. Towns were first developed as commercial centres where African traders had regular contacts with European merchants for business. Hence the amenities in towns caused some premeditated urbanization by adventitious and regular traders, workers and artisans. Dissatisfaction with patriarchal control and restrictions in the village compelled young men and women to move into towns to enjoy their new freedoms to seek employment with the colonial and mercantile establishments. But limited opportunities in this direction caused unprecedented migrations from town to town even across the colonial frontiers in search of greener pastures. In the process Africans directed their creative energies to all sorts of occupations to earn a living. Thus in towns, women took to prostitution while young men engaged in such crimes as theft, robbery, currency counterfeiting and dishonest practices in medical services. Some studies have demonstrated that the remittances of Nigerian prostitutes in the Gold Coast supported their relations in Nigeria as a form of social security service.[8]

The reactions of colonial subjects to the British currency 1912–1918

Within the first 10 years of the currency revolution in West Africa, the British colonial officials gleefully celebrated an historic success of their experiment, to judge from the reports from the Gambia, Sierra Leone, the Gold Coast and Nigeria. The popularity of nickel penny, half penny and tenth penny in the Gold Coast and Nigeria was commended. However the local people rejected the imperial bronze coin because of its dullness. They preferred a bright coin. To them, the farthings were not bright when minted. They had to rub them in fine sand until they became bright and were fond of showing the bankers to ask why they could not be issued in the acceptable condition.[9]

West Africa nickel coins had a round hole in the middle for Africans to string together in a rope or twain. The hole enabled African carpenters, mechanics and smiths to use the 'tenths' as washers for nails and screws when fixing galvanized iron sheets in the building industry. For its brightness and intrinsic value, the silver coin was admired for making ornaments. As this practice adversely affected the circulation of coins and local trade, silver bullion was shipped to West Africa in increasing quantities for African silver smiths to boost their business. However several diviners in their localities used both cowries and silver coins in their rituals.

Any change in the design of a coin quickly provoked people's reactions. They looked at the coin with suspicion if it bore the embossed image of a dead British monarch and thereby rejected it, in preference for a new coin bearing the image of a new monarch. In their calculation the old coin was valueless on account of the dead monarch and was tagged 'the money of the dead' or 'owo oku' in Yoruba (Southwest Nigeria). Of course it would be wrong to suggest or affirm that Africans quickly dispensed with their commodity currencies. Rather they were treasured as stores of value, objects of worship and materials for herbal medicine. By 1918, in the riverine areas of Southern Nigeria, the 'rods' and 'wires' were used for mending and strengthening the canoes, as these communities had only water transport.[10]

It was in 1916 that the West African Currency Board (WACB) began to issue notes in three denominations of 20 shillings, 10 shillings and 2 shillings (20s, 10s, 2s) to Nigeria,

the Gold Coast and Sierra Leone, where they were popular among the educated elite, school teachers, European commercial class and colonial civil servants. The majority of illiterate farmers, labourers, traders and artisans preferred coins which they could handle well for local purchases. Apart from their inability to decipher the symbols on the notes in various denominations, notes were easily lost, damaged or destroyed in their poor living conditions. On the other hand, coins could not be destroyed by insects or rain. But the notes could be destroyed during fire outbreaks in the rickety huts or houses with thatched roofs that the majority of people lived in: only a small number of elite and successful business men and traders could afford to cover their houses with corrugated iron sheets.

The fishermen and fishmongers in the above mentioned riverine areas lost a great deal of currency notes during the rainy seasons that resulted in the notes being torn to shreds. Having learnt their lessons they henceforth preferred coins.[11]

Another general practice was hoarding of coins in homes rather than saving them in the banks. Hoarding, from an African perspective, is a misnomer for saving their daily earnings in the traditional culture. For safety and security, coins might be buried in the earth but could unfortunately be washed away during heavy downpours. Others kept coins in small earthen wares, like pots, with holes on top. These were hidden in an obscure part of their houses.

Africans were (and still are) in the habit of keeping money at home or always carried cash because they distrusted the European banks and bankers. How could they save their stores of values with strange Europeans, whose names, addresses and language they never knew, spoke and understood? They feared they would be cheated and even detested the banking processes that required their mandatory credentials for withdrawals. Their misconceptions and misperceptions of these rituals compelled them to either adhere to the pre-existing thrift societies or keep their money at home. Indeed the collectors of daily contributions of these thrift societies did not save the collections in the banks in compliance with the unwritten constitutions by members. Another major reason was the distances to be covered from their dwelling places to the banks. Some had to trek for two or three days to transact banking business as motor transport was a rarity. Only a few people with bicycles could visit the distant banks frequently.

The impact of First World War and currency in Sierra Leone

Prior to the war, the trade of Sierra Leone was dominated by both Britain and Germany. But by 1917, all German traders were totally excluded from the colonial trade and the vacuum was filled by France, the United States, Belgium and Switzerland in exporting palm kernels, groundnuts, ginger, colanuts and palm oil. But trade was hindered by the war especially by attacks on the trans-Atlantic shipments by German U-Boats, hence the local shortage of British currency.

This development occasioned the use of the 5-franc pieces of France, Belgium, Italy and Switzerland, in addition to the imperial and the West African coinage as legal tenders, the value of each being fixed at 3s: 10½d. This new arrangement caused a lot of confusion among the colonial subjects. Even British traders, having been stirred by economic nationalism, condemned the economic disadvantages of permitting foreign coins to circulate as legal tender at a fixed rate of exchange which local producers of export crops did not understand. Herein lay an unpremeditated paradox in the official prohibition of commodity currency and the introduction of British currency. Ironically the war conditions and the new trade relations with some European countries now permitted the circulation of their coins to strengthen diplomatic ties at the expense of the economic interests of local traders.[12]

On account of inadequate quantities of British currency, local buyers of European and African merchandise resorted to the barter system. The general shortage of coins restricted their freedom of choice and caused some stagnation of trade. Those who possessed the French coin with the current exchange rate of 3s: 5½d. *Vis-à-vis* the British coin, inevitably had reduced purchasing power when later the French coin depreciated to 3s:5½d. They thereby had to pay more in pound sterling (British coins) for consumer items. To them therefore British goods were more expensive. To alleviate their plight, the colonial subjects resorted to smuggling and the black market, which further aggravated the colonial trade. This development precipitated recurring, relentless protests from the local chambers of commerce in the local and foreign press with a request for an immediate prohibition of foreign coins.

Meanwhile the British currency notes for £1 and 10shillings issued under the Currency and Bank Notes Act, 1914 were also legal tender in Sierra Leone. Out of them, notes to the value of 18, 500 were withdrawn in 1917, leaving notes valued at 6,500 still in circulation. As usual, such a withdrawal was because the notes were not so popular with majority of people, who expressed their preference for British coins but which were inadvertently in short supply. An alternative was to supplement the remaining paper currency in circulation with the introduction of West African currency notes, issued in Nigeria, in denominations of £1 10s to the value of £6000. Although not officially legal tender in Sierra Leone, the colonial government gave a guarantee to accept the Nigerian notes in payment of dues. With the tacit agreement with the Bank of British West Africa, the notes were redeemable at the Bank face value.[13]

British currency in the mandated territories

The wartime scarcity and shortages of British coins and European goods had severe adverse effects on the local economy. The mandated territories of Togo and Cameroons, were seized from Germany and shared between Great Britain and France. Thus British and French Togo as well as British and French Cameroons shared common borders. Although our attention is on the experience of the local population in the British sphere, it is inevitable to discuss the problems of trans-frontier fiscal policy in terms of cross-border trade, taxation, movement of goods and people and exchange rate of one currency with another.[14]

Hitherto, the peoples of the British Cameroons had been exchanging the German mark for 1 shilling without any demur in their trading activities. But the exigencies of the war and the exercise of mandatory powers to regulate socio-economic activities in the mandated territory accounted for the issue of an official order for the exchange of one German mark for 9 pence with immediate effect in 1918.

This deviation from the existing parity exchange rate generated some unprecedented argument and protests among the local population against the untoward depreciation of the German currency in their possession.[15] By arguing that the German mark had an equivalent purchasing power of 1 shilling, they expressed an ingrained degree of Germanomania which could only be erased by British propaganda, liberal democratic ideas, programmes of modernization and re-orientation with the ultimate objective of gradually cultivating Anglophilic sentiments.

But the law must have its free course and the people lamented the depletion of their capital by one quarter. Indeed they were ignorant of the complicated processes of exchange between countries. Those that possessed large stocks of rubber and cocoa to sell to the merchant firms discovered with great disappointment and shock that their value was worth only three quarters of the expected turn-over. When they added the transport cost for delivering their produce to the facilities of the merchant firms, they discovered a further reduction in their profit margins.[16]

To promote an instant Anglomania, the importation of marks was prohibited and about half a million sterling worth of marks in circulation were withdrawn, melted down and re-coined into British shillings on a par with the coinage in Nigeria. It was expected that this arrangement would foster the economic integration of the British Cameroons into Nigeria and the consolidation of British control. With the total eradication of traces of German influence, free trade between the peoples of Nigeria and the Cameroons, was expected to flourish, to mutual benefit.

To cover the cost to the British Treasury, 5% was charged on remittances of money from the Cameroons to Nigeria by European and African traders, colonial civil servants and plantation workers. With this measure, the British government could offset any losses on the question of free trade as opposed to trade monopoly. But the 5% charge was a heavy burden on both European firms and African traders in Nigeria, as well as their counterparts in the Cameroons who transmitted money to Nigeria in payment for the goods obtained there. Also those who purchased goods in Nigeria to be conveyed to the Cameroons had to pay 5% more on the goods. The general hardships caused by this fiscal policy impelled the local people to lodge a serious complaint with the League of Nations through the Permanent Mandates Commission after the war.[17]

Thousands of African labourers on about 30 plantation farms in the Cameroon, were initially unwilling to receive their wages in marks, having discovered that they got less than they expected when making purchases in the local markets. This nasty way of being short-changed could hamper labour productivity and cause a general decline in the economy. Only an increase in labour income could stimulate higher agricultural productivity and production of export crops. But the challenges of the war prevented the adoption of any liberal measures to ameliorate the similar economic hardships experienced in the Ivory Coast and Dahomey (now Republic of Benin) owing to the lamentable shortage of silver and paper money. The complaints of African and French businessmen about inadequate supply and circulation of 5-franc or 3-franc pieces (paper money) was the subject of the meeting of the French Colonial Union in 1918, in course of which, lack of transport was identified as the major cause.[18]

Along the Nigerian boundary, in the immediate vicinity of Mamfe (in the British Cameroons), in 1923, the shilling was the predominant coin, but east of Mamfe the further one travelled towards Bamenda and Chang, the higher the value of the mark, while the rarer British currency became. Around Menka, brass rods were more common than marks, whose conversion into British currency during tax collection was a complicated and expensive process. For example the Banyang traders charged 6 pence in the pound as commission. According to the 1923 annual report, sufficient British currency could only be introduced into the area by employing large forces of labour on the plantain farms and encouraging produce-purchase by European firms.[19]

Bangwa, which was in the British sphere, also lacked trading facilities for the sale of produce to European firms. But Nkongsamba in the hilly terrain of the French zone happened to be a more popular and profitable produce-buying centre than Mamfe or Ikom, with the German mark predominantly used in commercial transactions. Indeed, some villages such as Akwun, a two-day journey from Ikom, traded regularly with Nkongsamba about an eight-day journey. Lack of trading facilities also inevitably exposed the Kumba Division to the same scarcity of British currency and the predominance of both French and German currencies. While the farmers were forced to pay customs duties on their export crops of cocoa and palm kernels, and later on their imports, they had to receive French money in payment for their produce which was of doubtful value in the British territory and usually led to further loss when exchange was effected. Basically, the customs barriers and lack of trading facilities between Kumba Division and the French area accounted for the general dilemma confronting the local people who concluded that the British deliberately discouraged the establishment of trading facilities because the collection of customs duties was deemed to be more profitable to the government. In 1923, German silver marks equivalent to £2,787 was in circulation in the Cameroons Province.[20]

Cross-frontier fiscal policy and people's reactions

The colonial subjects also experienced some hardships on account of the fiscal boundaries fixed by the French and British authorities by which two different import and export duties were collected from traders intending to cross from one border to another. The problems of trans-frontier migrations and control measures on smuggling and crimes have been well researched and do not warrant any further articulation. But it must be stressed that the two colonial powers appeared to be strange bedfellows on account of their rivalries and conflicting fiscal and monetary policies, in the mandated territories of Togo and the Cameroons.[21]

According to a report submitted by the Permanent Mandates Commission to the Council of the League of Nations in 1924, the two colonial powers had imposed dissimilar import duties on spirituous liquors imported into the mandated territories to the effect that while the liquor was cheap in the French sphere, it was more expensive in the British sphere. This being so, the local population within the borderlands resorted to smuggling, which hampered colonial trade. The League of Nations recommended the introduction of an *ad valorem* duty to stem the rising waves of smuggling. Both French and British governments were expected to meet and deliberate on the modalities for adopting uniform import duties on alcoholic liquors imported into West African including the former colonies.[22]

But the French were confronted with the depreciation of the franc in terms of its exchange rate to the pound sterling. The implication was the resultant lower import duties on spirituous liquor of equal strength imported into the French possessions and the mandated territories contiguous to Nigeria i.e. the Gold Coast and the British spheres of the Cameroons and Togoland. This depreciation was attributed to an increase in the British rate of duty above the minimum required by the convention signed at St. Germain-en Laye on the 10 September 1919. By article 4 of the convention, a minimum import duty of 500 francs per hectolitre of pure alcohol must be levied on all spirituous beverages imported into the areas covered by the convention. This was alcohol of standard strength i.e. 50% alcohol, which attracted an import duty of 15 shillings *per* gallon in British West Africa and the British spheres of the mandated territories. But the British increased the duty to 25 shillings per gallon in case of spirits containing more than 50% of alcohol. This is equivalent to 4,950 francs per hectolitre of pure alcohol taking the franc at 90 to the 1 pound sterling. These figures were based on the speculations of British officials that were close to the French officials. While ignorant of the current rate of duty on spirits imported into French territory, they were of the opinion that the rate was below the above figure.[23]

While anticipating a deadlock in the Anglo-French negotiation of uniform duties, the Permanent Mandates Commission suggested that the two colonial powers could agree on the same rate of duty expressed in gold francs per unit of pure alcohol so long as the gold value of the pound sterling remained stable. The French government was expected to undertake a frequent review of its actual rates of duty (in paper francs) in view of the fluctuations in the gold value of the paper Franc. The Commission insisted on the substitution of *ad valorem* duty for the current specific duty which was economically detrimental to the British possessions and mandated territories in West Africa. When two elephants fight, it is the grass that suffers. As long as the diplomatic negotiation was unresolved because neither party was ready to concede to the other, the colonial subjects, rather than endure any stress on cross-frontier trade, resorted to cross-border smuggling and black market as their survival strategy.[24]

Thus the erection of two walls of conflicting fiscal frontiers by the French and British in West Africa inevitably led to the imposition of the prevailing irreconcilable export and import duties which constituted a heavy burden on African traders involved in cross-frontier commerce. While a law-abiding minority used the official trade routes and submitted to border checks and payment of mandatory duties, the majority charted new escape routes in the porous borders through which European goods and produce were smuggled in the day and at night. Both British and French personnel patrolled the borders to arrest smugglers. In the process, they encountered armed smugglers with whom they exchanged gun shots that resulted in the death of smugglers and patrol men.[25] Even though official reports affirmed the arrest and prosecution of culprits and the confiscation of their merchandise, the phenomenon of cross-border crimes have remained a recurring concern in the West

Africa Economic Community (ECOWAS) since its formation in 1975.

The early years of modernization and colonialism also compelled the populace to direct their ingenuity to evolving anti-colonial practices that guaranteed relief and comfort during short-term or sustained trade cycle as soon as they realized that new fiscal and monetary policies dmamaged their interests. For example, the colonial concept of taxation (in any form), exchange rate, devaluation and customs duties, were inimical to their commercial and material interests and profit margins. They could not understand the essence of taxation as a compulsory civic obligation. In their thinking, tax proceeds were spent on the provision of amenities to European residential areas to the detriment of their own welfare, hence the frequent widespread tax revolts, tax evasion, avoidance and dodging, in trans-frontier migration.[26]

This study also gives a hint about the evolution of unofficial currency exchange business at the various border towns or posts by Africans across West Africa. Quite often in contemporary times, the prevailing official exchange rates in each country help the money changers to determine their rates which are a little higher. Yet they attract patrons. Payment is made on the spot in cash. Despite the well-established modern banking system, the majority of African traders and travellers still carry cash in inter- and intra-African trade: a carry-over from the colonial period. The only snag in the unofficial currency exchange (tagged black market) is the risk of receiving counterfeit currency notes, which may not be detected on the spot. Many patrons have been victims of dishonest money changers over the years[27] and, to date, no country in the sub-region has successfully eradicated the black markets, which have remained a vibrant segment of the informal sector since colonial days. So also in trans-border trade, which economists believe has contributed substantially to economic growth, even though lack of reliable records handicap any attempts at determining the extent of the contribution. Similarly, the operations of the black markets have allegedly been held responsible for heating up national inflation and distorting the configuration of the external annual remittances to each country on account of unrecorded transactions.

Conclusion

A key segment of the colonial scheme was the monetization of the colonial economy in West Africa, by which the use of African traditional currencies was prohibited for the substitution of the newly-introduced British coins and notes. Wage labour, sale of land, taxation and the European banking system were introduced to facilitate the much expected change and the integration of the colonial economy into the global capitalist market. In other words, colonial administration and the establishment of judicial, military, economic and political structures were integral to the programme of modernization and processes of social change. There was an assurance of the emergence of new social organizations and new values among the populace which overshadowed the pre-existing traditional social structures and political institutions. These new structures must be similar to those in the industrialized countries and orchestrated by social mobilization to revamp old social, economic and psychological behaviour for exposure

to the use of European machinery, buildings, consumer goods, modern life, mass-media, change of residence, urbanization, industrialization, literacy and growth of *per capita* income.[28]

Crucial to these changes were the functions of money and wealth, which were to be acquired by the colonial subjects through wage labour, services and engagement in the production of export crops and sales of domestic and imported goods in the local markets. New markets and banking institutions functioned as regulative and allocative mechanisms in the economic life of the populace with many problems of adjustment, hence the colonial application of coercive measures. In the perception of the populace, capitalism was synonymous with inequality, discrimination, injustice and exploitation of labour and resources, as exemplified by wage differentials between African and European workers, the well furnished but segregated residences of the latter and their standard of living, all in the name of modernization. It was therefore natural for the colonial subjects to identify a number of contradictions between the European ideals and social reality,[29] hence the rising waves of direct and subtle anti-colonial revolts and protests in the form of tax evasion, hoarding and counterfeiting of coins and smuggling. However, modernization is an ongoing process of change and progress, with problems to be confronted and solved later. Nevertheless its benefits outweigh its curses.

Notes

1   Johnson 1970, parts 1 and 2; Johnson 1968; Hogendorn and Johnson 1986; Hopkins 1966; Herbert 1973; Curtin 1975; and Hopkins 1973.
2   Osuntokun 1979, 169-205 AND 237-269.
3   Curtis, Feierman, Thompson and Vansina 1978, 451–471; Webster and Boahen 1969, 228–256; Growder 1973, 116–162.
4   Joshi 2007 and Sanderson 1995.
5   Anonymous 2007.
6   Ofonagoo 1979, 283, 284 and 290.
7   Railway transport facilities were extended to areas noted for export crops and minerals for exploitation and shipment to Europe.
8   Naanen 1991.
9   *West Africa*, 26 January 1918, 871.
10 *West Africa*, 26 January, 1918, 871.
11 *West Africa*, 26 January, 1918, 871.
12 *West Africa*, 1 December, 1917, 736.
13 *West Africa*, 1 December, 1917, 736.
14 For details, Asiwaju 1984, 29–50.
15 *West Africa*, 18 May, 1918, 244.
16 *West Africa*, 18 May, 1918, 244.
17 *West Africa*, 18 May, 1918, 244.
18 *West Africa*, 25 May, 1918, 266.
19 National Archives, Ibadan, CSO 26/2 File no. 11556.
20 National Archives, Ibadan, CSO 26/2 File no. 11556.
21 Hargreaves 1984.
22 National Archives, Ibadan, CSO 26/2 File no. 13977.
23 National Archives, Ibadan, CSO 26/2 File no. 13977, Enclosure in Foreign Office (F.O.) Letter no. A 7016/4960, 4 December, 1923.
24 *Ibid.*
25 For ethnic groups and impact of the Anglo-French Boundary see Fanso 1982.
26 For colonial policies and distant migrations, see Fanso 1982, note 25, 356–370; Asiwaju and Crowder 1977, 3, 5; Asiwaju 1974; Asiwaju 1977.
27 Author's recent personal experience traveling from Nigeria to Ghana by road.
28 Eisenstaat 1965.
29 Collin 1997.

Bibliography

Anonymous 2007, 'Modernization theory'. http//.en.wikipediae.org/wiki/modernizationtheory (accessed 14 October, 2007).

Asiwaju, A.I. 1974, 'Anti-French Resistance Movement in Okori-Ije (Dahomey), 1895–1960', *Journal of the Historical Society of Nigeria* 7(2).

Asiwaju, A.I. 1977, 'Migrations as Revolt: The Example of the Ivory Coast and Upper Volta before 1945', *Journal of African History* XVII, 4.

Asiwaju, A.I. and Crowder, M. 1977 (eds), Protest against colonialism in West Africa, London.

Asiwaju, A.I. 1984, *Partitioned Africans: Ethnic Relations Across Africa's International Boundaries, 1884–1984*, Lagos.

Collin, F. 1997, *Social Reality*, London and New York.

Curtin, P.D. 1975, *Economic Change in Pre-Colonial Africa. Senegambia in the era of the slave trade,* Madison.

Curtis, P., Feierman, S., Thompson, L., and Vansina, J. 1978, *African Years: West Africa Since 1800,* London and Harlow.

Eisenstaat, S.N. 1965, 'Social change and modernization in African societies South of the Sahara', in W.H. Lewis (ed.), *French-Speaking Africa: The Search for Identity*, New York, 223–224.

Fanso, V.G. 1982, 'Trans-Frontier Relations and Resistance to Cameroon-Nigeria Colonial Boundaries, 1916–1945', Ph.D. Thesis, University of Yaoundé, 149–157.

Growder, M. 1973, *West Africa Under Colonial Rule*, London.

Hargreaves, J.D. 1984, 'The Making of the Boundaries: Focus on West Africa', in A.I. Asiwaju, *Partioned Africans*, Lagos, 19–28.

Herbert, E. W. 1973, 'Aspects of the Use of Copper in Pre-Colonial West Africa', *Journal of African History* XIV, 179–194.

Hogendorn, J. and Johnson, M. 1986, *The Shell Money of the Slave Trade*, Cambridge.

Hopkins, A.G. 1966, 'The Currency Revolution in South-West Nigeria in the Late Nineteenth Century', *Journal of the Historical Society of Nigeria* III(3), 471–483

Hopkins, A.G. 1973, *An Economic History of West Africa*, Harlow, UK.

Johnson, M. 1968, 'The Nineteenth-Century Gold Mithqual in West and North Africa', *Journal of African History* IX(4), 547–569.

Johnson, M. 1970, 'The Cowry Currencies of West Africa', Pt 1, *Journal of African History* XII(1), 17–49; Pt 2, XII(3), 331–353.

Joshi, S. 2007, 'Theories of development: modernization *vs.* dependency'. *http//www.infochangeindia.org/devp* (accessed 14 October, 2007).

Naanen, B.B.B. 1991, 'Itinerant Gold Mines': Prostitution in the Cross River Basin of Nigeria, 1930–1950', *African Studies Review* 34(2), 63.

National Archives, Ibadan, CSO 26/2 File no. 11556, vol. I, Annual Report, British Cameroons, 1923.

National Archives, Ibadan, CSO 26/2 File no. 13977, vol. I, 1923.

Ofonagoo, W. I. 1979, *Trade and imperialism in Southern Nigeria, 1881–1929*, New York-Lagos.

Osuntokun, A. 1979, *Nigeria in the First World War*, London.

Sanderson, S.K. 1995, *Macrosociology: An Introduction to human societies*, New York.

Webster, J.B., and Boahen, A.A. 1969, *The Growth of African Civilization: The Revolutionary history,* Boston-Toronto.

West Africa, 1 December, 1917, London.

West Africa, 18 May, 1918, London.

West Africa, 25 May, 1918, London.

West Africa, 26 January 1918, London.

The Adisi Case: Currency Counterfeiting in Interwar Colonial Gold Coast

Ayodeji Olukoju

Introduction

The discussion in this chapter is set within the context of the inter-war period, especially the economic crisis of the late 1920s and early 1930s, which highlighted the fragility of indigenous entrepreneurship in the face of the vagaries of the global economy.[1] A striking feature of the period from the perspective of the British colonial administration was the high incidence of foiled and successful counterfeiting and uttering of colonial currencies. Much has been written on this subject, especially in the Nigerian context. Toyin Falola,[2] and Falola and Akanmu Adebayo,[3] have located currency forgery in the context of culture and politics of money in Yorubaland (south-western Nigeria), while Ayodeji Olukoju has added the dimension of counterfeiting and uttering as an ambiguous illustration of self-help criminality as resistance against the colonial order.[4]

Falola and Adebayo have attempted to explain the incidence of currency counterfeiting in terms of a 'get-rich-quick' mentality that can be understood in the context of the attitude of the Yoruba to money. Although the society traditionally frowned at ill-gotten wealth, the wealthy (*olowo* or *olola*) were accorded respect in society and this encouraged money-making enterprise in the society. Adebayo has also deepened our understanding of the Yoruba attitude to money by highlighting the people's characterization of money as 'Kose-e-mani' (The Indispensable One).[5] The colonial context simply accentuated such tendencies and attitudes toward money and money-making (among the Yoruba and other colonized peoples) and provided new opportunities for money-making, including illegal ones such as counterfeiting. Olukoju's study on the other hand while agreeing that counterfeiting was a product of the colonial context placed it in the framework of inter-regional trade between northern and south-western Nigeria (which facilitated the uttering or distribution of the fake coins) and, more importantly, explained it in terms of an implicit alienation from (and resistance to) the colonial order, coupled with a drive for accumulation.

It may be deduced from the Nigerian case studies that a combination of any of cultural pressure for accumulation or the privileging of the wealthy, the context of inter-war depression and underlying alienation from, coupled with ambiguous resistance to, the colonial order was responsible for the upsurge of inter-war currency counterfeiting in West Africa. But more case studies are required for a clearer understanding and better explanation of the phenomenon in colonial Africa. Consequently, the following discussion of developments in the late-1920s Gold Coast and the adjoining French Togoland colony provides another perspective on the subject of currency counterfeiting in the wider, West African context.

Incidence of forgery of financial instruments in coastal West Africa in the 1920s

By the end of the First World War, a combination of circumstances had made the introduction of currency notes necessary.[6] First, there was a shortage of silver currency, which needed to be augmented with alloy coinage or notes, if a serious currency crisis was to be averted. Second, the brief post-war boom of 1918–20 had engendered an atmosphere of optimism that was, however, reversed in the next two years, when an equally brief and drastic economic slump dislocated the colonial economies.[7] The Gold Coast colony had emerged as a major cocoa-exporting economy, which expanded the space for the emergence of African entrepreneurship in a colonial economy that was dominated by expatriate interests.[8] It is being suggested that the incidence of currency counterfeiting and the involvement of a certain class of Africans in the act derived from the peculiarities of the political economy of the 1920s, especially the dislocating aftermath of the post-war boom.[9]

Attempts to counterfeit colonial currency on the Gold Coast might have had a longer history but the earliest case of inducement to counterfeit the notes was in 1924. In that year, a Gold Coast *indigene*, known as J. Miles Oppon, using a post-office box address in Coomassie (Kumasi) had approached a German jeweller in the Cologne area to make a mould for making counterfeit 5- and 10-penny coins. He also requested information about the composition of the alloy (mixture of copper and brass) to facilitate his own reproduction.[10] It is instructive that he promised to pay his prospective accomplice in the product of the Gold Coast:

> if you so desire, I will ship you cocoa beans of the best quality to cover the cost of the machine and your charge in analysing the coin, or otherwise remit you money in payment.[11]

Realizing the criminality of his proposal and its consequences, Oppon warned his German contact to 'keep this matter strictly confidential between ourselves only, and you will see how we both will be benefited [*sic*] by.'[12]

While Oppon was interested in making fake coins for circulation, other Gold Coast indigenes attempted to print currency notes. A German police report of September 1925 stated that:

> the Niggers Josef Samuel Solomon, Mechanic, born 15/8/92 and Joachim Benjamin Coblima Acken, Trader, born 11/5/86 in Elmina were arrested here on the 22/9/24 for attempting to arrange for the printing of forged '20/- Notes' of the Island of Lagos, in British West Africa.[13]

They were sentenced to four months imprisonment and released on 22 February 1925 on completion of their terms. The police could not trace them afterwards.

A different request came from a Mr Schmeck, based in Accra, capital of the Gold Coast to a German trader, Albert G.

Richard Gossow, requesting the forgery of 1,000 copies of Customs entry forms, receipts and other financial instruments of 20/- and 10/- each. The West African demanded confidentiality and promised to pay for the printing by bank draft to cover costs, freight, packing and other incidental expenses once an agreement was reached.[14] Gossow approached a Leipzig printer, Messrs Vereinigle, for the printing of the Customs Declaration forms only. The latter reported the matter to the Police, who arrested and prosecuted the German, Gossow. He claimed that he had not committed any offence as he thought the printing of the Customs entry and I.O.U. forms – a financial instrument – (the latter in water-colours) was in order and that was what he took to the printer on behalf of the customer in Accra. In any case, he argued further, the enquiry concerning the price did not contain an order. However, the German printer declined the job since he did not do steel engraving but did not warn Gossow that the request was criminal in intent. In the final analysis, the charges were dropped as currency notes were not involved.[15]

Colonial records of the 1920s are replete with cases of foiled attempts at forging postage stamps and colonial currency notes by young literate indigenous Africans. As stated in **Table 1** below, such attempts took place in Nigeria and the Gold Coast, the leading colonies of British West Africa. With few exceptions, the incidents took place in major coastal commercial towns of these colonies. Most of the prospective counterfeiters had had a smattering of formal education and had served a form of apprenticeship under some expatriate traders. Others, such as, Ernest Adisi, the subject of this study, were promising indigenous traders. All had requested German printers to aid them in the production of the forged notes. In virtually all cases the Germans reported them to the police, who took appropriate action. Several of these prospective counterfeiters were duly convicted (see **Table 2 below**). But, as we shall see, the case of Ernest Adisi was exceptional in several respects.

The examples above indicate the prevalence of the attempts by Gold Coast citizens to procure European printers to aid them in the forgery of security instruments, especially coins and currency notes. By March 1926, after convictions had been obtained in several cases, the Gold Coast Inspector-General of Police enthused that though there were 'several outstanding cases' under investigation, 'I hope I have stopped this sort of thing for a time'.[16] His optimism was based on the reports of convictions contained in **Table 2 below**. This was later belied by the scale and daring of the scheme masterminded by Adisi, as detailed in the rest of this essay.

Colonial officials welcomed the co-operation of the European would-be collaborators of the West African counterfeiters who had aided police prosecution. But officials of the West African Currency Board (WACB.) were dissatisfied with the seemingly light sentences imposed on the offenders. They felt that two years' imprisonment with hard labour was,

> inadequate if such crimes are to be prevented... [given the] numerous attempts [that]... have been made by natives of the Gold Coast to defraud the country by means of counterfeiting, and it is evident that such efforts will continue to be made unless they are put down with a strong hand.[17]

Events were to show that the sentences did not discourage prospective coiners, the most celebrated of whom was Ernest Adisi, whose activities will be examined later in this piece. Meanwhile, financial inducement had helped in getting prospective European collaborators to co-operate with the colonial and imperial governments in West Africa to foil many of these bids. After due consideration, it was decided that a sum of £25 would be paid to an informant as soon as the first notification was lodged, followed by enquiries about the credibility of the source and the balance of £25 paid upon receipt by the WACB. of a report from the affected colony whether or not the culprit was traced or conviction secured.[18] **Table 1** indicates the success of such collaboration motivated by financial rewards.

In all, the cases of attempted counterfeiting in the early/mid-1920s as indicated in the Tables reveal some discernible patterns. First, the prospective counterfeiters sought to exploit their limited artisanal knowledge to forge currency notes, as in the case of Narking (alias 'E.T. Nyedemey') of Akuse, who deployed his skills in photography to that criminal end. Second, the counterfeiters nonetheless admitted their technical disability by seeking collaboration with European printers (**Table 2**). Hence, virtually all of the counterfeiting schemes had international dimensions. Third, they appear to

Table 1: Particulars of informants and suspects in counterfeiting cases in West Africa in the 1920s

Informant and address	Attempt made by
Dr Trenkler & Co. Leipzig	Joseph Dabuanu of Koforidua, Gold Coast
Messrs Schumann of Berlin	George A. Whyte of Kumasi
Maschinenfabrik C. Thomas (in conjunction with Max Doeller of Neustadt an der Haarolt)	Shalman Godfrey of Calabar, Nigeria
Rothschild & Co. of Eisenbach I Thuringia	Jayeola Coker of Lagos, Nigeria
Secke & Devrient of Leipzig	Gold Coast Stores, Ltd., Accra
Steenbergen & Co. of Schandauer Strasse 24, Dresden	M.P. Armye, Gold Coast
Frederick Metzger of Elise Averdieckstr 12, Hamburg	F.O.C. Horsfall of Abonnema, Nigeria
E.A. Gaile of Riga, Latvia	Mensah Bros & Co. of Koforidua, Gold Coast
Heinrich Wigge of Unna	Shalman Godfrey of Calabar
C. Henke Gesellschaft fur Bahn und Industrie Bedarf M.B.H., Dortmund	-ditto-
J.A. Morin of Hamburg	Abousam Amuhuba and Epiphone Regis Tate of Ivory Coast; and N.P. Frankson of Attuaboe, Gold Coast
Joseph Jegeb of Dresdenerstr 18, Berlin	K. Wadjo Bonn, Tafo, P.O. Box. 13, via Accra, Gold Coast; Joseph Arkansas c/o Swanzys Transport, P.O. Box 31, Koforidua, Gold Coast; R.S. Seraphim of Koforidua, Gold Coast

Source: National Archives of the United Kingdom, London, CO 554/73/4, 'Counterfeiting of West African Currency,' Secretary, WACB. to Commissioner of Police, New Scotland Yard, 26 January 1927, enc. in Sec., WACB to Undersecretary, Colonial Office, London, 4 February 1927

Table 2: Convictions for counterfeiting currency notes on the Gold Coast, 1925–26

Name	Place of offence	Date of conviction	Sentence	Remarks
Emmanuel Twinty Narkrong alias E.T. Nyemedey	Akuse	30.4.25	5 Years Imprisonment with Hard Labour (I.H.L)	Notes were forged in the colony by photography
Sam John Ocansey	Akuse	27.5.25	10 & 5 Years I.H.L, to run concurrently	-ditto-
Kweku Brenyah	Saltpond	21.8.25	2 Years I.H.L.	-ditto-
Kobinak Gyimah	Saltpond	9.9.25	5 Years I.H.L.	-ditto-
K.E. Hausou	Saltpond	9.9.25	4 Years I.H.L.	-ditto-
Kauko Arthur alias J.K. Arthur	Accra & Sekondi	8.10.25	5 Years I.H.L.	An attempt to import from England
F.D. Dukun	Half Assini	281.26	5 Years I.H.L.	An attempt to import from Germany (Hamburg)
Aggrey	Prestea	4.3.26	5 Years I.H.L.	An attempt to import from Manchester, U.K.
Oseni Latunji	Tarkwa	4.3.26	5 Years I.H.L.	An attempt to import from Germany (via F.R. Schmidt, Torgau)
Walter K. Kofie	Tarkwa	4.3.26	5 Years I.H.L.	-ditto-

Source: National Archives of the United Kingdom, London, Encl. In IGP, Gold Coast to Bevin, 27 March 1926, CO 554/69/2, 'Counterfeiting of W[est] A[frican] Currency and Postage Stamps'

have identified Germany and the United Kingdom as likely sources of collaborators, as indicated by the target and destination of their overtures.

'A very big fraudulent scheme': the Adisi case, 1927

On Sunday, 5 June 1927, one Joseph K. Mamattah, Agent of the United Trading Company (UTC) at Keta, Gold Coast, was arrested for uttering a fake £1 WACB note in the Motor Accessories shop of Messrs G.B. Ollivant, Lome. The Police discovered in his premises 37 new fake notes of the same denomination in a small leather handbag and a leather suitcase 'of considerable weight' containing £3,717 in fake notes. The suspect confessed under interrogation that he had received the consignment from one Edward Bruce, a resident of Anecho in French Togoland, who had also been arrested. A sum of £40,000 in fake notes was found in Bruce's premises. Mamattah further implicated Bruce's brother, Emmanuel, who was based in Nuremberg, Germany.

The Police had thought that the notes had been printed in either of the Gold Coast or Togo, especially as Mamattah had a lithographic establishment in Keta, which he had sold in 1924/25 to one Titus Glover of the Scottish Mission printing department, Accra. They dismissed the supposition that Glover had printed the notes in Accra and then smuggled them across the border through Mamattah, who was a frequent visitor to Accra. This was because Glover's failure to pay for the printing press had strained relations between both men. But it was later concluded that the notes were printed in Germany since Mamattah had recently cabled £200 to Bruce in Nuremberg. Moreover, Edward Bruce had also received a consignment of beds, mattresses and motor oil from Germany under the name of Goldsmith Kwawuvi. Strangely, the papers for the goods (consignment notes and invoices) were sent to the Bank of British West Africa (BBWA), Keta, where they were called for and paid for by Mamattah. Initial Police investigations concluded that the fake notes were imported by means of the mattresses in the consignment. The notes were described as 'excellent forgeries except for the lack of a watermark.'[19]

The British Vice-Consul in Lome provided a detailed description of the technical defects in the notes, which might have been unknown to the untrained eye. In addition to the lack of a watermark, the paper was slightly glazed; the notes were slightly wider than the genuine ones; the black printing was too accentuated and showed through on the other side; the red printing was not distinct enough and paler than in the genuine note.[20] Apparently, the forged notes were shipped to Lome in the upholstery of a sofa and in a large false-sided tin of motor grease. The writer advised the Gambia colony to examine mails from Germany to check for further importation of the fake notes.

Colonial officials and those of the WACB were alarmed by these developments, which posed a great threat to the colonial currency system. The fact that the notes had been manufactured and uttered (that is, put into circulation)was particularly worrisome. This necessitated inter-departmental and, more significantly, inter-colonial co-operation in West Africa and Europe. First, efforts were made to apprehend Emmanuel Bruce, who was reported to be making his way to West Africa from Hamburg with more consignments of the fake currency notes. The French authorities in Lome, Togo counselled secrecy especially over the arrest of his accomplices, Edward Bruce and Mamattah, so as not to scare him off.[21] The WACB, which was eager to halt the circulation of the notes, suggested that the French should get the German police to arrest Bruce in Nuremberg but feared that news of local arrests might hinder the apprehension of the masterminds behind the scheme. Conversely, the Sierra Leone colonial government thought that a public warning would check the spread of the fake notes.[22]

The earliest hint that a bigger mastermind was behind the Bruce brothers and Mamattah was given in a terse telegram sent by the Currency Officer, Accra to the WACB as follows: 'Ernest Kweku Adisi importing counterfeit West African currency notes of 20/- denomination... travelling by... [the S.S. Wadai]'.

The suspect was described as being 38 years old, 5 feet 4 inches tall, black and hailing from the Gold Coast. The intelligence report was sequel to the discoveries of further consignments of the fake currency notes in Accra, which were strikingly similar to those already seized in Togoland.[23] Adisi was arrested and charged at Bow Street Police Court, London under the Fugitive Offenders Act, with importing counterfeit currency notes within the jurisdiction of the Gold Coast Colony and Togoland. As much as £4,000 was suspected to have been so imported. Adisi demanded to read the warrant and then refused to make any statement even in Court, and was, therefore, remanded. A banker's draft for £450, £16 in English money and some money in foreign (presumably German) currency was found on him.[24] Adisi had been described by a Gold Coast official as 'a well known Accra man, a cocoa dealer who has handled large sums of money in produce dealing in the last few years.'[25]

A clearer picture of the scam was now emerging, with Emmanuel Bruce, based in Nuremberg, identified as the key figure in the actual manufacture of the fake notes. He was described as a native of Anecho (German Togoland) and was agent for Mr. Kubukanapfs of Keta, from whose employ he resigned to start his own business in Germany. Before relocating to Europe, he had been agent for G.B. Ollivant at Keta but he barely escaped conviction for embezzlement and falsification of books, having been acquitted only on a technicality. The judge had said that in spite of the reprieve, there was ample proof of his culpability. Bruce was nevertheless engaged by the German shipping firm, Woermann Linie, as its agent at Lome and Keta.[26]

An official of the BBWA in Hamburg submitted a later report on Emmanuel Bruce after the suspect had been arrested. It stated that Bruce was well known to the bank in the city, having been educated in Germany, 'which he regards as his 'spiritual home''. Though he often visited West Africa, he resided mostly in Nuremberg, at 34 Bauerngasse. Bruce was reported to have had dealings with several Hamburg firms, 'some of whom have lost money on him while the others have only avoided losses by means of legal proceedings and garnishee orders'. He was, in the opinion of the bank official, 'an exceptionally able scoundrel'.[27]

The French in Lome desired to apprehend Emmanuel Bruce who was being expected from Nuremberg, but did not wish to seek German diplomatic assistance to achieve this aim. Yet, it was important to arrest him with the fake notes in Germany for the dual purpose of getting a conviction and of leading the police to his printer. The British too were eager to have him in custody but preferred that he should face trial in French territory because the French police and legal systems were more draconian. 'The French authorities are not kind to forgers and others in custody as ourselves', the Gold Coast Inspector-General of Police stated, 'and it is possible that Edward Bruce ('Goldsmith Kwawuvi') will disclose information that may implicate certain persons in British Territory'.[28] Hence, he had not given publicity about the counterfeit notes lest Emmanuel Bruce should be warned off and abscond, but banks, treasuries and Chambers of Commerce were duly warned. Accordingly, the Accra Chamber passed a resolution asking the government to withdraw the notes or have them perforated.[29] The BBWA, Keta was excited by a report that the police in French Togoland had made 'a big seizure of 46,000 exceptionally good counterfeit West African Currency Board Notes' which might deceive 'a native' but should have been detected by a bank cashier 'as the colouring is slightly blurred and although the printing is exceptionally good, there is no water mark'. The

report added that the French had 'wrung a confession' from Mamattah, which implicated the Bruce brothers, and enthused that the French government 'have the situation well in hand and have no doubt nipped in the bud a very big fraudulent scheme'.[30]

The Nuremberg Police finally moved against Emmanuel Bruce but a search on his house on 30 June 1927 yielded nothing, presumably because he had received sufficient warning. He was, however, placed under surveillance and was to be searched if he ventured to travel. The German Police did not commit themselves to any further action since no evidence had been found to implicate him. However, under pressure from the British Consulate in Hamburg, the Germans detained Bruce.[31] It was reported that Bruce and his German companion had gone to the harbour in Hamburg on 27 January to board a ship for West Africa. But on learning from a cook that Adisi had been arrested in Southampton, they reportedly left the harbour in haste! The German police then apprehended one Paul Herden, who had printed the notes for Emmanuel Bruce, who was also arrested apparently on the strength of evidence supplied by Herden. Bruce claimed to have printed the fake notes under Adisi's instructions.[32]

On the Gold Coast, Edward Bruce and Mamattah admitted under interrogation that only they and Emmanuel Bruce had been responsible for the illicit activity. Not satisfied, the Police searched the cable communications of the period and discovered that a consignment of two cases of bedsteads and bedding, and a drum of oil had reached Accra by the *S.S. Djojca* by the end of May 1927 and had been cleared. They searched Ernest Adisi's premises in Accra, where they discovered a 'drum of grease containing counterfeit notes packed in metal containers and oiled paper.'[33]

Conclusion of police investigation and trials in Germany, the United Kingdom and the Gold Coast

Police investigations in Germany and the Gold Coast had reached a critical point by July 1, 1927. In Germany, Bruce's host family (the Knolls) and his female companion, Frau Baer (Herr Knoll's sister) co-operated with the detectives. Bruce's companion disowned and threw him out of the apartment. Frau Mathilde Knoll admitted that she saw him loading what he had called 'advert materials' inside beds and mattresses. As she 'did not want to have any more unpleasantness,' she deposited three large trunks of his belongings at the forwarding agents Strauss in her name. Bruce, who had been arrested at an inn, and Herr Knoll took police to Herden's shop, where the latter admitted to have manufactured 100,000 'advert forms' for Bruce. He submitted all the heliographic plates in his possession.

Herden, an elderly German in a precarious financial state, claimed to have had doubts from the beginning but had been assured by Bruce that the 'forms' were not for circulation as currency. Bruce had explained that they did not need to have a watermark, as they would be sent in single pieces to individual customers![34] Bruce later brought the Arabic letters for inclusion on the blank obverse side of the 'advert forms' after Herden had received the order. When queried, Bruce had explained it away as the logo of his company! Herden stated that when he voiced his apprehension, Bruce assured him that he could not engage in forgery or swindling, as that would jeopardise his 'large export business.' For the 100,000 notes that he printed, Herden received 3,000 marks in several instalments, a price that the police agreed was too low a remuneration if he was a conscious accomplice. This was because the forgery entailed three series of colour printing, which, with the material used, left a narrow profit margin.

Bruce's testimony corroborated Herden's and implicated Ernest Adisi as his principal in the criminal act. He admitted that he had 'done something which I ought not to have done and which is punishable.' Bruce explained that he gave piece-meal orders for the printing of the fake notes so that Herden would 'not demand so much money for the printing.' Moreover, he needed to avoid arousing the printer's suspicion. He exonerated the Knolls and explained how he met Adisi and the manner of the packing and despatch of the consignments of fake money.[35]

As preparations were being made to try the accused persons in court, Bruce retracted his earlier statement and secured the services of a German barrister. Apparently acting under instructions, he refused to make any statement and no incriminating evidence had actually been found when the police searched his premises. The defence counsel stuck to the claim that the fake notes had been made as 'advert materials' but this was undermined by evidence that they had been uttered in West Africa. The court took notice of Herden's advanced age and relative poverty as predisposing him to throwing discretion to the winds when he was approached to print what he should have known were fake currency notes. Notice was also taken of his low charges and the fact that Bruce had not paid him the balance for the job. Herden's conduct was described as being 'as unbusinesslike as it was imprudent.' As for Bruce, the evidence was not considered strong enough to warrant his extradition but he was tried nonetheless under German law.[36] The court sentenced Bruce to four years 'penal servitude and … the loss of civil rights for a further five years' and Herden to 18 months imprisonment.[37]

While the trial of Bruce and Herden was proceeding in Germany, Adisi's too was making slow but steady progress through the British and Gold Coast courts. On 23 July 1927, Adisi appeared before Sir Chartres Biron at Bow Street Court and was defended by Mr. Christmas Humphreys, instructed by Mr. E.F. Hunt of 6 Gray's Inn Place. Adisi was committed to Brixton Prison for 15 days pending appeal against his extradition.[38] A newspaper report stated that the presiding Magistrate had ruled that there was 'a clear *prima facie* case, and he therefore made an order for the accused man to be returned to West Africa for trial.'[39] Adisi lost his appeal and was duly extradited to the Gold Coast, where he arrived on 24 August 1927.

The trial of E.K. Adisi, E.J. Afwireng, E.T. Amoah, J.E. Lokko, Mrs Afwireng, Beatrice Dankwa, Q.L. Crabbe, Mercy Matheson and Yaw Sao – 'all Africans' – before His Worship Captain J.K. Dickinson, M.C., was full of drama. The accused persons were duly represented by counsel: Mr Francis Dove for Adisi; Mrs H.F. Ribeiro and Mr K. Quartey Papafio for the Afwirengs; Messrs R.S. Sackey and Owoo for Amoah; Mr Charles Renner for Lokko; Quartey Papafio for Yaw Sao; and Mr. R.S. Sackey for Crabbe. As no evidence was offered by the Crown against Beatrice Dankwa, Q.L. Crabbe, Mercy Matheson and Yaw Sao, they were all duly discharged. The others faced

trial at the District Commissioner's Court, Accra from 30 August to 9 September 1927. 'Considerable interest was shown by the public,' it was reported, 'and the Court was crowded daily.' The case was transferred to Cape Coast because of 'the many relatives and acquaintances of the accused persons in Accra.' Adisi, in particular, was said to have been 'an intimate friend of several lawyers in Accra.' It was feared that a trial by jury in Accra would favour him for the Inspector-General of Police declared, 'I distrust Accra juries.' The Chief Justice of the Gold Coast refused Adisi's plea for a change of venue (back to Accra).[40]

There was 'considerable legal argument' as to whether the accused persons should be tried together or separately. The judge, Mr Justice Michelin ruled that all should be tried together by assessors. The trial then commenced on 18 October before Michelin and three assessors: one European (Mr Thomas) and two Africans (Messrs Hammond and Mensah). The accused were charged with possessing and uttering counterfeit currency contrary to Section 303, subsection 2 Cap. 16 of the Laws of the Gold Coast Colony; importation with intent to defraud contrary to Section 1 of that Law; importation contrary to Section 50 and Section 303 subsection 1 of Cap. 16; and for conspiracy to commit these crimes. The actual trial lasted from 14 October to 22 December 1927; 43 witnesses being examined, 26 on behalf of the Crown and 17 for the defence; and 156 exhibits were tendered and received in evidence. After the evidence for the prosecution closed on 8 November 1927, the Chief Justice ruled that there was no case against Loko, who was accordingly discharged. Adisi was found guilty on all counts and was sentenced to 15 years on the first and five years each on others, all sentences running concurrently. Afwireng (in whose mother-in-law's cellar at Mangoase, some 50km from Accra, was found £40,000 counterfeit notes) was found guilty on the third count but not on the first two. After a 'strong recommendation for mercy by the assessors,' he was jailed for three years with hard labour. Amoah was found guilty on the first, second and third counts, and got six years for the first and five years each for the other two counts, all running concurrently. Mrs. Afwireng was not found guilty and was duly discharged. This was the end of the Adisi case, which the Police chief described as 'one of the biggest known cases of the actual importation of counterfeit currency notes in the Empire.'[41]

The police handling of the investigation of the case and the trial of the accused in the Gold Coast generated its own controversy. As the Inspector-General of Police in the Gold Coast admitted, the police were criticized for its handling of the trial.[42] It was alleged that Scotland Yard officers (Messrs Mansergh, Moorman and others) 'secreted or destroyed a most important document' (an agreement) to obstruct Adisi in his defence. Second, either of Messrs Mansergh or Simmons 'deliberately fabricated the whole of the statements made by one of the accused persons' (Afwireng) after he was arrested. Third, the three British police officers were said to have 'lied with respect to 5th accused's (Mrs Afwireng) knowledge of English.' Fourth, the police had interfered with witnesses for the defence. Fifth, there was an inter-departmental conspiracy between police and Customs Officers to fabricate evidence to support prosecution. Sixth, that police concealed material papers found during the searches. Seventh, that preferential treatment was meted out to the accused Amoah and, finally, that it was 'not a police prosecution but a persecution'!

The Inspector-General of Police absolved his men and colleagues of these serious charges. He argued that the Gold Coast police 'have received excellent instruction and training and have acquired a mass of information about persons in this country which is invaluable.' He added a note of racist paternalism, typical of the age, by commenting that: 'I considered it necessary to keep the investigation in the hands of European Officers as far as possible.' The defence of men and operatives by officers is to be expected but we have seen above that French police investigators and interrogators were already notorious for their strong-arm tactics. But, on balance, it cannot be denied that there was a near-successful and daring attempt to counterfeit and utter colonial currency by desperate colonial subjects. If the element of nationalism cannot be found in this saga, the contributions of formal education and exposure to international trade, as well as the likelihood of influences by others (Syrians were the usual suspects) played a great role in this misadventure. As the police chief commented while clamouring for tougher sanctions: 'I maintain that the punishment now provided by law is an insufficient deterrent for the more subtle type of criminal that education and prosperity have produced'.[43]

Conclusion

The significance of this case study stems from its manifold novelty. First, we have concrete evidence for the provenance of the equipment (moulds) used in the making of forged currency. Second, unlike previous cases of local counterfeiting, this was a clear case of foreign manufactured and imported fake currency. Third, this was the first instance of the forgery of currency notes as opposed to coinage, which was counterfeited in many parts of West Africa, especially Southern Nigeria. Fourth, the Adisi case provides a unique illustration of a transnational crime network in a colonial context. It is significant how the case engendered a multinational European effort (British-French-German) to crack. Fifth, this was organized crime of a type that was probably unknown in early 20th-century British West Africa. Most striking is that it involved two sets of brothers: Edward and Emmanuel Bruce, and Ernest Adisi and E.J. Afwireng, who were said to be 'blood brothers' though they bore different surnames. This suggests that criminal enterprise, like licit entrepreneurship, was seen to thrive on social solidarity and that a thin line separated the two in the desperate situation of the 1920s. The kin-based solidarity was probably seen as ensuring security or secrecy, or was a device to keep the profits in the family. Sixth, the preference for the Germans as accomplices suggests that the West Africans were conscious of differences between the Germans and other Europeans (arising from the post-World War I settlement) and thought that they could exploit German disgruntlement for their purpose. Of relevance is the fact that the Germans had lost their colonies in Africa to the French and British, and it is instructive that Emmanuel Bruce, the lynchpin of the actual forgery operation, was a German-speaking African based in Germany who hailed from a former German colony. It also suggests that German reputation for precision and expertise in fabrication or manufacturing endeared them to the West Africans.

Finally, in comparative terms, the Gold Coast case-study presents striking parallels to the earlier Nigerian studies. The inter-war colonial context was a shared experience both in terms of economic vicissitudes and the self-help strategies of African entrepreneurs, who were marginal actors in the colonial economy. From the correspondence of the would-be counterfeiters and colonial sources, Africans in both Nigeria and the Gold Coast shared a drive for money-making and a readiness to cut corners based on the suspicion that expatriate entrepreneurs (British and Levantine) also engaged in shady deals. Such assumptions were reinforced by the produce adulteration and sharp practices that characterized the export and import trade of the period. However, unlike the Nigerian case-study, the evidence for the Gold Coast did not stereotype any group (like the Ijebu-Yoruba of Western Nigeria) as being preponderant actors in the counterfeiting saga.

Acknowledgements

Material for this paper was collected while the author held the British Academy, Henry Charles Chapman, and Leventis Visiting Research Fellowships at the Institute of Commonwealth Studies and the School of Oriental and African Studies, University of London in 1998 and 1999. Comments by Dr Funke Adeboye and participants in the British Museum Conference on 'Money in Africa', 9–11 March 2007 on an earlier version of the paper are gratefully acknowledged. The author remains culpable for any subsisting errors in the paper.

Notes

1 For the literature on West African economic history, with particular reference to the inter-war period, see Hopkins 1966, 1970, 1988; for a case-study of the vicissitudes of colonial-era entrepreneurship, see Olukoju 2002a.

2 Falola 1997.

3 Falola and Adebayo 2000.

4 Olukoju 2000. While Falola 1997, Falola and Adebayo 2000, and Olukoju 2000, focus on fake coins and on Nigeria, this piece deals with a successful case of the manufacture and uttering of currency notes in another British West African colony.

5 Adebayo 1999.

6 See Hopkins 1970, Ofonagoro 1979 and Olukoju 1997, 2002b for studies of the Nigerian currency system during the period. For other British African colonies, see Hogendorn and Gemery 1988 and Maxon 1989.

7 For a Nigerian case study see Olukoju 2004.

8 For a study of the Gold Coast colonial economy see Austin 2005.

9 See Olukoju 2004 and 2002a.

10 National Archives of the United Kingdom, CO 554/69/2, 'Counterfeiting of W[est] A[frican] Currency and Postage Stamps.'

11 CO 554/69/2, J. Myles Oppon, P.O. Box 43. Coomassie, Gold Coast to C. Becker, Esqr., Jeweller & Goldsmith Drususgasse, 1, Köln-am-Rhein, Germany, 4 December 1924, enc. in Walter D. Ellis, Downing Street to Sec., WACB, 11 February 1926.

12 CO 554/69/2, J. Myles Oppon, P.O. Box 43. Coomassie, Gold Coast to C. Becker, Esqr., Jeweller & Goldsmith Drususgasse, 1, Köln-am-Rhein, Germany, 4 December 1924, enc. in Walter D. Ellis, Downing Street to Sec., WACB, 11 February 1926.

13 CO 554/69/2, Report by Dachsel, Criminal Detective, Criminal Detective Department, Leipzig, 4 September 1925.

14 CO 554/69/2, Agent, Gold Coast Stores Ltd., c/o Box 166, Accra to Messrs Richard Gossow & Co., 15 August 1925.

15 CO 554/69/2, Statement made to the Police by Albert G. Richard Gossow on 16 September 1925; F. Oliver, British Consulate General, Hamburg to Principal Secretary of State for Foreign Affairs, 24 March 1926.

16 CO 554/69/2, IGP, Gold Coast to Bevin, 27 March 1926.

17 CO 554/73/4 'Counterfeiting of West African Currency', Sec., WACB to Currency Officer, Accra, 4 February 1927.

18 CO 554/73/4, Secretary, WACB to Commissioner of Police, New Scotland Yard, 26 January 1927, enc. in Sec., WACB to Undersecretary, Colonial Office, 4 February 1927.

19 CO 554/73/4, Capt. H. Mitchell, Assistant Commissioner of Police, Keta to IGP, Accra, 7 June 1927.

20 CO 554/73/4, R.C.F. Maugham, British Consul, Dakar to Principal Secretary of State for Foreign Affairs, 22 June 1927, enc.: W. Darwall, Ag. British Vice Consul to Governor, The Gambia, 8 June 1927.

21 CO 554/73/4, Enc.1, Telegram, Currency Officer, Accra to WACB, 15 June 1927, in Wickhart, Sec., WACB to Undersecretary, Colonial Office, 22 June 1927.

22 CO 554/73/4, enc.2: Sec., WACB to Currency Officer, Accra, 17 June 1927, in Sec., WACB to Undersecretary, CO, 22 June 1927.

23 CO 554/73/4, enc. 3: Currency Officer to WACB, 20 June 1927.

24 'Forged Notes in West Africa: Gold Coast Merchant Arrested', *The Times* (London), 27 June 1927.

25 CO 554/73/4, Sec., WACB to Undersecretary, 5 July 1927, enc. 1: IGP to Currency Officer, 17 June 1927.

26 CO 554/73/4, Sec., WACB to Undersecretary CO, 23 June 1927, enc: Confid. Rpt. By Head Office, B.B.W.A., London, 20 June 1927.

27 CO 554/73/4, Sub-Manager, B.B.W.A., Hamburg Office to GM, Head Office, 6 July 1927, enc. in Sec., WACB to Undersecretary CO, 12 July 1927.

28 CO 554/73/4, Lt-Col. H.M. Bamford, IGP, to Currency Officer, Accra, 10 June 1927.

29 CO 554/73/4, Sec., WACB to Undersecretary, CO, 5 July 1927, enc.2: African & Eastern Provinces, Chamber of Commerce, Accra to Treasurer, Victoriaburg, Accra, 17 June 1927.

30 CO 554/73/4, L.C. Chilley, BBWA, Keta to General Manager, Head Office, London, 15 June 1927.

31 CO 554/73/4, Code telegram, 1 July 1927 from Addison, Berlin to CO.

32 CO 554/73/4, F. Oliver, Consulate-General, Hamburg to Chargé d'Affaires, British Embassy, Berlin, 2 July 1927; Code telegram, Addison, Berlin to CO, 9 July 1927.

33 CO 554/73/4, Sec., WACB to Undersecretary, 5 July 1927, enc. 1: IGP to Currency Officer, 17 June 1927.

34 CO 554/73/4, Chargé d'Affaires, Berlin to Principal Sec., Foreign Office, 13 July 1927, enc. 2: Ruckdaschel, Criminal Kommissar, Muggenhoferstrasse no. 26, 5 July 1927.

35 CO 554/73/4, Sec., WACB to Undersecretary, 5 July 1927, enc. 1: IGP to Currency Officer, 17 June 1927.

36 CO 554/73/4, Asst Comm., New Scotland Yard to Undersecretary, CO, 5 August 1927, enc: Rpt by ComPol of the Metropolis.

37 CO 554/73/4, Wickhart, Sec., WACB to Undersecretary, CO, 22 November 1927.

38 CO 554/73/4, Asst Comm., New Scotland Yard to Undersecretary, CO, 5 August 1927, enc: Report by Commissioner of Police of the Metropolis.

39 *The Times*, 25 July 1927.

40 CO 554/77/10, 'Counterfeiting of West African Currency, 1928', Bamford, IGP to Col. Sec., Victoriaburg, 5 January 1928, enc. in Gold Coast Confidential of 21 January 1928.

41 Ibid.

42 CO 554/77/10, Bamford to Col. Sec., 5 January 1928, for the quotes and information in the following paragraphs.

43 CO 554/77/10, Bamford to Col. Sec., 5 January 1928.

Bibliography

Adebayo, Akanmu G. 1999. 'Kose-e-mani: Idealism and Contradiction in the Yoruba View of Money,' in E. Stiansen and J.I. Guyer (eds), *Credit, Currencies and Culture: African Financial Institutions in Historical Perspective*, Stockholm, 146–174.

Austin, G. 2005. *Labour, Land and Capital in Ghana: From Slavery to Free Labour in Asante, 1807–1956*, Rochester, New York.

Falola, T. & Adebayo, A. 2000. *Culture, Politics & Money Among the Yoruba*, New Brunswick, New York.

Falola, T. 1997. '"Manufacturing Trouble": Currency forgery in colonial Southwestern Nigeria,' *African Economic History* 25, 121–146.

Hogendorn, J.S. and Gemery, H.A. 1988. 'Continuity in West African monetary history?: An outline of monetary development,' *African Economic History* 17, 127–146.

Hopkins, A. 1966. 'Economic aspects of political movements in Nigeria and in the Gold Coast, 1918–1939,' *Journal of African History* 7(1), 133–152.

Hopkins, A. 1970. 'The creation of a colonial monetary system: The origins of the West African Currency Board', *African Historical Studies* 3, 101–132.

Hopkins, A. 1988. *An Economic History of West Africa*, London.

Maxon, R.M. 1989. 'The Kenya currency crisis, 1919–21 and the imperial dilemma,' *Journal of Imperial and Commonwealth History* 17(3), 323–348.

National Archives of the United Kingdom, CO 554/69/2, 'Counterfeiting of W[est] A[frican] Currency and Postage Stamps.'

National Archives of the United Kingdom, CO 554/73/4 'Counterfeiting of West African Currency.'

National Archives of the United Kingdom, CO 554/77/10, 'Counterfeiting of West African Currency, 1928.'

Ofonagoro, W.I. 1979. 'From traditional to British currency in Southern Nigeria: Analysis of a currency revolution, 1880–1948,' *Journal of Economic History* 39(3), 623–654.

Olukoju, A. 2004. *The 'Liverpool' of West Africa: The Dynamics and Impact of Maritime Trade in Lagos, 1900–1950*, Trenton, New Jersey.

Olukoju, A. 2002a. 'The impact of British colonialism on the development of African business in colonial Nigeria,' in A. Jalloh and T. Falola (eds), *Black Business and Economic Power*, Rochester, New York, 176–198.

Olukoju, A. 2002b. 'The Colonial Monetary System in Northern Nigeria, 1903–1939', in T. Falola (ed.), *Nigeria in the Twentieth Century*, Durham, North Carolina, 183–199.

Olukoju, A. 2000. 'Self-help criminality as resistance?: Currency counterfeiting in colonial Nigeria,' *International Review of Social History* 45(3), 385–407.

Olukoju, A. 1997. 'Nigeria's colonial government, commercial banks and the currency crisis of 1916–1920', *International Journal of African Historical Studies* 30(2), 277–298.